KNIGHTS OF THE REICH

*The Twenty-Seven Most Highly
Decorated Soldiers of
the Wehrmacht in World War II*

KNIGHTS OF THE REICH

GÜNTHER FRASCHKA

Translated from the German by David Johnston

Schiffer Military/Aviation History
Atglen, PA

Bibliography

Galland: *Die Ersten und die Letzten*, Schneekluth Verlag, Darmstadt
Rudel: *Trotzdem*, Plesse Verlag, Göttingen
Nowotny: *Walter Nowotny*, Druffel Verlag, Leoni Starnberg
Clostermann: *der grosse Arena*, Alfred Scherz Verlag, Stuttgart
Ramcke: *Fallschirmjäger*, Lorch Verlag, Frankfurt am Main
Rommel: *Krieg ohne Hass*, Verlag Heidenheimer Zeitung, Heidenheim
von Manstein: *Verlorenen Siege*, Athenäum Verlag, Bonn
Jochim: *Oberst Hermann Graf*, Pabel Verlag, Rastatt
Toliver-Constable: *Holt Hartmann vom Himmel*, Motorbuch Verlag, Stuttgart
Walter Görlitz: *Model*, Limes Verlag, Wiesbaden
Höhne: *der Orden unter dem Totenkopf*, Bertelsmann Verlag, Munich
G.W. Schrodek: *Geschichte des Panzerregiments 15*, Schild Verlag, Munich
Fraschka: *Der Panzergraf*, Pabel Verlag, Rastatt
K.J. Walde: *Guderian*, Ullstein Verlag, Frankfurt/Main
David Irving: *Hitler und seine Feldherren*, Ullstein, Frankfurt
Herzog-Schomaeckers: *Ritter der Tiefe – Graue Wölfe*, Verlag Welsermühl, Munich-Wels
H. Busch: *So war der U-Boot Krieg*, Deutscher Heimat Verlag, Bielefeld).

Book Design by Robert Biondi
Translated from the German by David Johnston.

This book was originally published under the title,
Mit Schwertern und Brillanten,
© 1989 by Universitas Verlag, in F.A. Herbig Verlagsbuchhandlung, Munich.

Printed in the United States of America.
ISBN: 0-88740-580-0

We are interested in hearing from authors with
book ideas on related topics.

Published by Schiffer Publishing Ltd.
77 Lower Valley Road
Atglen, PA 19310
Please write for a free catalog.
This book may be purchased from the publisher.
Please include $2.95 postage.
Try your bookstore first.

Contents

Foreword   7

Dedication

To my three fallen brothers
Gerhard
Fritz
Richard

as a reminder to both my sons
Wolfgang and Ulrich

FOREWORD

I n the 1950s I began researching those soldiers of the last world war who had been decorated with the Knight's Cross of the Iron Cross with Oak Leaves, Swords and Diamonds, until December 31, 1944 the highest German decoration for valor.

At the end of 1944 Hitler created the Golden Oak Leaves as the ultimate decoration. *Oberstleutnant* Hans-Ulrich Rudel was awarded the decoration on January 1, 1945. It was intended that it be awarded to twelve outstanding individual fighters. Rudel, who was simultaneously promoted to *Oberst*, was an exception.

I gathered names and addresses and began the laborious job of tracking down each recipient or the survivors of those who had been killed or were still prisoners. The objective of this undertaking was not to restore a cult of heroes; I simply wanted to write about these outstanding personalities of recent history, and recall what they had achieved as representatives of millions of soldiers. I had no intention of evaluating their worth, as the main thrust of my considerations was the question "who was the man?"

I received willing support wherever I turned, and was able to publish *Mit Schwertern und Brillanten* in 1958. At that time it created something of a sensation in the book market. Names which it seemed had long been forgotten were brought to life again. It was reviewed by the specialist and daily press, by magazines and illustrated papers all over the world, and by historians such as Liddell Hart, Professor Pandit Tarachand

Roy and Walter Görlitz. The fate of the most highly-decorated German soldiers of World War Two was described for the first time since the war. A new edition appeared eighteen years later – reworked, supplemented and compressed.

At that time nine of the twenty-seven wearers of the Diamonds were still alive. The question "What has become of them?" was often asked, and the first edition had long since sold out. Now, with only two of the most highly-decorated still living (Erich Hartmann and Adolf Galland), the Universitäts Verlag presents the eighth edition, 43 years after the most terrible and tragic event in German history. (Note: Since the release of the eighth German edition in 1989, Erich Hartmann has died. The update appears in this edition.)

The primary objective of my writings is to prevent those twenty-seven men from being forgotten. Without exception they selflessly risked their lives – out of belief in a good cause. As soldiers and as men they were irreproachable individuals, who never hesitated to intervene on behalf of what was right and proper. And in the cases where several of them did commit errors, it was not out of inability or carelessness, but tragic circumstances. Their deeds, however, are indisputable.

Examples of bravery, courage, readiness to take action, will, comradeship and loyalty are more necessary than ever in a time when millions of young men in the western world volunteer for military service, to defend freedom and if need be give their lives for the existence of their democratic homelands. German history is rich in men who gave everything for the existence of their nation. It is immaterial whether the acts of these men led to victory or were incapable of preventing defeat. The military accomplishments of the twenty-seven wearers of the highest German decoration for valor will always be acknowledged.

CHAPTER I

OBERST WERNER MÖLDERS

November 23, 1942, twelve noon. The German radio network announcer introduces the news and the armed forces communique. At lunch tables in apartments, boarding houses and workers canteens conversations fall silent. People look at one another inquisitively and expectantly. In recent days the armed forces communiques have spoken of heavy fighting between German troops and desperately defending Soviet armies. What will the armed forces report bring today? Something is in the air, one can almost physically feel the tension. The people look at each other with concern – in the endless expanses of Russia, winter has arrived with unheard of fury. It has been snowing for days without pause. After the autumn's muddy period the front-line troops must now battle ice and snow.

Millions wait for the voice of the newscaster, then he begins to read; the armed forces communique for November 23 reports German successes: "... more than one hundred Soviet tanks destroyed ... thousands of prisoners taken ... heavy fighting ... our troops repulsed every enemy attack ..." And suddenly the announcer's voice wavers and stops short. It loses its cool, factual, impartial tone. The men at the loudspeakers listen intently. In the past years they have developed a special feeling for such artificial pauses. An announcement of special importance almost always follows such a pause – only seconds long. Now the voice of the announcer sounds calm and clear again:

"The Armed Forces High Command has announced that the Inspector of German Fighters, Oberst Mölders, has been killed in a airplane crash. The crash occurred in an aircraft not flown by him. The Führer has ordered a state funeral for this wearer of the highest decoration for bravery, the Knight's Cross of the Iron Cross with Oak Leaves, Swords and Diamonds."

The people collectively hold their breath. Mölders! Dead!

There is only one topic of conversation: the death of Germany's most successful fighter pilot, the death of the idol of German pilots, of German youth. The people cannot comprehend it. Most can't explain the terse announcement by the OKW: "in an aircraft not flown by him . . ." Later, there is no commentary on the accident, no naming of the crash site. Only the ceremonies of the state funeral are carried by every radio station.

There is sadness. It has been obvious for a long time that all is not going smoothly on the Eastern Front. The death announcements in the newspapers speak of this; each day the news must give up more space to them. Black mourning-borders . . . and now Mölders, too, is dead.

The people cannot comprehend that the popular Mölders, survivor of more than a thousand air battles and Germany's top-scoring fighter pilot with 115 victories, is no longer alive. They still see the face of the young *Oberst*, familiar to every German, smiling from the title pages of the illustrated papers, while his physical remains have long since been buried. Who was this *Oberst* Werner Mölders, at age twenty-nine the Inspector of Fighters, role model for a generation?

Werner was two in 1915 when his father Viktor Mölders, a *Leutnant*, was killed in an attack on the Western Front. His mother struggled to raise four children, but she nevertheless enabled him to attend high school, where he passed his final examinations at the age of seventeen and a half.

The young man had a desire to become an officer. When he applied for this career in the infantry of the "hundred thousand man army" he was one of sixty-one applicants. A large selection considering that only three would be accepted. One of those chosen was Werner Mölders. After a brief period of pioneer training with the 2nd Infantry Regiment in Allenstein, East Prussia, he quietly reported to the Luftwaffe, which was being developed in secrecy. It wouldn't have been the first time that future experts failed and returned home with the assessment "not suitable." That is exactly what happened to Mölders, who was rejected after undergoing suitability tests and examinations. After his first flight he staggered from the machine with a white face; his stomach revolted. In subsequent flights he was overcome by terrible headaches and dizziness when the aircraft entered a turn.

It appeared that Mölders was in fact unsuitable. But then something awakened in him, something which no method of testing, no matter how sophisticated, could detect: his iron will! The will to overcome his rebelling body, the will to succeed in spite of everything, the will to take things in hand. And this will won out. Werner Mölders requested a new examination. It was granted. He took off, flew, completed the program. It took all his strength. The Luftwaffe doctor's assessment: "Conditionally suitable." This assessment resulted in a transfer to the commercial flying school in Cottbus, where he was to begin training. There the doctors once again decided against him.

But Mölders did not give up. He wanted to, had to, become a pilot; flying was his destiny. He would overcome his rebellious stomach and the dizzy spells. He asked the *Gruppenkommandeur* to go on a test flight with him. This time it was a success: Mölders conquered his stomach and banished the feelings of dizziness. He was quite calm. He had become master of himself. The *Gruppenkommandeur* was an understanding man. He overturned the doctor's decision and allowed *Leutnant* Mölders to continue with the training course. Mölders didn't disappoint his superior; he led the class and completed his training with an outstanding assessment.

Leutnant Mölders, former combat engineer, was more than a little surprised when the job of setting up a dive-bomber *Geschwader* was given to him and several more senior officers.

There followed a transfer to the *Immelmann Geschwader*, which included the future fighter aces Wick, Öesau, Tietzen and Bertram. Mölders remained there only a year before being ordered to Wiesbaden to help in the formation a new *Geschwader*.

Then, in 1936, civil war broke out in Spain. People in Germany followed the events on the Iberian Peninsula with great interest. An unprecedented campaign by the German press and radio, directed from the Reich Ministry of Propaganda, stirred up the population with headlines such as: White against Red! Spain cannot be allowed to fall into the hands of the communists! The freedom of Europe is at stake!

Germany's sympathies lay with a young Spanish general: Francisco Franco. He was made out to be a symbol of freedom and social order. Germany identified with this man and his campaign against the socialists and republicans, the communists and anarchists, which was very much in step with the views of those politicians who feared the threat to Europe posed by world communism. The military, which smelled an opportunity to intervene in the battle against the "reds", also endorsed the stand of the German government. It was in the best interests of a free Europe that Spain not be lost!

It was no secret that the Soviet Union desired and supported a communist revolt in Spain. She provided the republicans and communists with military advisors, weapons and munitions. Soviet-supplied *Rata* fighters ruled the skies. The situation became more difficult for Franco's ground forces as the weeks passed. International brigades, formed in France, fought against the Nationalists. Socialists and communists all over the world were called upon to join the battle in Spain.

This was the moment for Germany's leadership to take the decision to intervene in Spain. Its objective was to prevent Spain from being swamped by a "red flood" and the subsequent establishing of a communist bastion in Western Europe. The military, on the other hand, saw it as a unique opportunity to engage in "maneuvers with live ammunition," test its air force and anti-aircraft weapons, and at the same time amass valuable experience.

As time went on, Mölders became increasingly suspicious, for several of his comrades had disappeared without saying goodbye. This continued until, one day, he learned that German fliers were fighting in Spain on the side of General Franco.

The *Legion Condor* was formed in the Reich Air Ministry. It saw action in Spain, at first disguised as a civilian company, then openly as a combat unit. Its reputation was legendary, its actions forever linked with General Franco's victory. "Secret" or "non-secret," the young *Oberleutnant* Werner Mölders volunteered for combat service in Spain. He had no way of knowing that he would return home as the *Legion Condor*'s most successful pilot.

One man had already come to the fore in Spain, a man whose name was spoken with respect by the Nationalists and with fear by the "Reds": Adolf Galland. When Mölders took over his *Staffel*, which was equipped with Messerschmitt fighters, on May 25, 1938, air superiority was assured wherever the "Condor fighters" put in an appearance.

Mölders shot down an enemy aircraft on his very first flight in a Messerschmitt. The next day a second Curtiss followed, and on the flight home from this sortie he encountered a formation of the barrel-shaped, but very maneuverable *Ratas*, one of which he shot down.

Following an early promotion to *Hauptmann* at the age of twenty-five, Mölders, the most successful German fighter pilot in Spain with 14 victories, received the Spanish Cross in Gold with Diamonds. His "Spanish experiences" made him one of the "old hands" of the Luftwaffe fighter arm. In March 1939 he assumed command of a *Staffel* of JG 53, the *Pik-As* (Ace of Spades) *Geschwader*, which contained the elite of the Luftwaffe.

Over France on September 19, 1939, Mölders shot down his first enemy aircraft or World War Two. The victim was a French-flown Curtiss Hawk 75A. For this victory he was awarded the Iron Cross, Second Class. The Iron Cross, First Class followed his seventh kill, and after his twentieth *Generalfeldmarschall* Göring presented him with the Knight's Cross. Mölders was the first member of the fighter arm to be so honored. By then his *Gruppe* had shot down 81 enemy aircraft.

Then came June 5, a beautiful, sunny day which almost proved to be Mölders' last. He shot down a French reconnaissance machine that afternoon following a long running fight.

The pilot of the enemy aircraft was an outstanding flier and Mölders had to work hard to shoot him down. Afterward the young *Gruppenkommandeur* was in a depressed mood. "I would have preferred to have got to know this pilot personally. For anyone who can fly like that doesn't deserve to be shot down," he said to his comrades. By now Mölders had shot down his 24th and 25th enemy aircraft.

At 17.15 hours the *Gruppe* was placed on alert and took off. The Messerschmitts came upon a group of enemy fighters. This time Mölders wanted to instruct and guide his inexperienced young pilots in the best way to attack the enemy. He stayed back, keeping their tails clear and directing them by radio. "Move in . . . still closer . . . don't get nervous . . . don't fire yet . . . do you have him in your sights . . . ? Go . . . open fire . . . !" Seconds later a burning enemy machine fell toward the earth trailing a banner of black smoke.

An unconcerned Mölders watched from 800 meters as his charges earned their first laurels. Suddenly there was a loud banging and crashing as bullets struck his cockpit. Hit! To his horror he found that his speed had fallen drastically, the throttle lever had been shot away and the aircraft was incapable of maneuvering. He looked about frantically for the enemy but saw none.

Mölders looked down. Should he try for a forced landing? He held out very little hope that his aircraft would glide that long. Furthermore he was over enemy territory, 60 kilometers behind the front in the vicinity of Compiègne. He had only one chance: get out of the aircraft! Far below French soldiers stood and stared at the white mushroom of his parachute as it slowly descended toward the ground.

Mölders had no notion of giving up. As soon as he had landed and released his parachute he ran away. The French opened fire, but failed to hit him. Finally, however, they caught him. An officer took his Knight's Cross and other valuables and led him away to be interrogated. Along the way the soldiers tore off the captive's shirt and struck him in the face. The French officer did not intervene until Mölders asked for protection from further abuse.

After a short drive in a car Mölders was brought before Colonel Dessous of the French Army. The officer helped the bloodied German wash up and returned his Knight's Cross and other valuables. Over a glass of red wine he apologized for the way his countrymen had behaved. And Mölders, who held fairness above all else, accepted.

In the unit war diary Colonel Bassous noted the following concerning the parachute landing by *Hauptmann* Mölders:

> "Parachuted from an aircraft on June 5, near Chateau Blincourt, which is under the command of Commandant Bassous, commander of the 195th.
>
> R.A.L.T. This young officer's behavior is exemplary.
>
> Found in his papers was the Iron Cross with a congratulatory message from his fellow fliers. It is my responsibility to return to him his decorations and the personal letter."

Colonel Bassous saw in *Hauptmann* Mölders the ideal of a chivalrous officer, an example for all young men no matter to which nation they belonged. Colonel Bassous and Werner Mölders stayed in touch even after the German was released from the officer camp at Montferrat near Toulouse and returned to his comrades. The friendship-comradeship between the two families continues to the present day, even though both officers have been dead for many years.

Mölders' ascent was swift. Ambition and skill balanced each another. On July 19, 1940 he was promoted to *Major* and assumed command of the *Geschwader*. Flying from bases on the English Channel, Mölders had the opportunity to prove that he was in fact a master of aerial combat. Now his opponents were the fast and maneuverable Spitfires and Hurricanes flown by the courageous pilots of the RAF.

On his very first mission over England Mölders shot down a Spitfire but was himself wounded in the knee by a bullet fragment. He was lucky, and instead of coming down in the Channel was able to nurse his shot-up aircraft back to base.

Four weeks later, just as the Battle of Britain was beginning, Mölders was awarded the Golden Flying Badge with

Diamonds. He and his men fought against British Spitfires, Bristol Blenheims and the barrage balloons which guarded Britain's port cities and London. Victory followed victory for the *Geschwaderkommodore*. Daily the newspapers reported on the competition between the three aces: Mölders, Galland and Wick. *Oberleutnant* Wick, a former student of Mölders', flew with JG 2 *Richthofen* and very quickly developed into a top-ranking ace. On September 21 Mölders reported his 40th kill.

The men at the airfield loudspeakers forgot about their soup, when one day the Wehrmacht communique announced: "Today in the Reich Chancellery, the Führer and Supreme Commander of the Armed Forces personally presented the Luftwaffe's most successful fighter pilot, *Major* Mölders, with the Knight's Cross of the Iron Cross with Oak Leaves, which was awarded him following his fortieth air victory."

As said, the men forgot to eat their soup – after all their *Kommodore* had been among them only a few minutes earlier. They had just seen Mölders on the airfield! None of them knew anything about it. And while they thought about the bulletin and its significance, their *Kommodore* was already on his way to Berlin, where he landed and was received by Hitler exactly one hour after the reading of the Wehrmacht communique. What the men didn't know was that Mölders – wanting no fanfare – had slipped away quietly. When he returned,he found that his officers had hung the text of the congratulatory telegram over the mess entrance in large letters on a transparency: "In grateful acknowledgement of your heroic actions for the future of our people, I award you, as the second officer of the German Armed Forces, the Knight's Cross of the Iron Cross with Oak Leaves on the occasion of your fortieth air victory."

"... as second officer of the German Armed Forces ..." The first was *General* Dietl, commander of the mountain infantry, who had been decorated for his personal actions, bravery and command skills in the battle for possession of Narvik. And now Mölders! At this point his *Geschwader* was the most successful in the Luftwaffe. He was thus not just an individual success, in which case one could have assumed that it was just a matter of the *Kommodore* assuring himself the first opportunity to fire before all others. No, Mölders and his men pursued the enemy after their own methods, and he had come away the victor on forty occasions.

But who was to be the next wearer of the Oak Leaves? Who would be next to reach 40 victories? Then, four days later, the radio announced that Adolf Galland had shot down his fortieth enemy aircraft and that he was becoming the third member of the armed forces to be awarded the Oak Leaves.

This is how it was: Galland was competing with Mölders, who at that moment was Göring's guest in the Rominten Heath where he shot a magnificent stag. When he heard of Galland's fortieth he flew back straight away, climbed into his aircraft, took off and shot down his 41st enemy aircraft. When he landed, his technical officer, *Oberleutnant* Claus, greeted him with the words: "Well that was a good beginning."

It was a good beginning. In November Mölders became an *Oberstleutnant*, his total of downed enemy aircraft climbed, and Hermann Göring, Commander-in-Chief of the Luftwaffe, decided to appoint the young officer to the post of "Chief of Fighters." But Mölders declined when they first spoke of the matter. "There's still time, *Herr Reichsmarschall*. I would like to stay with my Geschwader for the time being. The boys still need me."

Werner Mölders was one of those pilots who participated in aerial combat with the enthusiasm of a competitor in a sporting event. His performance as a pilot corresponded to his will to give his all. On June 21, 1941 his adjutant told him: "Yesterday Galland became the first German soldier to receive the Swords." Two days later the Wehrmacht communique announced that, following his 72nd victory, *Oberstleutnant* Mölders had become the second German soldier to be awarded the Knight's Cross with Oak Leaves and Swords.

That was one day after the start of Operation "Barbarossa," the hardest and most costly campaign fought by the German Armed Forces in the Second World War. At that time no one knew or suspected that it would be so. Not even Mölders. His orders: "Destroy the Soviet fighter and bomber fleet in the first assault."

When the code-word for the attack was issued in the early morning hours of June 22, 1941, Mölders led his men over the demarcation line, which had been drawn on Polish soil by the German and Soviet authorities. The enemy air force was taken by surprise. It defended desperately against the German fighters which attacked the Soviet airfields, destroying parked aircraft and shooting down hundreds in the air. The great success enjoyed by Mölders' *Geschwader* spoke for the quality of his pilots as fliers and fighters. All told they shot down 96 enemy aircraft in a single day! Eleven of these were credited to Mölders. The Soviets so feared him that they instructed their fighters to avoid all combat with JG 51. The effort was in vain.

On July 15 Mölders shot down his 98th through 101st enemy aircraft. One hundred aircraft shot down, destroyed! Mölders had surpassed the achievements of von Richthofen, Boelcke, Immelmann and Udet. *Oberstleutnant* Mölders had become the first fighter pilot in the world to shoot down 100 enemy aircraft. With this feat came a promotion to *Oberst* and the awarding of the Diamonds. Mölders received the decoration the same day he shot down his 100th, becoming the first German soldier to be so decorated.

A few days later Hitler asked him if he had a personal request. Mölders thought, and after a short pause said, "I ask, *mein Führer*, that you end the persecution and defamation of the Bishop of Münster. Some time ago I wrote a letter to the *Reichsmarschall* and later requested during an audience that Graf Galen not be persecuted on account of his criticisms. The *Reichsmarschall* promised me his support. But I know that attacks against leaders of the church continue from certain sides. It is my wish, *mein Führer*, that this be prevented."

Göring, who was standing behind Hitler, could scarcely conceal his agitation. More than anything he would liked to have sunk into the floor, and the other generals present felt the same. But – and this was their greatest concern – how would Hitler react? Hitler gazed at the young *Oberst*. The answer came slowly and calmly: "You may rest assured that the Bishop of Münster will remain unmolested. I have heard about the excesses of some party offices. These people have been called to account."

There followed a brief pause, after which Hitler said, "But I have also heard about the bishop's pastoral letters. His business is providing spiritual comfort. But it's not good when a man like Graf Galen meddles in the politics of the Reich. Nevertheless I have understanding for the bishop." Hitler smiled as he continued. "And . . . there is something else I would like to say, my dear Mölders. I know that I can rely on you and your men. You are the bravest soldier the Wehrmacht has. I am proud of you."

Mölders took his leave. Scarcely had he closed the door when he was approached by Göring. "You know Mölders, you shouldn't be allowed to do that to me. You of all people whining about something to the Führer. The Führer has other worries now, as if he could concern himself about such trivialities, which are certainly exaggerated anyway."

Mölders' face narrowed. "I don't find it a triviality when threatening letters are sent to the house of the Bishop of Münster, and when the Gestapo interrupts services and questions churchgoers. I also know that they are making life difficult for other religious figures. Or is it not true that a number of clergymen of both denominations are being held in prison?"

"Göring struggled to retain his composure. "Mölders," he said softly, trying to smooth things over, "What you are doing is nonsense. Most probably you were misinformed. I say to you once again: nothing is happening to the churches. Nothing at all. And you can depend on that."

But Mölders remained skeptical. Then Göring impulsively stuck out his hand. "Here, you have my word. The word of the *Reichsmarschall!*"

What was Mölders to do? He was too trusting and decent to doubt the word of the Reichsmarschall. Taking Göring at his word, he shook hands. "Perhaps I see things too negatively," he said. "For I would consider it a crime if what they told me were true. As well it would be totally unnecessary for the leadership of the Reich." Like the pilot Werner Mölders, the devout Christian Werner Mölders remained a loyal soldier. Nothing could have made him change his mind, nothing could take away his belief in victory. He believed like millions of others. But he also couldn't know that there was a file with his name on it in the Reich Central Security Office.

The "Mölders Case" was extremely embarrassing to *SS-Obergruppenführer* Ernst Kaltenbrunner, this as a result of his protest against an action which was supposed to be directed at Mölders. Kaltenbrunner inveighed against the zealous and narrow-minded "lowbrows" in his department, who were eager to earn their spurs by trying to prove that the most popular, most successful and most highly-decorated German soldier was "a danger to the state." The Gestapo accused Mölders of intervening on behalf of Bishop Graf Galen and openly protesting against the state's interference in church affairs. Once the "Mölders File" had passed through the office of *Reichsführer-SS* Himmler, there was nothing to stop Hitler from learning about it. "I don't want the churches harassed," Hitler said to Bormann, the actual wire-puller in the battle against the clergy. "A clarification and separation of state and church will take place after the war. But until then I want peace. If Mölders has heard of infringements and opposes them, I can only respect him for it. He is a devout Christian, a guileless man. Keep your fingers off this decent soldier!"

Hitler turned and left the room quickly. Soon afterward Mölders was appointed Inspector of Fighters on his order. This was much to Mölders' regret, as he was happiest with his *Geschwader*. But he saw the reason for the move. With 115 victories to his credit he took leave of his friends.

Mölders' new duties included visiting the air fleets on the Eastern Front and listening to the wants and suggestions of their commanders. After only a few days in his new position, Mölders, the patient listener and expert, saw the bottlenecks and deplorable state of affairs in which the Luftwaffe and German industry found themselves. He worried about all that he had heard, experienced and seen. And all of a sudden he realized that the war in Russia would be no blitzkrieg campaign as he had initially believed. The losses suffered by the units disturbed him, and the shaky supply situation, which in no way corresponded to the needs of the front, seemed to be the key to all evils. After drawing up the first balance sheet, he knew that it was vitally important that he, the young *Oberst*, succeed in his mission, lest Germany's success in Russia be threatened.

November 21 brought snow and an unexpected cold snap to the entire Eastern Front. So too near Simferopol, where Mölders had established temporary headquarters in order to carry out his inspections in the southern sector of the Eastern Front.

The adjutant stepped into the room without knocking and passed Mölders, who saw the grim face of the young officer, a teletype message: "Chief Air Inspector General Udet killed in accident while testing new machines. State funeral November 24. Führer and Reichsmarschall expecting you."

Without waiting for his superior's reaction, the adjutant informed him that the air fleet chief had put a Heinkel He 111 at his disposal for the flight to Berlin. For a moment Mölders stared dumbstruck at the piece of paper in his hands. Now Udet too, he thought.

The next morning Mölders drove to Kherson, where the aircraft was waiting for him. They flew to Lvov. The following day the He 111, now loaded with additional mail and packages, continued on its way. Aboard the aircraft with Mölders were a young *Major* and an *Oberstleutnant*. The aircraft was piloted by the experienced *Oberleutnant* Georg Kolbe, who still wore the uniform of an *Oberfeldwebel*. Kolbe, who had only recently been promoted (skipping over the rank of *Leutnant*), was to receive his officer's kit in Berlin. Before takeoff from Lvov airport the meteorologist reported: "Visibility poor." But Mölders insisted they continue. The He 111's pilot was unable to get on top of cloud. The aircraft droned on through one cloud bank after another. The pilot refused to take responsibility for continuing and insisted they reverse course. But Mölders ordered: "You will fly on. I must be in Berlin on time."

If things weren't already bad enough, one of the aircraft's two engines now failed. "Head for the nearest airfield," ordered Mölders.

"I'm just over Schmiedefeld . . . near Breslau," responded the pilot.

Then it happened. It was eleven thirty. A dull thump shook the earth. The workers in the Martin Quander poultry farm at Breslau 32, Flughafenstrasse 132, were startled. A supervisor flung open the door and waved. "Come on, out – there's a

German aircraft outside! Come quickly!"

Meanwhile the farm's wheelwright ran to the aircraft and tried to free the occupants from the wreckage. But help came too late. A man in the uniform of an *Oberstleutnant* lay dead on the ground. Beside him lay an *Oberst*. He wore a Luftwaffe uniform and was highly decorated. The wheelwright paused. He knew this officer, he had once seen his face. Once? No, a hundred times! Then the name came to him. "Mölders! Mölders is lying here!" he shouted. The other workers hurried to the scene and stared at the two dead men. *Oberst* Mölders' neck was broken.

The pilot, *Oberleutnant* Kolbe, lay in the shattered machine, with injuries to his arms and legs. He screamed in pain as the workers lifted him from the aircraft. Kolbe died on the way to hospital. Both Mölders' adjutant and the radio operator, who lay whimpering on the grass, survived. The latter had jumped from the plunging aircraft at an altitude of thirty meters. He escaped with a broken arm and several bruises. What had happened?

With one engine dead, the He 111 flew toward Schmiedefeld airport, which was shrouded in fog. The pilot had established contact with the ground station. As he turned onto final approach ground control advised him not to land. But the machine had already lost too much height and speed. The pilot tried to climb the aircraft, but then the second engine failed. The He 111 stalled, fell like a stone and crashed to earth. The fuselage broke in two aft of the cockpit.

A simple memorial plate on the ground floor of the Martin Quander poultry farm commemorated the death of the first wearer of the Diamonds. After Soviet forces overran Silesia, Poles removed the plate and threw it into a nearby bog. Later the German inhabitants recovered the plate and buried it. They wanted to extinguish all memories of the previous years. But *Oberst* Werner Mölders is part of the history of the last war. He has not been forgotten. Not only was he an outstanding soldier, but an exemplary man as well. A gentleman in uniform.

CHAPTER II

GENERALLEUTNANT ADOLF GALLAND

T he black cigar and the black moustache are his trade marks. There is scarcely a photo that shows him with out one; he is Adolf Galland, one of the most photo graphed and filmed soldiers of the last world war. At the age of twenty-nine he became Inspector of Fighters, and at thirty the youngest General in the German armed forces.

Adolf Galland belonged to that group of soldiers who viewed aerial combat from the perspective of the classical du-elist. His concept of the air war was significantly influenced by his great respect for the World War pilots Richthofen, Immelmann and Boelcke. The duel, not killing or destroying, remained the decisive factor for this outstanding flier, fighter and tactician.

Flying was his greatest passion. Adolf Galland was supposed to take up a "respectable" occupation, as his father, the goods director for the Count of Westerholt auf Westerholt, wished, but the young Galland got his way. He seemed to have been born with this ability to get his own way: Adolf Galland's ancestors were Huguenots and he was born in Westerholt near Gelsenkirchen-Buer. French and Westphalian characteristics gave him the flair of the charmer with a touch of stubbornness. He learned to see the world from above in a glider. The impressions he gained through gliding reinforced his desire to pursue a career as a pilot. Small wonder then that written on his school leaving certificate were the words: "Galland wants to become a pilot!"

At that time, in 1932, there were eight million unemployed in Germany. Only the lucky young ones obtained an apprenticeship. In most cases the parents had to make monthly payments as well. And Galland wanted to become a pilot! In order to do so he had to graduate from the Civil Aviation School in Braunschweig. He applied for admission, even though he knew that he was only one of about 4,000 applicants. Eighteen passed the admission test. Adolf Galland was one of them.

After training in gliders came powered flight and aerobatics training "with all the trimmings." Then, in 1933, Galland received the opportunity to train as a fighter pilot in Italy, under the strictest secrecy of course. For under the terms of the Versailles Treaty Germany was not permitted to have an air force in addition to its 100,000-man army.

After his Italian excursion Galland joined Deutsche Lufthansa as a volunteer pilot. Afterward he was urged to become an officer. In February 1934 he joined the 10th Infantry Regiment in Dresden as a recruit and by the and of the year, after graduating from officer candidate school, he had been made a *Leutnant*, effective October 1, 1934.

Germany soon began creating the Luftwaffe, secretly at first. Well-trained pilots were already available to fly the relatively modern aircraft. In March 1935 Adolf Galland was transferred to I *Gruppe* of *Jagdgeschwader* 2 *Richthofen*, which was based in Döberitz. In the hangars sat the new He 51 fighters. For Galland this was the fulfillment of a dream. Now he could fly, fly, fly. But in October 1935 he crashed during aerobatics training. His nose was deformed and the vision in one eye was significantly impaired. It was no wonder that the medical officer declared: "Galland, you are no longer fit to fly."

Had all his efforts been in vain? Galland sought advice from his older comrades. Finally his commanding officer informed the medical officer that the young man could fly. And so Galland was once more allowed to sit at the controls of an aircraft.

A year later, 1936, civil war in Spain. The Iberian Peninsula became a testing ground for the great powers. The Soviet Union assisted the Republicans, socialists and communists who, although in the minority, soon gained power in large areas of

Spain. Germany and Italy backed the young General Franco. From that point on it was a race between white and red.

German officers in Spain examined the situation there in great secrecy. Then the cards were laid upon the table. The *Legion Condor* fought in Spain for Franco. *Oberleutnant* Adolf Galland was there. As leader of the "Mickey Mouse" *Staffel*, he achieved outstanding success. After 15 months in Spain he was relieved by Werner Mölders. Following the victorious conclusion of the civil war Göring awarded him, along with Mölders, Harder, Schellmann, Lützow, Oesau, Balthasar and Harlinghausen, the Spanish Cross in Gold with Diamonds. Earlier Galland had received the *Madalla de la Campaña* from Franco.

During the war against Poland in 1939 Galland was able to make good use of the experience he had gained in Spain. He flew fifty missions with his *Staffel*, primarily in the Kutno, Warsaw and Modlin areas.

War against France. Adolf Galland scored his first three aerial victories on May 12, 1940. At that time he had no idea that this was the beginning of a rapid rise to success. In short order he increased his total to seven kills. Galland received the Iron Cross, First Class from *Generaloberst* Milch in recognition of his success.

It wasn't long before Galland suddenly found himself facing an enemy whose aircraft and flying skills were on a par with those of the Germans: the Royal Air Force and its Spitfires and Hurricanes. On May 29, 1940 Galland shot down a Spitfire over Dunkirk. He will never forget this combat, for his opponent was a pilot who forced Galland to call upon all his skill. Finally the enemy aircraft went down in flames. Galland hoped that the enemy pilot would escape by parachute, but nothing happened. The Spitfire crashed and exploded. Galland performed a loop over the crash site, a salute to his fallen foe.

Galland was unexpectedly transferred to *Jagdgeschwader* 26 Schlageter. There he assumed command of III *Gruppe*. Galland introduced himself in fine fashion. On June 14, the day he assumed command, he shot down two Morane fighters. Combats against ten and twenty enemy machines were the order of the day, and the French as well as the British began to fear Adolf Galland.

On July 18, 1940 Galland was promoted from the ranks to *Major* and on July 29, at the age of twenty-eight, he received the Knight's Cross in recognition of his seventeen kills.

In spite of the success enjoyed by the German fighters, which was surely trumpeted too loudly to the public, Göring was angry over the fighter arm's performance to date in escorting the bombers. During a meeting with Galland and Mölders at Karinhall, when he presented them with the Golden Pilot's Badge with Diamonds, Göring urged the two young officers to instill more vigour into fighter operations. He declared candidly that more youth had to be brought to leadership positions and informed Galland and Mölders that he intended to appoint each of them to command a *Geschwader*. Galland expressed a wish to be allowed to remain with his *Gruppe* but Göring refused.

On September 24, a few days after being named *Kommodore* of JG 26, Galland achieved his 40th victory. Afterward he was awarded the Knight's Cross with Oak Leaves, becoming the third member of the German armed forces to receive the decoration.

Galland's *Geschwader* was still on the Channel Coast in 1941. Late on the afternoon of May 10 Göring called Galland and ordered him to take off at once with the entire *Geschwader*. Galland couldn't comprehend the reason for the order. After telling the *Reichsmarschall* that no inbound enemy aircraft had been reported, he asked the reason for the order. An excited Göring stated: "This time you're to prevent an aircraft from flying out. The Führer's deputy has gone mad and is flying to England in a Bf 110. He absolutely must be brought down!"

The *Kommodore* assessed the situation and came to the decision that he could not give the order to take off, as it was already too late and there were too many German night fighters – most of them Bf 110s – in the air. And who could tell which machine was being flown by Rudolf Hess? Furthermore Galland considered the undertaking senseless, for he didn't believe that Hess would reach England unscathed. And lastly the English air defenses were extremely watchful.

But contrary to expectations Hess succeeded. On arriving over his objective in Scotland he bailed out. Galland wrote in his book *Die Ersten und die Letzten*: "Whatever reasons lay behind the flight – at the last moment someone had attempted to pull the emergency brake on a train racing down the wrong track."

June 21, 1941, the day he received the Swords, nearly marked the end of Galland's career. He shot down two Blenheim bombers within four minutes and was forced to crash-land his fighter with a dead engine. That same afternoon, after shooting down his 70th enemy aircraft, Galland was wounded. Hit hard, Galland's Bf 109 caught fire at an altitude of 6,000 meters.

Get out! he told himself. But push and strain as he might against the cockpit hood, it refused to budge. Impacting bullets had jammed the hood. The heat and flames made it almost impossible to breathe. Meanwhile the Bf 109 fell earthward and began to break up. And Galland was still stuck fast.

For the first time he felt panicky fear. But seconds later the thought of being burned alive gave him superhuman strength. Faced with the prospect of a horrible death, he once again strained against the cockpit hood – and it gave way. Galland jumped clear, or at least he tried to. There was a strange, sharp jolt, and he saw that he was hung up on the last third of the cockpit canopy.

The Messerschmitt, which by now was ablaze, fell toward the earth with Galland. Any chance of escaping with his life appeared to be gone. But miraculously the trapped parachute freed itself and he fell away from the spinning machine like a stone. Galland wanted to pull the rip cord quickly; he had practiced it countless times. But in his excitement he mistakenly grasped the quick-release handle. He had already released the safety catch when, to his horror, he realized that instead of saving himself he had almost caused his own death. Galland almost fainted from fear, and he was still at 5,000 meters. He fell and fell, racing toward the earth. The speed became ever greater, more heart-stopping. Another pull and he would have fallen to earth without a parachute. However his oft-quoted flyer's luck was with him – he landed safely.

The English had many excellent fighter pilots, but one stood out from the ranks of outstanding, fearless pilots and his name was well known to the German Luftwaffe: Wing Commander Douglas Bader.

The man with the German-sounding name was a sensation, for he flew with two artificial legs. Both of his legs had been smashed below the knee in a flying accident in 1931. From that day on Bader was determined to fly again. For he supported the point of view that the heart was the decisive factor for a fighter pilot, then the legs.

One day the telephone rang in Galland's command post in France. A breathless *Gruppenkommandeur* informed him that British Wing Commander Douglas Bader had been shot down in the most recent engagement. He went on to say that Bader had come down by parachute and been captured. Galland considered the matter briefly and then sent a staff officer with his car to the hospital and invited the astonished Wing Commander to tea in the *Jagdgeschwader's* headquarters.

Immediately after his capture Bader had asked: "Hopefully I wasn't shot down by an LAC?" No one knew for sure. Certainly it was no *Obergefreiter* (LAC). It was more likely that it had been an *Unteroffizier* (sergeant-pilot), one of those who had earned reputations as outstanding fighter pilots and who flew no worse than the best pilots of the officer corps. But even this NCO wouldn't have been able to console Bader over his defeat. And so Galland and his officers decided to select an *Oberleutnant* to present to the British officer, who very much wished to meet the man who had bested him. The *Oberleutnant* felt rather uncomfortable when he faced the Wing Commander. "I congratulate you . . ." was all that the vanquished pilot had to say.

As he took his leave Bader asked one more favor: "Might I ask you, Kommodore Galland, to have my two replacement prostheses sent from England?" At first Galland thought it was a trick, but the Englishman's face showed that he was bitterly serious. "I'll see what can be done, Commander. First I will have to speak with my superior," answered Galland. As soon as Bader had left, Galland got in touch with Göring. The *Reichsmarschall* agreed enthusiastically: "We will help the Englishman. That's the rule of fairness. You know, Galland, it was the same with us in the First World War. Exactly the same."

Galland then ordered contact made with the British using the international air-sea rescue frequency. At first the English were suspicious. But when they were assured that Bader was well, but that he couldn't walk without the two leg prostheses, which were in his apartment, they agreed to the plan to deliver the artificial legs.

Bader also knew how to make use of the two prostheses which had been repaired by German mechanics, for he used them in an escape attempt. He escaped out a hospital window using bed sheets knotted together, but he didn't get far.

Years later as a prisoner of war, Galland was astonished to see Douglas Bader again. The Wing Commander greeted Galland with a box of good cigars and saw to it that his fair German opponent had it no worse than he had once had when the roles were reversed.

There wasn't a newspaper, illustrated magazine newsreel that hadn't featured pictures of Galland. This dashing and capable officer, who had shot down 21 Spitfires, three Blenheims and one Hurricane in the summer of 1941, had a reputation of being fair and chivalrous, even in a life and death struggle. One day Göring asked him what he would think of an order to shoot English pilots in their parachutes.

Galland: "I would consider it murder, *Herr Reichsmarschall*! I would never carry out this order, would not pass it on and would oppose it with every means."

Göring was satisfied: "That's exactly the answer I expected from you. It's the same as in the First World War. We would never have carried out such an order."

On November 22, 1941 *Oberst* Werner Mölders, the first *General der Jagdflieger*, was killed in a flying accident near Breslau. Adolf Galland, who had meanwhile been promoted to the rank of *Oberstleutnant*, stood guard at the open grave. He thought of what the optimistic Mölders had said at the beginning of the war against the Soviet Union: "We'll soon have it (the USSR) too."

Then he recalled Göring's words: "First Mölders comes with his *Geschwader* to the front. The Russians have superior numbers, but they can't fly. One shoots down the unit leader and then the illiterates don't know what to do. When Mölders has done enough you'll come, Galland, and take care of the rest."

Galland thought about these things at the open grave of his friend. After the burial ceremonies the *Reichsmarschall* waved the *Oberstleutnant* to him and appointed him Mölder's successor as *General der Jagdflieger*.

What might the twenty-nine-year-old *Oberstleutnant*'s thoughts have been when he was handed this difficult and responsible post? At twenty nine years of age the *"General der Jagdflieger"*, that meant responsibility for the entire fighter arm, for the technology, the logistics, technical development, production, for the replacement of fallen or wounded unit leaders, for the overall situation. And all this at a time when the campaign against the Soviet Union was not unfolding as the German command had envisaged. The Russian winter had revealed for the first time the weaknesses and shortcomings of the German Wehrmacht and its command. And for the first time the casualty lists were endlessly long. The shock struck the German command to the core.

For Galland, who had previously commanded a *Geschwader*, it was a matter of "changing gears." he had to dive, "head-first" as it were, from the combat-tactical field into the strategy of aerial warfare. At the age of twenty-nine! Technically he was subordinate to the Luftwaffe Chief-of-Staff, while disciplinarily he was under the direct command of the Luftwaffe Commander-in-Chief (Göring). He therefore had only two direct superiors: Göring and Jeschonnek.

For the new *General der Jagdflieger* Adolf Galland it was no easy task to take his leave of his *Geschwader*. A close comradeship had been formed in times good and bad. Galland told Göring this. The *Reichsmarschall* understood, but his decision stood. Galland did succeed in extracting a promise from the *Reichsmarschall* to be present for his departure from the *Geschwader*.

On December 5 Göring came to Abbeville to lay a wreath at the grave of his nephew, who had been killed in aerial combat while flying with Galland's *Geschwader*. He used the opportunity to announce in Hitler's name Galland's promotion to *Oberst*. Afterward they drove to Audembert, where the *Geschwader* was on parade to bid farewell to Galland. A difficult, responsible task now awaited him as *General der Jagdflieger*. It was a task which Galland was to master.

Galland's office was located in Berlin. He assembled a staff of proven and trusted compatriots to help him. Galland established his command post in Goldap, near Hitler's and Göring's headquarters. His superiors held the view that his most urgent task was the rapid defeat of the Soviets. To this end the Luftwaffe was to be employed in concentration. In the meantime, however, the first advance detachments of the American air force had arrived in England. Roosevelt hadn't waited long. Preparations were already being made for the bomber offensive – and Galland sensed what lay in store for him.

It came as a surprise when, on February 28, 1942, the young *Oberst* was awarded the Diamonds following 94 victories. Mölders hadn't received the award until after his "hundredth", but Hitler observed that Galland's 94, which had been achieved exclusively in the West, "weighed heavier." It was more likely, however, that he wanted to underline the significance of Galland's new position.

The baptism of fire came sooner than expected. In January, under conditions of the greatest secrecy, Galland was given the task of providing air cover for Operation "*Donnerkeil*." The battle cruisers "Scharnhorst" and "Gneisenau" and the heavy cruiser "Prinz Eugen", which were at anchor in Brest Harbor, were to be moved. So far their mission had been to tie up the Royal Navy. In doing so they relieved the pressure on German-Italian shipping traffic in the Mediterranean and indirectly eased Rommel's difficult situation in Africa.

The basis for the operation was Hitler's fear that his plan for 1942, to destroy the Soviet forces once and for all, was being threatened: deliveries of Anglo-American aid to the Soviet Union would strengthen their resistance. As well, he was convinced of a new British-Scandinavian-Soviet offensive on the northern flank. Information from the intelligence service had led him to this conclusion. For this reason he demanded the transfer of the three warships from Brest into Scandinavian waters. The commanders of the *Kriegsmarine* were of a different view. Luftwaffe Chief-of-Staff Jeschonnek also disagreed. But Hitler stuck to his decision.

This operation gave Galland an opportunity to display his organizational talents. Control of the fighter umbrella was precise. Working closely with the *Kriegsmarine* posts responsible for the breakthrough and the captains of the warships involved, Galland presented his plan for Operation "Jagdschutz" at a major situation briefing. Hitler was impressed, and privately asked Galland if he believed the operation would succeed, especially since everything depended on the aerial umbrella over the warships. Galland did not hesitate long. "Everything depends on how much time the English will have to mobilize the Royal Air Force against the task force. We need total surprise and luck as well. My fighters will give their utmost if they know what's at stake."

Hitler once again swore the participants in the briefing to strict secrecy. Galland assembled the necessary units. He knew that the operation represented a great risk. But the task also excited him, the opportunity for him and his fighters to play a decisive role in an operation which demanded the utmost of everyone. Galland came through his baptism of fire as *General der Jagdflieger* with flying colors. Minutely-detailed plans were worked out and confirmed with the *Kriegsmarine*, and then were weighed, assessed, rejected and recalculated. A close eye was kept on the weather situation. Fighter operations were worked out on the drawing board, almost to the point of using a stopwatch.

In spite of the strict secrecy measures, the Allied intelligence service was aware that something special was going on in Brest. Operation "Donnerkeil" was supposed to get under way during the night of February 11/12. Galland now had 252 machines at his disposal. What had Hitler said: "Everything depends on the air umbrella . . ."

The air umbrella functioned perfectly.

The Royal Air Force was on alert, but no one on the island believed a report from a British reconnaissance aircraft that a large fleet had been sighted sailing up the Channel at high speed. They didn't credit the German *Kriegsmarine* with that much cheek and daring. Not since 1690 had the English experienced enemy warships sailing through "their" Channel. Now confronted with the facts, the British tried to prevent the German breakthrough with all the means at their disposal. The Channel was thick with mines; nevertheless the ships succeeded in breaking through – albeit with some mine damage. The Royal Air Force threw itself desperately at the cruisers. But Galland's fighters were ready. On February 13 the Wehrmacht communique reported: "During the air and sea battle in the Channel area on February 12, 1942, a British destroyer was damaged and set on fire. After breaking through the channel narrows between Calais and Dover, German naval forces under the command of Vice Admiral Ciliax reached their destination ports, losing only one picket boat. 49 British aircraft were shot down. The air units of *Generalfeldmarschall* Sperrle, under the command of *General* Coeler (bomber and reconnaissance) and *Oberst* Galland (day and night fighters), especially distinguished themselves."

It was not until the operation was fully over that the public learned the true extent of the undertaking. The tactical success had been extraordinarily great, losses remained extremely low. The number of downed British aircraft climbed to over 60. The moral shock had a paralyzing effect on the Allies. The performance of the young "*General der Jagdflieger*" impressed Hitler. On November 19, 1942 he promoted Adolf Galland to the rank of *Generalmajor*. A sensational career had reached its apex. At thirty years of age Adolf Galland was the youngest general in the German Armed Forces!

As he wrote in his book, the responsibility of his position was a heavy burden. It was inevitable that disputes arose between the young general and Göring. The *Reichsmarschall* unfairly reproached Galland harshly for the alleged "failure of the fighters", which were unable to increase their successes against an increasingly powerful enemy.

Galland never held back in the course of the frequent verbal confrontations. He spoke his mind whether it suited Göring or not. Since as *General der Jagdflieger* he had no direct command authority, he was unable to exert any direct influence on important operational or organizational decisions. Naturally he was heard out in all these decisions – and he used the opportunities to express his opinions and views. In many cases his suggestions and advice were accepted. As said, it was not easy for the young general to get his way in a circle which consisted largely of more senior "colleagues."

In autumn 1942 Galland was charged by Jeschonnek with the improvising of night fighter operations on the Eastern Front, in order to counter the nocturnal supplying by air of Soviet partisans. In the meantime the so-called *Reichsverteidigung* (Reich Defense) was formed. Nevertheless Galland's warnings of expected bombing attacks were dismissed out of hand by Göring.

The allied strategy for the defeat of Germany was clear: the German armaments industry was to be destroyed from the air. When this produced no decisive success, the Allies began destroying German cities. Millions of tonnes of bombs were dropped on Germany. Armadas of bombers, consisting of 800 to 1,200 machines, flew into German airspace day and night. The German fighters were powerless against this tremendous armada of heavily-armed Flying Fortresses and their escort fighters. In spite of this they threw themselves against the bomber fleets unconditionally and without regard for themselves. A grinding battle against windmill wings had begun.

The German fighter arm was to achieve one more triumphant success. On August 17, 1943 the Americans lost sixty four-engined bombers in an attack on Schweinfurt. In spite of these heavy losses they repeated the attack on October 14. Galland assembled 300 day fighters and 40 twin-engined fighters to intercept the 226 Flying Fortresses. This time the German fighters shot down 61 bombers and damaged 140. This success was not to be repeated, for after this defeat the bomber units only flew with heavy fighter cover.

Adolf Galland expressed his concerns to his superiors whenever the opportunity arose. In April 1943 he flew the prototype of the new Me 262, the world's first jet-powered fighter. Galland was enthusiastic. He told Göring that every *Jagdgeschwader* should be equipped with the aircraft. But Göring had other ideas: "The Führer intends to employ the Me 262 as a Blitzbomber over England and later over the invasion coast." What madness! The German command had been presented with an opportunity to reverse Germany's fortunes in the air with this aircraft, as was confirmed by experts from all over the world after the war.

Working with Göring was now unbearable at times. More and more the *Reichsmarschall* was falling out of grace with Hitler. The Luftwaffe's success rate against enemy bombers was low in comparison to its numbers. This annoyed Göring, who raged and rebuked the courageous fighter pilots. In reality they had not failed. That was Göring's excuse and a way of easing his own conscience. During a lively discussion in the officer's mess at Schleissheim airfield, which Göring had ordered all unit leaders to attend, the *Reichsmarschall* lost control and accused the fighter arm of failure and cowardice, even during the Battle of Britain. When he went so far as to accuse the most highly-decorated officers of having obtained their Knight's Crosses by lying, an outraged Galland ripped the decoration from his throat and threw it on the table. Galland: "An icy silence hung over the room. I looked straight into the eyes of the *Reichsmarschall*, who was speechless in the truest sense of the word, ready for anything. But nothing happened. Speaking in a normal voice, Göring quickly concluded his statements. From that day it was more than half a year before I wore my war decorations again."

In January 1945 Galland was relieved from his position as *General der Jagdflieger*. Finally Göring ordered him to form a fighter unit equipped with jet fighters. Galland brought in old friends and successful fighter pilots to join the experimental unit. It flew the famous Me 262, an aircraft which made a name for itself during the final months of the war, inflicting considerable losses on the enemy. Flying the Me 262, of which he said, "Building this machine at the beginning of the war could have been decisive for us," Galland fought against the superiority of the Anglo-Americans. In one sortie he destroyed two Marauder bombers with one rocket salvo. The number of victories achieved by the unit was surprisingly high in relation to the number of machines employed. The enemy feared and avoided the Me 262s, aware that they were far inferior in speed and firepower.

In those days, when everything was staked on the last card, the jet-powered Heinkel He 162 *Volksjäger*, or people's fighter, was supposed to enable the Luftwaffe shoot down the enemy bombers. There was a shortage of trained fighter pilots however. To fill the gaps it was proposed that the *Volksjäger* be flown by sixteen- and seventeen-year-old members of the Hitler Youth and by glider pilots. Operating in concert with the *Rammjäger*, they were supposed to force the enemy to cut back his bombing raids. Operations were limited, however, and unsuccessful. The war came to an end.

Adolf Galland was in Bavaria when his meteoric military career was abruptly ended. He had no worries about his future. He wanted to be treated no differently than the millions of other soldiers. But before he surrendered to the Americans he had all the Me 262s put to the torch.

As a prominent fighter pilot, Galland was flown to England by the Americans. He was shocked when one of the interrogating officers introduced himself as an "old acquaintance." The American had been a correspondent in Berlin during the early years of the war when Goebbels had held a press conference at which Galland was the guest of honor. The propaganda machine was running in high gear at that time and the famous German fighter pilot was there to provide a vivid account of his impressions of the air war to the foreign press. Then the young journalist had interviewed Galland the pilot – now he was interrogating Galland the prisoner.

Galland spent two years as a prisoner of war. And during those two years, between interrogations, discussions and exchanges of experiences, the pilot made plans for the future. He could no longer fly in Germany. The country was destroyed, millions of refugees wandered about the cities. A great migration of people from East to West was under way.

When Adolf Galland returned to Germany he tried to build an existence. In early 1948 he received news from Argentina that that nation's air force was interested in his wartime experiences. In November of the same year Galland went to Argentina, where he met many acquaintances, among them the successful bomber pilot Werner Baumbach and Focke-Wulf's famous chief designer Professor Kurt Tank. He concluded an agreement with the Argentine Air Ministry, advising the Argentine Air Force in questions of air defense and training. After six and a half years he returned to Germany. Galland might perhaps have stayed, for he felt very much at ease with that country and its people. But political developments led him to make a different decision.

In the Federal Republic the "climate" had changed. The country was on the verge of forming new armed forces, which of course included an air force. The man in charge of building the armed forces, Theodor Blank, got in touch with Galland, outlined his plans and listened to Galland's ideas. Theodor Blank was soon convinced that Galland should become Inspector of the new Luftwaffe. But this was not to be the case. The planned European Defense Alliance (EVG) foundered at the last minute at the instigation of the French government. And thus the decision was made against Galland. Theodor Blank was later replaced and in 1956 F.J. Strauss became Defense Minister of the Federal Republic of Germany. Strauss named Josef Kammhuber, former commanding general of the Night Fighter Corps, to the post of Luftwaffe Inspector.

Looking back, Galland did not regret the decision. "I couldn't have followed the chosen course. Everything was done much too precipitously, too quickly, without clear guidelines. Concessions to politics, especially the primacy of politics over the building-up of the Luftwaffe, often stood too much in the way." "The Luftwaffe was created without preparing the population psychologically. Lessons from the war no longer counted, desk strategists had the upper hand. Not until Steinhoff, Trautloft, Rall, Panitzki, Krupinski and the other successful fighter pilots gained influence did it get better. But the beginning was not to my taste . . ."

For Adolf Galland the question was: what to do now? The answer was nothing. He had already established contact with the aviation and space industry. He was a partner in a Düsseldorf firm but left after two years and went his own way. Since then he has been an industry advisor and a member of the board of directors of three general aviation concerns – Luftbild, Charterflug, and a significant helicopter operation, which carried out pipeline and high-tension wire patrols and training as well as casualty evacuation in Germany and Africa.

Few officer fliers of the last war enjoy an international profile as high as Galland's. He is among the most prominent in the world, appearing as a guest of honor and speaker at many aeronautical gatherings. He is an honorary member of the exclusive international flying club "The International Order of Characters." In the Federal Republic he is an honored member of the Fighter Pilots Association. He flies his single-engine Beechcraft Bonanza, because, as he says, he has always flown on one engine.

He has changed little: the once dark hair is streaked with grey but the black moustache, the cigar and the youthful laugh are characteristic of the sixty-four year old who once served as a model for millions of young men.

CHAPTER III

OBERST
GORDON M. GOLLOB

March 1975. Kitzbühel courthouse jail, Cell 8. The tourist looked about with great interest. Every thing was as it had been. He leafed through the register of inmates and stopped short when he found his name. Prisoner number 318/1945. There was the list of his personal belongings, from the stool to the Kübelwagen. It was almost thirty years to the day since retired *Oberst* Gordon M. Gollob, then a civilian, had been imprisoned by the American CIC. Thirty years ago! The memory overwhelmed the visitor with the unusual first name, Gordon Mc. A man called Gordon Mc must be something special. He was . . .

The candles had burned down to stumps. The flickering light cast eerie shadows on the walls of the large room. Seated in an armchair was *Reichsmarschall* Hermann Göring, Commander-in-Chief of the German Luftwaffe, master of Karinhall. A young *Oberst* had taken his place opposite him.

"You're late my dear fellow," said Göring, a little short-winded.

"I expected you sooner, we have little time."

The *Reichsmarschall* played with a golden tobacco box which lay before him on the desk.

"I couldn't come any sooner, *Herr Reichsmarschall*", replied the visitor. "These constant air raid alerts! The devil seems to be loose again." He had struck Göring's most sensitive spot, as the *Reichsmarschall* had once sworn on his name that no enemy aircraft would appear over the Reich. Now this was something he would just as soon have forgotten, for almost all the aircraft in Germany's skies now belonged to the Allies. Things were going badly for the Reich in those January days in 1945.

Göring got up. He supported himself with his fists on the surface of the heavy desk and looked seriously at the man opposite him. "I've had you called here, because you're to take on a new job. The Luftwaffe isn't finished yet, it can't be. Gollob, you must help me. I therefore appoint you *General der Jagdflieger*, to take effect immediately!" Impulsively he extended his hand to the *Oberst*, who had likewise stood up. "You will do it! It must be done! It doesn't bear thinking about if . . ."

He said nothing more. But the *Oberst* knew without further words that the situation was extremely threatening: the Soviet armies were advancing on Silesia, the Americans were on German territory, and allied air forces ruled the skies. And he, *Oberst* Gordon M. Gollob, was supposed to help? "I will do my best, *Herr Reichsmarschall*."

"I know that. Now sit down my dear Gollob. I would like to speak with you a little more." Göring smiled and gazed at the situation map with an empty look. Suddenly, without raising his eyes from the map, he asked, "Tell me, how did you come by your English first name, Gordon? I've long wanted to ask you about it. I've also heard that you're very musical and play several instruments very well – violin, piano, cello. And of course you can fly too, and how!" He laughed.

"*Jawohl, Herr Reichsmarschall*, replied Gollob, "But that is a long story." The *Oberst* paused. He closed his eyes for a moment and the film of Gollob's life rolled.

A moving film.

His parents' house stood in Graz. Mother and father were artists. Grandmother Zoe Reininghaus had been born a von Karajan. Both parents studied in the Academy of Fine Arts in Vienna and Munich and in the National Art School in Graz.

When their son was born on June 16, 1912, they named him Gordon Mc. They had to spell out the name for the city official. He had no way of knowing that the parents had borrowed the name from a student friend, Gordon Mallet McCouch, an American of Scottish ancestry and the boy's godfather.

Young Gordon wanted to become an engineer and pilot. The son of two gifted artists wanted to fly! Understanding and help came from an unexpected source: from grandmother Zoe. In 1930, while a high school student, he built his first training glider, which in 1931 he flew from the old airfield near Innsbruck. He earned his A- and B-Class gliding certificates and soon became a flight instructor as well as a construction and airframe inspector. During this time he studied mechanical engineering for four semesters at the Technical High School in Graz.

When, in 1933, Gollob joined the Austrian National Army as an artilleryman, it was only a tactical detour on his way to becoming a pilot. For it was predestined that Gordon M. Gollob would become a pilot and an officer. The first decisive stage in Gollob's successful military career was three years of officer training at the Theresian Military Academy in Wiener Neustadt, probably the most famous military school in the German-speaking world, which had a reputation of turning out outstanding officers.

On September 1, 1936, as a *Leutnant* in the Austrian Air Force, Gollob assumed responsibility for the training of new pilots. He loved aerobatics and earned an excellent reputation as an aerobatics pilot. His activities as an instructor bore their first fruit with Austria's "*Anschluss*" (joining) to Germany. The German Luftwaffe was then forming a cadre of young and dependable men. Officers such as Gollob were most welcome. On June 1, 1938 he became an *Oberleutnant* and several months later *Staffel* Officer in *Zerstörergeschwader* 76. Then came the war. The morning of September 5 was clear. The heavy fighters of ZG 76 were over Polish territory. Gollob was already on his way home. Suddenly he saw a tiny dot silhouetted against the sun below him. He pointed his Bf 110 toward it; in less than half a minute he would be able to identify the type and then . . . It was time. The Polish aircraft, a PWS 56 biplane, tried to escape by flying low. A terrific chase ensued, over hedges and trees, fences and sheds, the small, extremely maneuverable biplane in front, behind the twin-engined Bf 110, which weighed almost five tonnes. Then the Polish pilot flew straight and level a second too long; a burst from the

Messerschmitt's four cannon blew the biplane apart. The next day Gollob attacked a Polish airfield and destroyed several aircraft on the ground, for which he received the Iron Cross, Second Class.

It was not until December 18 that Gollob achieved his second victory. The *Geschwader* had been transferred to Jever to defend against British air attacks. On this day a formation of Wellington bombers approached the German Bight. While still over the sea they were intercepted by a *Schwarm* of Bf 110s led by Gollob. He positioned himself behind one of the British bombers. There were flashes as the tracing rounds from the Bf 110's cannon disappeared into the Wellington's fuselage. Seconds later the British aircraft plunged toward the sea, a blazing torch.

Gollob flew as a *Staffel* leader in the occupation of Norway. Over Newcastle, over the Shetlands, over Trondheim, over Narvik – he was successful everywhere. In recognition of this success he was awarded the Iron Cross, First Class.

But Gordon M. Gollob's sole wish to become a fighter pilot. As a *Zerstörer* pilot he couldn't develop as he wanted and as he knew he could. What he longed for was the "sabre duel" at 6,000 meters. His outstanding eye, impressive coolness, confidence and great piloting skill made him a natural fighter pilot. After a brief period of night fighter training he was assigned to a day fighter unit. He achieved his first objective when he reported to *Jagdgeschwader* 3 (Udet) on the Channel Coast. It was from there that the great air war raging over Great Britain was being conducted. The German fighters and bombers met a determined and clever enemy.

At last Gollob was sitting in a Bf 109 E.

A number of incidents during operations and several unexplained crashes caused him to have second thoughts about this German "wonder" aircraft. Why did pilots go into ever-steepening dives until they crashed? Why did the weapons fail to fire so often for no obvious reason?

Gollob's weapons failed too. He determined that this always happened at high altitudes, but not at low altitudes or on the ground. In an effort to find the cause, one day he climbed to 11,000 meters and stayed there until the machine was completely cooled off. The weapons refused to fire. Then he placed the Bf 109 on its nose and in less than 60 seconds he was taxying to a halt in front of his armorers. The machine was white with rime ice, for it was still at the temperature prevailing at 11,000 meters, minus 30 to 40 degrees.

The surprise: instead of gun oil the "black men" found a coarse green powder which couldn't have been a lubricant. The mystery of the weapons failures had been solved. And the unexplained crashes? Gollob's suspicion that it must have something to do with a trim problem was soon confirmed. His superiors took notice of the young *Oberleutnant* who confidently and persistently gathered his information and then filed a report. The result was a temporary posting to the Rechlin Testing Facility.

War with the Soviet Union. Gollob had become a *Hauptmann* and *Gruppenkommandeur*. He had no way of knowing that "his time" had come: the time of the sure-shooting hunter, victor in many air battles. His masterly accuracy was soon legend among the units on the Eastern Front. In spite of shooting down large numbers of enemy aircraft his expenditure of ammunition was very low. Usually he fired from extremely close range and therefore often shot down enemy aircraft with less than twenty rounds from his aircraft's engine-mounted cannon. He generally ran out of fuel before ammunition. Once, when he shot down five Soviet aircraft in one sortie, he came home with enough ammunition for three further kills.

On July 21, 1941, following his 24th victory, Gollob received the Honor Goblet for outstanding success in aerial combat. Six weeks later, on September 18, 1941, he was awarded the Knight's Cross. On October 18 he shot down nine Soviet fighters. Three days later he downed his 81st enemy aircraft and was awarded the Oak Leaves (October 26, 1941). A transfer to Germany was imminent, but first a senior post ordered him sent to Rechlin.

On December 10 Gollob wrote a detailed report on the comparison flights involving the Bf 109 F-4 and the Fw 190 A-2. He admitted that the Focke-Wulf possessed several advantages, but he spoke out against the machine, for in his opinion the development of aviation equipment must lead from the air-cooled engine back to the liquid-cooled in-line engine because of the demand for higher performance.

The report, which was intended for Göring, never reached his hands. It remained in a safe in the Rechlin Testing Center, for it did not suit the concepts of the senior command.

On May 20, 1942 Gollob was made *Geschwaderkommodore* of JG 77. Within four weeks he brought down his 101st enemy aircraft. On June 24, 1942 he received the Oak Leaves with Swords and soon afterward was promoted to *Major*.

Gollob was more than an outstanding fighter. His ability as a commander was also proved when he took command of JG 52, whose commander, *Major* Ihlefeld, had been lost to injury. The commander of the air fleet, *Generaloberst Freiherr* von Richthofen, placed him in overall command of German fighter forces during the Battle of Sevastopol. Gollob handled this task with such success that von Richthofen brought him in to help prepare for a planned German assault on Leningrad, which in the end did not take place.

August 30, 1942 was an important day in the life of *Major* Gollob. Only thirty-one years old, he became the third member of the German armed forces to receive the Diamonds. By that time he had also become the first fighter pilot in the world to achieve 150 victories. Proud as he was of the high decoration, Gollob was equally proud of the fact that he had never lost a wingman. Indeed, most of them were highly decorated.

Gollob was not happy about the ban on flying which came with the awarding of the decoration and which was not to be lifted until 1944. Hitler and Göring both cut him short: no more dogfighting! Instead, in October 1943, he was transferred to the staff of Fighter Commander 3 on the Channel Coast, and soon after was named to the post of Fighter Commander (*Jagdfliegerführer*) himself. When he became "Jafü 5" (Fighter Commander 5) he frequently turned to his superiors, the "Senior Fighter Commander West" and "Air Fleet", requesting more as well as better machines. In a report on the operational suitability of the Bf 109 in the West he wrote:

"In its present state the Bf 109 G-3 to G-6 is the worst product of a modelling hour. In my opinion this aircraft type is no longer fit for operations in the West . . . Our Fw 190 and Bf 109 fighters are vastly inferior to the enemy machines."

This report, characterized by its blunt frankness, went to the "Senior Fighter Commander West" in Chantilly Castle near Paris. Perhaps it went farther, perhaps to the air fleet in Paris, to the OKL or to Göring. Perhaps it made its way to the trash basket. In any case it went unanswered.

Gollob pushed unreservedly for the quantity production of the Me 262 and its employment as a fighter. It was the only aircraft which could still influence the air war. However he was forced to watch helplessly as the senior staffs simply failed to recognize the worth of this outstanding machine. They intended to use it, not as a fighter, but as a "Blitzbomber." A shaken Gollob read the teletype message which conclusively decided the air war in favor of the Allies.

"War council, 5. 12. 1943, 16.35 hours: The Führer once again referred to the tremendous importance of jet aircraft for use as fighter-bombers. The Luftwaffe absolutely must succeed in bringing a number of jet fighter-bombers to the front in early 1943 . . . The Führer considers any sort of delay in the jet aircraft program as an irresponsible misunderstanding of the facts. Written reports concerning the production status of the Me 262 and Ar 234 are to be submitted every 14 days."

Hitler had become fixated on the idea of using the Me 262 as a fighter-bomber. The experts were unable to convince him that, as the fastest aircraft in the world, only the Me 262 could provide effective protection against enemy bombing attacks. Hitler was thinking of bombing raids on England instead! He misinterpreted the state of the air war and the resulting constraints. Hitler failed to see the real combat value of the Me 262, bestowed upon it by its technology and performance. Gollob flew the Me 262, an aircraft which could reach the 1,000 kph mark with ease, at Lechfeld. Like everyone else he was fascinated by the machine. Enthusiastically he told Göring: "This is the only machine that can bring about a change, *Herr Reichsmarschall*. Only with it can we regain aerial superiority."

Göring argued: "This machine flies much too fast. It is therefore impossible to shoot down anything with it."

"At least give it a chance," responded Gollob.

"No! Do you understand? No! If the Führer hears that you want the Me 262 as a fighter he'll throw you out." The conversation was over.

Unfortunately for Gollob the Me 262 lay far beyond his area of activity in Northern France. Night after night the allied bombers passed over this area on their way to targets in Germany. Gollob wanted to try something new. He was not one of those who resigned himself or fatalistically gave in to fate – Gollob was a man always in search of new possibilities.

Among those under his command was engineer Karstensen, a member of an avionics research institute. Gollob spoke with him and one day a plan was born: a radar search device was needed, one which would enable the fighters to find and shoot down enemy bombers by night. This would require pilots trained in instrument flying and a reliable radio control organization.

The men set up a workshop in a barn. After several weeks of hard work, under the most primitive of conditions, they had built the first radar search device for a single-seat fighter. It was called "Neptun J" and may have been the first device of this type.

Gollob was spurred on by the success of "Neptun." In short order a *Staffel* was equipped with the device. The new equipment enabled the fighters to hunt enemy bombers in any weather. The necessary high standard of training was guaranteed by the energy and personal efforts of the *Staffelkapitän* involved, *Oberleutnant* Haberland.

The Allies were no longer safe in the night skies over Northern France. The small, fast fighters repeatedly made surprise attacks and then disappeared as quickly as they had come. Any aircraft in the fighter's forward sector could be detected out to a range of six kilometers. The new device's efficiency was demonstrated by the growing number of night kills.

Those in Berlin began to take notice. The OKL recognized the value of the new device. However certain influential posts succeeded in banning its use on the Channel Coast, ostensibly to prevent the enemy from learning which frequencies were being used and developing an effective method for jamming the equipment.

A similar device was under development by Siemens, but it was much less effective and unfit for service use. Nevertheless, less-interested bureaucrats decided that the Siemens device, which never reached the front, was the better of the two. There was never again a German single-seat night fighter. The Allies had been saved from a potentially worrisome development.

During the formation of a new radio listening service Gollob was transferred to the staff of the *General der Jagdflieger*. The invasion was imminent. For the third time Gollob requested that the flying ban imposed by Hitler after his 150th victory be lifted. The response, contained in a teletype message dated January 14, 1944, read: "... flying ban for *Oberleutnant* Gollob not lifted by the Führer, instead it remains in effect."

Generalfeldmarschall Sperrle summoned Gollob to bid him farewell. Gollob, who had meanwhile been promoted to the rank of *Oberst*, gave the field marshall an unbiased situation report:

> "*Herr Feldmarschall*, go to the *Reichsmarschall*. Tell him how things are. We can no longer speak at all of a German Luftwaffe here. What the few battered fighter units are doing is nothing short of self-sacrifice. And when the invasion begins we'll have nothing more, nothing at all, to offer."

Sperrle replied. "Believe me, I've been there more than once. But I've had my fill of waiting in the outer office and being told after three days that he can't see me. I won't do that any more. And furthermore – it would have no purpose. We must see what we can do on our own."

As said, Gollob was transferred to the staff of the *General der Jagdflieger*. His initial impressions of the development, testing, and production sites were shattering. He turned to his duties. Gollob became involved with the Me 163 program and was responsible for all the technical and tactical issues concerning the type. Later he joined the "Fighter Staff" which, in October 1943, succeeded in raising fighter production to its highest levels ever in spite of round the clock bombing by the Allies.

The technology of the Me 163 and development of the Ju 248/Me 263 were challenging tasks. Gollob flew the Me 163 A and B in spite of the flying ban, the only member of the staff of the *General der Jagdflieger* to do so. Indeed no other officer above the rank of *Major* had flown it. That was gladly left to those obsessed with flying, men like Späte, Opitz, Olejnik, Schumacher and others. These were the actual Me 163 test pilots: fearless and unshakable in their belief in a new type of flying, in spite of numerous burn injuries and broken bones.

Gollob, too, wanted to experience the sixty-degree climb toward infinity. Two minutes to an altitude of 10,000 meters, that was simply fantastic.

On September 18, 1944 the *General der Jagdflieger*, Adolf Galland, used a minor incident as an excuse for a serious argument and the immediate release of *Oberst* Gollob from the fighter staff.

In the West the Ardennes offensive was under way and Gollob led an "aviation command squad" within the Sixth Army. The squad was equipped with the latest radio guidance equipment and its mission

was to guide German fighters from the ground when enemy aircraft appeared over the front. Gollob's efforts were frustrated, first by bad weather and then by the superiority of the Allies.

Even "Bodenplatte", the last mass attack by the Luftwaffe on the allied ground organization on January 1, 1945, was unable to turn the tables. The operation cost the German fighter arm most of its remaining unit leaders. The operation's objective was not achieved, and with the loss of 300 pilots, the back of the fighter arm had been broken.

Two days after "Bodenplatte" Gollob visited the command post of II *Jagdkorps*. There he was dismayed to learn that almost all of the flight paths assigned to the units on January 1 had crossed V 1 routes, and at altitudes between 50 and 200 meters. Gollob, who had often watched the tremendous anti-aircraft fire along the V 1 routes from high in the Eifel Mountains, had found one of the major causes for the high fighter losses. The fighter commanders admitted that they had overlooked this "slip-up."

It wasn't the time to talk about the past. Now he was in Karinhall and had been *General der Jagdflieger* for several minutes . . . Nothing could have been more unexpected than this.

Göring had stood up. He shook the *Oberst's* hand and looked at him long and hard. "You must do it. You know that the Luftwaffe's standing with the Führer must be raised again. See to it."

While Karinhall lay behind Gollob, the obstacles piled up in front of him. He knew that he would soon come into conflict with Göring if he pushed through the program he was formulating.

Time was short. The Soviet Army was driving toward Berlin, while the Americans and British were advancing on the Ruhr. The supreme command appointed commissars and special plenipotentiaries. As the Luftwaffe's representative, Gollob found himself facing *General* Kammhuber, the "Special Plenipotentiary for the Combatting of Enemy Four-engined Machines", and *SS-Obergruppenführer* Dr.Ing. Kammler, the "Führer's Special Plenipotentiary for Air Armaments", with whose approval Gollob ordered the arming of the Me 262 and Fw 190 with the 50mm R4M air-to-air rocket. This was done without consulting the RLM, as there was no time. The Me 262 was outfitted with 24 rockets on wooden racks beneath the wings. One of these rockets was sufficient to bring down a four-engined bomber. When fired in a single salvo, the rockets often hit and destroyed two bombers, which usually flew in close formation.

During the course of February 1945 it became apparent that at least seven heavy bombers would be shot down for each total loss of an Me 262 through enemy action or mechanical reasons; this was confirmed in March. With this aircraft and armament heavy losses could have been inflicted on the enemy – had the Luftwaffe been equipped with it.

With Kammler's agreement, JG 7 was ordered to send pilots to take charge of KG 51's Me 262s, which were being used as fighter-bombers. This action was intended to put a radical end to the jet fighter-bomber nonsense and achieve a short-term reinforcement of JG 7, which it badly needed. Hitler's sole Me 262 fighter-bomber unit was thus deactivated.

The next day saw Gollob and Kammler in Karinhall standing before the *Reichsmarschall*, who was furious and worried over Hitler's reaction. After a raging debate Göring forced the return of all the jet aircraft. KG 51 resumed operations, wasting more valuable fuel. Gollob's reaction was to assemble all the documents which proved the Me 262's enormous worth as a fighter as well as everything which spoke against the mistaken use of the Me 262 as a *Blitzbomber*. He wanted to make one more effort to overturn a suicidal decision. Evaluation of statistical sources enabled him to calculate the authorized strengths and numbers of Me 262 units necessary to inflict such serious, ongoing losses on the Allies that they would be forced to cease their daylight attacks. And the night raids? *Oberleutnant* Welter was already flying night sorties in the Me 262, achieving unexpected success in these difficult missions. The British night raids, too, would soon have become unbearably costly had the necessary training been carried out in time.

Armed with a packet of unassailable documents, Gollob hoped to be allowed to see Hitler. But to his astonishment he was prevented from meeting with the Führer. "The Führer doesn't want to hear anything about an Me 262 fighter!"

Under these circumstances Gollob had no wish to go on holding an office which no longer was one. On April 7, 1944 the wearer of the Diamonds submitted a written request to be released from the office of *General der Jagdflieger*. In the letter he wrote: "As I am no longer in a position to bring my views into line with yours, *Herr Reichsmarschall*, and given that I consider such a harmony of views an absolutely vital condition for successful work, especially at this time, I request that I be released from my present duties."

Although the letter contained an extensive, thorough analysis of the situation and a number proposals, it elicited no response. With its readiness to make decisions and thus assume responsibility, the OKL was in a sorry state.

Gollob had flown combat missions in spite of serious stomach problems, which repeatedly forced him to seek medical
attention. The previous months had been hard on his health.
He put off a needed operation. Gollob had also reported this
to Göring. There was no answer, but there was a response: his
proposed promotion to the rank of *Generalmajor* would not be
forthcoming.

Gollob left Berlin on April 10, following his staff which had
already left for southern Germany. Eight days later Dr. Burghart
Breitner operated on Gollob in Igls Hospital near Innsbruck.
On April 24 he had himself transferred to Kitzbühel Luftwaffe
Hospital. Gollob was now in the center of the "Alpine For-
tress."

Generalfeldmarschall Ritter von Greim, the Luftwaffe's last
Commander-in-Chief after Göring's dismissal, also came to
Kitzbühel, accompanied by Hanna Reitsch, the fearless, quite
extraordinary aviatrix. The pair had made a daring flight into
besieged Berlin to visit Hitler one last time in the Reich Chancellery Bunker. In the process von Greim had been wounded.

The last *General der Jagdflieger* stood before the bed of the
last Luftwaffe Commander-in-Chief and made his report. The
two officers knew each other well from Russia – the First World
War pilot with the Pour le Mérite and Gollob, almost exactly
twenty years his junior. It was an open and frank discussion
among soldiers and it ended with von Greim's declaration that
he intended to commit suicide rather than submit himself to
the treatment he expected to receive from the Americans. The
Feldmarschall refused to listen to argument.

Soon afterward the Americans occupied Kitzbühel. *Oberst*
Gollob voluntarily reported in uniform to the American division commander, General Dahlquist, and it immediately became evident that he was dealing with a gentleman. This officer treated Gollob in an almost comradely fashion; the German was handled fairly, indeed even with concern. General
Dahlquist's behavior toward all German soldiers and officers
stood out from those who believed it necessary to degrade the
defeated. Dahlquist was a chivalrous foe, of whom Gollob
spoke with respect. This was further demonstrated on May 4
when Gollob learned of Göring's arrival and his reception in

the Grand Hotel by General Dahlquist. The General also saw
to it that Gollob's family, which was living in Kitzbühel, was
not harassed.

This soldierly approach did not seem to fit the concept of
the Americans in General Eisenhower's entourage. Like the
legendary General Patton, who was likely of the same mind,
General Dahlquist and his division were soon relieved. The
next American unit to be stationed in Kitzbühel, the "Rain-
bow Division", and its commanding officer, General Collins,
soon extinguished the outstanding impression left behind by
General Dahlquist and his soldiers.

On June 1 Austrian auxiliary police acting on behalf of the
American CIC came for Gollob in his apartment. The wearer
of the Diamonds was taken to Kitzbühel prison, where he was
brought before an American Major. When asked if he knew
why he was there, Gollob replied: "No, I don't know." "Take
him away" was the American's answer. Other American offices looking for Gollob in order to use him in development
work with Professor Lippisch were told by the CIC that they
had no idea where he was. From Kitzbühel he was taken via
Pass Strub and other camps to Ludwigsburg in Württemberg,
then by aircraft to England where Gollob was reunited with
many former comrades from the OKL.

Gordon Gollob was released by the Americans in 1946, but
when he arrived in Kitzbühel he was "welcomed" by the
French. The Americans had handed Tirol over to the French as
part of their occupation zone. Gollob himself stated that he
had been stationed in northern France for one and a half years.
Monsieur Suchard replied: "We know you very well. You behaved correctly." The French now also behaved correctly. They
asked Gollob about the types of aircraft he had flown and technical problems encountered by the Luftwaffe and then flew
him to the Air Ministry in Paris. The French wanted him to
write down his recollections. Gollob refused courteously but
firmly and the French respected his position.

Almost thirty years later the Americans Toliver and Constable wrote the book *Das waren die deutschen Jagdflieger-Asse
1939-1945*. In it they praised the accomplishments of Gordon
M. Gollob, of whom those with knowledge of the subject said

that there was probably no other officer in the Luftwaffe in his age group who could boast such extensive training. Toliver and Constable wrote of Gollob: "But out of respect for the important contribution to the jet aircraft program made by *Oberst* Gollob. A temporary transfer to *Erprobungsstelle* Rechlin at the beginning of 1942 brought to light Gollob's talents in the field of fighter development. Although he later returned to the Eastern Front for an extremely successful tour as *Kommodore* of JG 77, he was obviously destined for more important tasks. In October 1942 he was appointed fighter commander on the Western Front and in April 1944 became a member of the fighter staff, which was set up in the armaments industry under Saur's direction. Gollob made a major contribution to advancements in the area of the modern fighter aircraft operations. Not only did he work on the development of the Me 262, but on the Me 163 and He 162 as well."

"Gollob's duties kept him away from front-line operations. He did however command a special fighter headquarters during the Ardennes offensive, when Hitler committed the remaining fighter reserves in a ground support role, resulting in heavy losses."

"Gollob succeeded Galland as *General der Jagdflieger* when the latter was dismissed from the post in early 1945. Gordon Gollob survived the war. His 150 aerial victories, including six over western pilots, were achieved in 340 combat missions. Gollob holds a much higher place in the hierarchy of German fighter pilots than his victory total would suggest. He is one of only nine fighter pilots to have been decorated with the Diamonds. Gollob can also be considered the Boelcke of the Second World War, and his contributions to the development of outstanding aircraft and weapons were noteworthy."

After the war Gollob initially wrote for aviation publications and lectured to support himself and his family. In 1948 he became General Secretary of the Association of Independents. In 1951, having meanwhile moved to his wife's home town in Lower Saxony, he became an employee of a leading motor vehicle concern. Later he became a works manager in the north German states, which included Berlin, in the fire-fighting field. The Gollobs had two sons and a daughter. Until his heart attack in 1975 he flew gliders and powered aircraft. In the gliding field he earned the Silver C to the C License he earned in 1932. Gollob, who had flown more than 100 types of aircraft in his flying career, including the first Thunderbolt fighter to be captured intact, needed to stay active: as a pensioner he found relief in his well-equipped workshop. His main preoccupation remained the evaluation of his experiences and memories. Gordon M. Gollob died on September 8, 1987.

CHAPTER IV

HAUPTMANN HANS-JOACHIM MARSEILLE

T he career of the young pilot Hans-Joachim Marseille followed a path like that of a comet, brilliant and short-lived against the background of a star-studded sky. The enemy called him the "Eagle of Africa", his friends the "Southern Star." His piloting ability was unique and his forte was aerobatics; his favorite trick was to pick up a handkerchief from the ground with the wingtip of his fast Bf 109. His youthful face bore soft, slightly melancholy, features, but his eyes had the gleam of one who knew his business. Seldom has there been such an outstanding flier.

On September 30, 1942, news of the death of Joachim Marseille raced through Germany. For much of the German people this pilot was the embodiment of the brave lone fighter, while German youth saw in Joachim Marseille its idol. He was twenty-two years old when he died.

The sun rose in the East like a fiery ball, while on the small North-African desert airfield the usual morning activity reigned. *Hauptmann* Marseille climbed into his machine in preparation for a patrol over the front lines and the enemy's rear. Surprising the enemy in the early morning hours was one of Marseille's specialties.

The *Hauptmann* blinked as he looked into the sun.

"It's going to be hot today" he said.

The mechanic mumbled a weary "*Jawohl*" and stifled a yawn.

"Then let's go . . . everything ready?" asked Marseille.

"Everything's ready and good luck." The *Feldwebel* laughed and raised his fingers to the brim of his forage cap.

"Will do, old chap. Let's go!"

Seconds later *Hauptmann* Marseille was racing down the landing strip. His aircraft lifted into the air, effortlessly and apparently feather-light, and climbed away. Soon it was a shrinking dot in the sky and finally it disappeared from sight.

Three Spitfires appeared over the front. They failed to spot the Germans. Marseille dove on the enemy patrol from a higher altitude and shot down the enemy machines in a matter of minutes.

Ground control called: "Come back, everything's ready for you to refuel." Marseille landed and stood by his machine as the Bf 109 was refuelled.

A few minutes later the *Geschwader* Adjutant was standing by the aircraft. "Enemy fighter formation approaching. They want their revenge because you shot down those three this morning," he called to Marseille, who was standing on the wing.

The *Hauptmann* looked in the direction from which the British must come, but there was no sound of approaching aircraft.

"How many?" he asked.

"No idea. About twenty."

Marseille ordered two other pilots to take off with him. He wanted to intercept the English aircraft before they reached the front.

They encountered the enemy aircraft over no-man's-land. The British broke formation and adopted their preferred tactic: the eighteen Spitfires flew a gigantic circle, preventing the Germans from approaching. There wasn't much the Germans could do against these "windmill fliers." But Marseille knew this maneuver. He acted as if he had fallen for the trick. Quick as lightning he climbed his Bf 109. Then, like a hawk in a henhouse, he dove into the enemy formation and poured bullets into the fuselage of his chosen target. The Spitfire caught fire and fell away. Soon three more aircraft were ablaze and the British circular formation had become a mass of confusion.

Marseille had no difficulty in shooting down four more enemy machines. The other two German fighters kept pace with their commander: eight more Spitfires crashed in the desert. Only two managed to escape.

After Marseille had landed, the *Geschwaderkommodore* called to him: "For sure the Tommies will leave us in peace today."

"I don't agree," replied the *Hauptmann*.

Marseille was soon to be proved right.

A half-hour later the observer reported another formation of Spitfires. Marseille and his two comrades climbed into their machines again and roared into the sky.

What madness, the stupid way the English fly, the *Hauptmann* thought to himself. They're shot down like hares and each time they come back instead of trying something different.

The Spitfires were still circling over the British front-line area when Marseille intercepted them. At once the British fighters began circling around the three Germans, firing without pause. Marseille's machine was hit several times before he could fire a shot.

"After them!" he ordered by radio. Straight away the Germans dove on the twelve British fighters. A wild dogfight developed, in which nine of the enemy aircraft were shot down, four of them by Marseille.

After this second major victory the other members of Marseille's *Geschwader* – there were only a very small number of fighters in action at that time – welcomed him with shouts of hurray and waving cloths. Marseille wiped the sweat from his face. Scarcely had he set his feet on solid ground when he was called to the telephone. "The *Feldmarschall*", said the NCO at the telephone exchange. Then Rommel came on the line.

"The British are circling above my command post as if they're on a pilgrimage. Can you come and clear the air?"

Marseille laughed and said, "Yes, I'll come straight away." Then he informed his commanding officer of his departure and took off in the direction of Rommel's headquarters.

Near the command post he spotted three Mustangs, American machines flown by British pilots. The enemy fighters repeatedly dove earthward, firing on anything that moved. It was no wonder that Rommel had grown nervous.

Marseille attacked immediately, and before the Mustang pilots realized what was happening two aircraft were diving toward the earth in flames. The third climbed away and disappeared.

Rommel called again as soon as Marseille had landed.

"Bravo, Seille," he shouted. "Terrific how you brought down those boys. I saw it all . . . thank you very much." Rommel, who was very fond of the young officer, simply called him "Seille." He worried about him like a father does about his son.

Following this conversation the *Kommodore* ordered an attack on a British airfield where a number of new aircraft were supposed to be based. Marseille and his *Staffel* took off once again. The German fighters raced over the English airfield at very low altitude, forcing the anti-aircraft gunners to take cover, and shot up a number of enemy aircraft, leaving them in flames. As the Germans headed for home they suddenly found themselves facing ten British aircraft.

"After them", ordered the *Hauptmann*.

The British were confident that the Germans had no ammunition left or at best very little. They attacked. While the opposing fighters turned wildly, Marseille observed a Spitfire flying to one side of the dogfight, apparently issuing instructions to the others. It must be the squadron leader. Marseille climbed quickly and attacked the suspected enemy leader. But the Englishman was an experienced pilot and tried to shake off the German. Marseille forced him into a spiral, let his aircraft drop, and then pulled the Bf 109 into a near vertical position and from there shot out the English fighter's engine.

"Home now, I'm out of ammunition," called Marseille. In the meantime the other members of the *Staffel* had shot down seven more Spitfires.

The British did not attack again that day, the most successful of *Hauptmann* Joachim Marseille's career. He had shot down seventeen enemy aircraft: seventeen skilled, experienced British pilots flying fast machines the equal of the German Bf 109.

A few days later the British command issued an order, in which it said:

"Marseille is the best the Germans have here. He flies a Bf 109 like the others, but he flies better than they. Always in the forefront. He attacks with only a few machines. Do not allow yourself to become involved in wild dogfights. Make your attacks quickly. You must see that you can attack him frontally or from the side before he is in a position to maneuver . . ."

The British feared him, this Joachim Marseille.

Among Marseille's opponents was a British Wing Commander who had formerly been based on Malta. Shot down by Marseille, he told the Germans after his capture: "I had just come from Malta and he was all I heard about. They told amazing stories about him in the officers mess and I longed to meet Marseille. Finally I declared high-spiritedly: Want to bet that I can get him? After all I was one of the best Royal Air Force pilots stationed on Malta. A few days later I got my chance. I took off with a squadron to attack German airfields. The devil knows, we were at about 4,000 meters, when one of my people reported: 'Germans from out of the sun!' And then they were upon us."

"There was a wild dogfight. My adjutant shot down a Messerschmitt. The pilot swung to earth beneath his parachute. I heard the voice of another of my men: 'There he is..! Watch out . . . ! Mar . . .' There was a crash. I felt my stricken aircraft lose height and I saw Marseille sitting behind me. A thought raced through my head: If he fires now I'm finished. But the fellow didn't fire. He just sat behind me, as if he would have enjoyed seeing me simply fly into the ground. For what could I do in this situation?"

Suddenly I saw him rock his wings. Now he's going to tear my wings off, I said to myself. More instinctively than deliberately, I threw back the cockpit hood and climbed out. At that moment I saw Marseille pull up. He circled round me a few times, waggled his wings again – I even think he waved – and then I landed. Yes, and now I'm here."

The Englishman took a deep breath. "A damned fair lad. He could easily have killed me . . . but he didn't do it."

That was Marseille: a chivalrous flier, fair and brave. On

September 2, 1942 he was awarded the Diamonds following his 125th victory. He was proud of this decoration. But there had been obstacles to overcome before he became a man feared by the enemy and a name known throughout the aviation world.

On December 13, 1919, when Joachim Marseille was born, political chaos reigned in Berlin. Charlotte, his mother, was nevertheless happy that she had a boy. But Joachim caused the young woman only worry. He nearly died of influenza, and after his illness he was so weak on his legs that at the age of three he had to learn to stand and walk all over again. But in spite of everything he was always a happy youth. This fact was confirmed by his schoolmates from the Prinz-Heinrich Elementary School in Berlin-Schöneberg. "Marseille was always there when there was mischief going on." His teachers observed that he could have done much better had he not been so lazy. But the boy wasn't one to strive. Following graduation, at which time he was seventeen and a half, he said to his mother: "Now I can finally fulfill my greatest desire. I'm going to become a flying officer."

In the labor service he learned to drain moorland, and in October 1938 he was ordered to report to Quedlinburg for infantry training. A year later, as an NCO Officer Candidate having completing his flight training, he flew defensive patrols in his Bf 109 over the Leuna works. In 1940 he arrived at the front in Leuwarden in Holland. It was from there that he was to take off on his first combat mission.

During his first day at the front he encountered an able British pilot, whom he shot down following a brief battle. Immediately afterward a formation of Hurricanes dove out of the sun – but Marseille was quicker and escaped the enemy fighters at low altitude.

Late that evening he confided to friends that he was bitterly sorry about the enemy pilot he had shot down. They laughed out loud at him. "If you don't fire quicker than the enemy then you're the victim. Here the law of quickness rules. You must realize that, my dear fellow." They clapped him on the shoulder. "It'll be alright," they said and left.

Joachim Marseille was left alone in the mess. In his thoughts he could see the Englishman in front of him. He had seen his face beneath the flying helmet, the face of a young man no older than himself. However he was to send 157 more opponents to the ground before he himself was killed.

Marseille took off on his second combat mission and again he shot down a British machine. He received the Iron Cross, Second Class on his second day in action and the Iron Cross, First Class on his fifth, when he shot down his third and fourth enemy aircraft.

The other members of his *Staffel* considered Marseille an extraordinarily gifted and clever flier who possessed the daring and aggressiveness to tackle a numerically-superior enemy. While returning from a bomber escort mission over Dover he suffered the misfortune of having to make a forced landing in the Channel on account of engine failure. Marseille drifted in the currents for three hours until, at the end of his strength, he was picked up by a rescue boat. Marseille was delivered to hospital suffering from exhaustion and nervous strain.

Marseille had a difficult time with his superiors. Although he was a successful pilot, he became the only officer candidate in the *Geschwader* not to be promoted to *Leutnant*. What had he done to prevent him being promoted?

The unit was still based on the Channel Coast. The British lay in ambush, waiting for the German machines. That morning they were determined to avenge the defeat suffered the previous day.

"Marseille, you'll fly as wingman, understood?"

The officer candidate said "*Jawohl*." He understood that he was not allowed to fire his weapons, rather he was to observe the enemy and warn his comrades of surprise attacks.

The English were ready for a fight. Eighteen German aircraft against forty British. It was soon obvious that the enemy pilots were just as skilled as the German. The dogfight was under way when suddenly the formation leader gave an order which Marseille could not comprehend: "Reverse course and get out!"

But why run away? There was plenty of fuel and ammunition left and the enemy hadn't been defeated.

Then a Hurricane raced after the German machines, intent on diving on the formation leader, who was flying straight and level, unaware of any danger. Marseille had no time for an explanation. He left the small formation and looped past the leader to attack the British aircraft. On his first pass he shot up the Hurricane's engine; the aircraft plunged into the Channel in flames. Scarcely had Marseille landed and jumped down from his machine, when the *Staffelkapitän* roared at him: "I'm punishing you with five days detention for failing to carry out an order."

"I don't know what I'm supposed to have done wrong," replied Marseille.

"You were supposed to fly on and were forbidden to fire, were you not? Why then did you shoot down the Hurricane? Someone else could have done that."

Marseille was unable to have the CO's decision overturned. He had always been sensitive to unfair treatment. And now he had shot down an enemy who was about to attack the unsuspecting formation leader. He couldn't comprehend that he was to be placed under arrest for lack of discipline because he had wanted to help. A few days later it was announced that several generals were going to visit the unit. The *Staffelkapitän* came up with a surprise: Marseille would put on a display of aerobatics.

"Now you may show what you can do. Go on, fly and give them a performance that will knock his hat off!"

Marseille was known for his trick flying. He was the master of his machine like few others. The generals were amazed at the skill of the young officer candidate and clapped in approval. Then the *Staffelkapitän* said: "And now comes the sensational part."

Marseille flew slowly over the airfield. The aircraft dropped lower, drawing ever closer to the ground. A bamboo stick had been stuck into the ground and a handkerchief tied to it about a meter above the earth. Marseille was going to pick it up with his wingtip. Astonished, the Generals stopped laughing. There was an outburst of applause when the young pilot took the handkerchief with the wing of his aircraft. The Messerschmitt pulled up and roared over the heads of the visitors at high speed.

After landing his aircraft a laughing Marseille climbed down from the machine. But a few minutes later his *Staffelkapitän* informed him that he would have to punish him with a further five days arrest because he flown under the five meter limit, thus endangering his life and a valuable aircraft.

Pale with anger and disappointment, and enraged at so much stupidity, he challenged the punishment. "I was only carrying out an order, and after all it was an aerobatics display," he said in defense of his actions. But his superior was a man who, in the jumble of regulations, used his own discretion in interpreting the concept of discipline.

A transfer to Africa followed in March 1941. The move pleased Marseille as he was no longer happy on the Channel. His superiors demonstrated little understanding, he received no promotions, and no one paid any heed to his abilities and talents.

"All they thought about was their own success and victories. To them I was mere officer candidate, nothing but a pitiful nobody," he said to his mother.

But in Africa Marseille's star ascended. His new *Geschwaderkommodore*, Edu Neumann, recognized his potential at once. Neumann knew how to handle young men; he employed them according to their abilities. At his insistence his young charge was promoted to *Leutnant* in June 1941. In December that same year Marseille received the German Cross in Gold.

Marseille made a name for himself by shooting down at least one enemy aircraft on each sortie. This was no mean feat, for the English never attacked alone as did Marseille and Müncheberg, who often took off solo to face an entire squadron of Spitfires. The enemy on the other hand always flew with at least five machines, which circled about forming an almost impenetrable ring. In many cases Marseille shot down all five aircraft; seldom did he shoot down less than two. On February 22, 1942, following his fiftieth kill, he was awarded the Knight's Cross. The most successful period of his career was about to begin.

Four months later, after his 75th kill, he received the Oak Leaves. Soon afterward he reported his 100th British aircraft shot down, and the awarding of the Swords was assured. He received the decoration on June 18, 1942. On September 2, 1942 Marseille was awarded the Diamonds following his 125th victory.

In Führer Headquarters Marseille was called upon to deliver a 45-minute situation briefing, in which he mentioned that the Allies were not as bad as uninformed observers suspected. "The enemy's materiel superiority is so great that we will soon feel its effects in a negative way," declared Marseille passionately. "We need more fighter aircraft. The English are growing stronger day by day. I'm of the opinion that bombers have long since been rendered superfluous in a war in which we have been forced onto the defensive."

More machines and munitions were promised for Africa. Marseille believed what he was told, but he was soon to be disappointed.

Several days after his visit to Führer Headquarters Marseille was received by Mussolini in Rome. Two honors were bestowed upon him with all the pomp of the Roman Caesars; the greater was the awarding of the Golden Medal for Bravery, a decoration which was given to only two foreigners, Marseille and Müncheberg, both German fighter pilots.

Mussolini was a great admirer of the young German pilot. "Not only is your fatherland proud of you," he said, "But the Italian people as well. Germany's allies consider you one of their own. Your victories are received by us with equal enthusiasm and are celebrated here as much as they are in Germany."

Several days later Marseille flew back to Africa, where the British were quietly and patiently preparing a major offensive. Only in the air were they active, indeed the RAF was growing stronger day by day.

The young *Hauptmann* related to *Generalfeldmarschall* Rommel the impressions he had gained in Führer Headquarters. These suggested that an enemy offensive was imminent. But it would be months before a single new machine or fresh company would be sent to the "Africans."

In the space of a few days Marseille shot down another 33 British aircraft, until he, too, was struck down by fate. Fate came not in the form of a better, more successful foe, but as a cruel, malicious accident.

It was September 28, 1942. Marseille had just returned from a combat mission. The telephone rang.

"The *Feldmarschall* wishes to speak to *Hauptmann* Marseille," said the operator.

"Listen Seille, I want to kidnap you . . . to Berlin. The Führer is speaking in the Sports Palace. You are to sit on his right, I on his left. What do you think of that? That would be an honor you couldn't pass up."

"But *Herr Feldmarschall*, I can't go on leave again already. The others sit here and slave away and I take more leave than the entire *Geschwader*."

"But what you are saying is madness!"

"I would like to go to Berlin for Christmas, *Herr Feldmarschall*. I became engaged during my last leave and we want to get married. I need my leave for that." He knew that it wouldn't stop at the speech in the Sports Palace; it would be followed by invitation after invitation. "I request, *Herr Feldmarschall*, that you not insist on this request, after all I'm really desperately needed here."

Rommel laughed to himself. Then he said: "As you like. If you think more of getting married than of the Führer, then in God's name stay."

On September 30, the day of the speech in the Sports Palace, Marseille flew his usual patrol. Suddenly the engine began to "grumble" and his aircraft lost height.

"Have engine trouble, am going to bail out," he reported to the ground station. His men watched as his cockpit hood flew away and the *Hauptmann* climbed out of his machine. They watched in horror as his parachute failed to open. Perhaps it's another one of his pranks, they hoped. But this time Joachim Marseille was not playing a prank. This time it was bitterly serious. Marseille was dead when they found him.

Joachim Marseille died, undefeated by the enemy, after 158 aerial victories. Experts consider him the best German fighter pilot of all. His skill was unique, his daring unsurpassed, and his modesty earned him friends everywhere.

His mother related: "His motto was: 'Don't turn around, always look ahead.' Perhaps this best describes his character. I was and am proud of my boy, who so well suited the ideas of an officer as I pictured them when I held that tiny bundle of humanity right after his birth. Brave, decent and loyal. That was my Joachim."

CHAPTER V

OBERST HERMAN GRAF

After the war Sepp Herberger, legendary trainer of the German national soccer team, helped his friend Hermann Graf: he got the retired *Oberst* a position in the electric welding industry. Herberger thus returned the many favors which the highly-decorated officer and passionate soccer player had done the former Reich trainer during the war. Highly-ranked national team players such as Fritz Walter, Franz Hahnreiter, Alfons Moog, Hermann Eppenhof, Zwickhöfer, Fritz Hack, Klagges, Klaffke and others played with Graf's famous "Red Fighters," and as well were available to the national team and clubs such as Schalke 04, 1st FC Kaiserslautern, the later 1st FC Cologne and Admira Vienna in decisive games.

General der Jagdflieger Adolf Galland was aware of this whim of Graf's, and at every change of command involving the *Kommodore* he went out of his way to say: "I know that he comes and goes with a whole string of soccer players."

Then the Reich Federation for Physical Training became involved. It wanted to prevent *Geschwaderkommodore* Graf from playing soccer. The league sent an appropriate letter to *Reichmarschall* Göring and asked that he forbid Graf from playing soccer because he wanted to introduce professionalism to the sport. But Göring wrote laconically in the margin: "If Graf likes playing soccer then let him play."

Not only could Graf play soccer – he was one of the best young German goalkeepers – but he could fly and fight as well.

He was the last commanding officer of the Luftwaffe's most successful fighter unit, JG 52, which shot down almost 11,000 enemy aircraft. As well, he was one of the best-known fighter pilots of the Second World War.

Graf was the first fighter pilot in the world to achieve 200 victories. On September 26, 1942 he shot down his 200th to 202nd enemy aircraft over Pitomnik airfield near Stalingrad. Afterward he was promoted to *Hauptmann*; Graf had already worn the Knight's Cross of the Iron Cross with Oak Leaves, Swords and Diamonds since September 16, 1942.

Hermann Graf, the outstanding fighter pilot with 830 combat missions and 252 kills, 212 of them confirmed, enjoyed a unique run of success when he achieved 200 kills in a period of 13 months. He received the Knight's Cross on January 24, 1942. On December 27 he shot down his 39th enemy aircraft near Azov and his 40th and 41st over Golodayevka a few days later. On May 17, 1942 he was awarded the Oak Leaves for 104 kills and two days later the Swords. Only once before had an officer of the Luftwaffe been so decorated.

On September 16, 1942, following his 172nd victory, Graf became the fifth German soldier to receive the Diamonds. He registered his greatest success eight days later, shooting down ten enemy bombers in a single day.

Graf was banned from further flying, and on September 26, 1942 was ordered to leave the *Geschwader* on orders from far up the chain of command. Before leaving he flew over Stalingrad once more and bade farewell to the unit headquarters and command post: "Good luck comrades of Stalingrad, Karaya 1 departing . . . on orders from above." (Karaya 1 was Graf's code name.) Then he flew his Bf 109, with which he had scored 75 kills, to his new base.

Who was this fighter pilot who had so distinguished himself in combat and who was such an outstanding pilot and comrade?

It was flying that excited Hermann Graf as a youth. Born in the small city of Engen im Hegau on October 12, 1912, he made his first glider flight at the age of twelve. He then completed a course in administration and, after passing all his tests as a glider pilot, reported for service in the Wehrmacht. That was 1936. He practiced as a reservist with the goal of attending the Karlsruhe flying school. After completing the course he returned to work as an employee of the city public assistance office. Not until 1939 did he take an NCO course and become a reserve officer candidate.

On July 31, 1939 Hermann Graf joined the Aibling fighter wing. His beginnings were no more successful than those of many later successful fighter pilots. He flew 21 sorties during the war with France without firing a single shot. It was not until much later, in the war against the Soviet Union, that he shot down his first enemy aircraft.

It was 06.20 hours on August 4, 1941, in the vicinity of Kiev. Hermann Graf got behind a *Rata* and opened fire. At least that's what he intended to do. Suddenly there was another enemy machine behind him. But he was intent on shooting down the one in front of him. He pressed the firing buttons but nothing happened. Then he noticed that he forgotten to arm his weapons. Suddenly there was a crash behind him. When he looked around he saw the enemy fighter going down. His wingman, "Kaczmarek" Steinbatz, had saved his life. Relieved, but now even more determined, he pursued the *Rata*, opened fire and shot him down. That was number one in Graf's long list of victories.

Graf's success had been made possible by Steinbatz, the only *Feldwebel* in the German armed forces to receive the Swords, awarded following his 99th kill. The award was posthumous and was soon followed by a promotion to *Leutnant*.

Graf's *Staffel*, the famous 9th, included such outstanding and well-known fighter pilots as Grislawski, Füllgrabe and Süss, Klein, Emberger, Köppen and Zwernemann, all wearers of the Knight's Cross and some of the Oak Leaves. With these men Graf hunted enemy aircraft, especially the Il-2 close-support machine, which inflicted heavy losses on the German infantry in its trenches and positions.

Once during the advance in the southern sector of the Eastern Front, Graf's *Staffel* sat idle for days on the Crimean Peninsula without operational orders, while infantry and tank units were involved in bitter fighting. Graf and his men had been given the job of protecting a rear-area airfield.

Graf, however, wanted to help at the front. He repeatedly asked for permission to take off but was refused. Then one afternoon he tricked the base commander, an older *Oberst*, and asked him for permission to fly to his operational airfield. The *Oberst* gave the order to take off.

The *Staffel* followed its *Kapitän*. But instead of going to the operational airfield he set course for the front. The fighters flew a wide circle over the area and then spotted artillery fire, bursting shells, tracer and fountains of earth: the front was ablaze. A layer of gray mist hung over the front line. Flying at an altitude of 2,000 meters, Graf's men searched the sky for Soviet aircraft. Suddenly several enemy fighters dove into the mist and disappeared. Graf ordered the *Staffel* to stay where it was while he went down to see for himself "what was going on down below." He dropped through the layer of mist and emerged 50 meters above the front line. What he saw took his breath away.

On the ground a German assault gun was crawling slowly over the terrain, followed by a swarm of soldiers. Four Soviet Il-2s were attacking the assault gun, firing bursts of machine-gun fire into the soldiers, who dove for cover. All would have fallen prey to the Soviets had Graf not arrived. He attacked immediately, but suddenly an Il-2 raced toward him. Graf pressed the firing buttons and the enemy aircraft exploded. Seconds later he was on the tail of the second Il-2. A single burst sawed off the aircraft's right wing. The Il-2 went down in flames. The remaining two Soviet aircraft tried to flee. One succeeded, the other was caught and destroyed by *Feldwebel* Steinbatz.

After landing Graf cut short his *Kommodore*, who was intent on punishing the disobedient *Staffelkapitän*. His superior's anger dissipated when he told him how important the mission had been and how his men had helped out the hard-pressed ground forces.

Such missions were characteristic of Graf. During his career as a pilot he made it a point to help the infantry first and only then to seek aerial combat. He engaged enemy anti-tank and machine-gun positions and destroyed nests of resistance and supply columns. If enemy aircraft were spotted, he attacked only if it became obvious that they intended to attack German ground forces.

Other well-known fighter pilots spoke highly of Graf's elegant flying, his boldness and selflessness in action. In Bertold K. Jochim's book *Oberst Hermann Graf – 200 Luftsiege in 13 Monaten*, Graf described his most difficult air battle, which he described as a "chivalrous duel":

"Füllgrabe was in trouble. The leader of the enemy formation flew like a number one pilot and had him in difficulties. Then I attacked. We locked horns. The second Russian lost his nerve and withdrew to a distance of several kilometers. I ordered Heinrich (Füllgrabe) to get out of my way."

"There now began one of my loveliest and most risky air battles in the East. It involved everything man and machine could give: loops with a radius of a good thousand meters, reversals, over and over again. Sweat was literally running down my body. My opponent was at least as good as I. It was fabulous how he repeatedly tried to trick me. One reversal followed another. Again and again we went nose to nose. Both of us fired. Only at the last minute did he pull up and flash past overhead, then it was my turn again. Once we came within a hair of colliding. Then the other Russian fighter came back. I had just gained some breathing room. The second man of the Russian flight dove away. My previous opponent was behind me again, but still at least 400 meters away. Seeing this, I fired on the second enemy aircraft. The machine pulled up abruptly and went into a flat spin, which continued until it struck the ground. Apparently I had shot the enemy pilot through the head."

"Füllgrabe reported everything by radio. I had no time for observations. The skilled enemy pilot was still behind me. By now he had closed again to within 200 meters. I dove to just above the ground. A quick look at the airspeed indicator: 600 kilometers per hour. That was enough. Hats off to Daimler-Benz. Safe at 1,200 meters, I climbed away from the Russian. We now raced for altitude. Then we were at 3,000 meters. My opponent attacked again, intent on revenge. A new struggle began. Another ten minutes passed. With each attack I mentally tipped my hat to my opponent. He must be their `top gun', I thought. It was a good thing that I had had years to practice this type of flying, otherwise I'd have been shot down already."

"Heinrich Füllgrabe radioed that he was heading home. He was out of fuel."

"Another five minutes and my warning light began to flicker. I thus had enough fuel in my tanks for about twenty minutes. I was a good 50 kilometers behind the front. Actually I should have broken off the combat at that point, but the thought of it pained me against such an opponent. If I beat it he would be the victor, at least symbolically. Furthermore he was still on my tail and was literally chasing me toward his own lines. Again we flew one circle after another or closed head on. Once I didn't fly toward him, but tried to fly past to one side. Oddly, he did the same thing and we raced past each other on opposite courses, only a few meters apart. What would he do now? Perhaps let me pass then turn round and fire the decisive burst? I lost him from sight for a few seconds. Then something incomprehensible happened: he flew on toward the East and I toward the West. I made my approach literally with my last drops of fuel. The engine quit as I landed . . ."

"My knees shook as I climbed out. That was an opponent! The congratulations offered for my two victories scarcely penetrated my consciousness. My thoughts were with the Russian fighter pilot against whom I had fought. I would liked to have sat with him some day and chatted. He was surely a splendid fellow . . ."

Reichsmarschall Göring valued Graf and thought highly of his skill as a unit leader. He made him the commanding officer of *"Ergänzungsjagdgruppe Ost"* (Replacement Fighter Group East), which was based in France. However after several months Graf assumed command of JG 11 at Rotenburg near Bremen. His mission: fly against the bomber streams. The air battle over Germany was in full swing. Graf was the only wearer of the

Diamonds to fly missions in the "*Reichsverteidigung*" (Defense of the Reich), in the course of which he was wounded several times.

For relief he played soccer. His *Geschwader* included some notable players whom he had either "liberated" or requested for his unit. The team for which Graf played goal called itself the "Red Fighters" and earned a legendary reputation. It was comparable with the best in Europe. Whenever Graf had a little spare time he could be found on the soccer field.

Graf injured himself in one match, as the result of which he walked with a limp. Then he received a report that American bombers were approaching Schweinfurt. With some difficulty he managed to climb into his machine. He took off from Wiesbaden, intercepted the enemy formations and shot up two B-17 Flying Fortresses, forcing them to drop out of formation. The engine of Graf's machine was hit by return fire, compelling him to make a forced landing. He came down in a tobacco field and the farmers lifted him from his machine. When they saw Graf limping they became concerned and asked if he had been wounded. "No," he replied with a laugh, "That came from playing soccer." The faces of those around him wore skeptical expressions; they thought the pilot was trying to pull their leg.

On March 29, 1944, he again shot down two Flying Fortresses and grappled with the many escorting fighters trying to drive away the German fighters. But Graf's men stuck doggedly to the bomber unit. Suddenly he was attacked by four enemy fighters which had separated him from his unit. In a witches cauldron of whizzing and exploding bullets, Graf thought himself lost. His ammunition ran out and he had just enough fuel for the flight home. But the Americans circled round him and refused to allow him to escape. Then he decided upon an act which characterized the soldier Graf: he raced toward an enemy fighter at maximum speed, then closed the throttle as he neared the enemy fighter and rammed it! The American machine's canopy was shaved off and it fell away in a steep dive. But Graf's machine, too, was now incapable of remaining in the air. The impact had been so great that the aircraft, its wings badly damaged, was turned about in the air and began falling toward the earth, spinning wildly. The other

American fighters dove after the mortally-wounded Messerschmitt and tried to administer the coup de grace. There was only one escape: bail out! The aircraft had already lost a great deal of altitude, but Graf had to try it. His parachute opened at the very last minute – 150 meters above the ground. Fortunately the impact was a gentle one. Graf came down in a marshy area, which saved his life. Nevertheless he sustained such serious injuries that he had to be hospitalized. His luck held: the doctor succeeded in sewing him up so well that it was not necessary to amputate his left arm.

Graf wanted to lead his unit from his sickbed, however Göring prevented this. Instead he told Graf that he wanted him to take command of his old unit, JG 52, following his convalescence.

In the days before assuming command of JG 52, Graf's greatest worry was the development of the Luftwaffe. The German fighters no longer posed a serious threat to the incoming Allied formations. The commanders of the fighter *Gruppen* consulted with each other and with the consent of *General der Jagdflieger* Adolf Galland a delegation of highly-decorated pilots went to see Göring. They presented their requests: a strengthening of the Luftwaffe, expansion of the jet fighter program, involvement of a capable expert.

Hermann Graf and his fellow unit commanders demanded of Göring that he "now finally do something to put an end to the Allied air superiority." But the *Reichsmarschall* hid behind "miracle weapons" which would yet enter service in time. The meeting ended; nothing happened.

The end was drawing near. *Jagdgeschwader* 52 fought on as part of Army Group Schörner, supporting the ground forces in Czechoslovakia and Silesia. On Easter Sunday 1945 Graf shot down a tethered balloon.

As of March the *Geschwaderstab* was located in Deutsch-Brod. The day Germany surrendered Graf had all remaining aircraft blown up to prevent them from falling into enemy hands. The General in command of the *Fliegerkorps, General* Seidemann, ordered Graf and *Gruppenkommandeur* Erich Hartmann, both wearers of the Diamonds, to fly out immediately and surrender to the British in Dortmund. Graf and

Hartmann refused. More than 2,000 women, children, elderly people and refugees had placed themselves under the protection of the soldiers. Graf couldn't and wouldn't abandon them. On learning that there were American troops near Pisek, about 100 kilometers away, he decided to drive there and surrender all together.

Along the way Graf and the others came upon five "King Tiger" tanks in a marketplace, whose crews were being held prisoner in a cellar by the Czechs. Graf's men freed them, and together with the tanks they drove to the Americans. The soldiers of the 90th US Infantry Division took charge of the Germans and delivered them to a camp containing 30,000 POWs. The officers were allowed to keep their pistols, everything seemed very honorable.

Then, on May 17, to Graf's disbelief, the Americans handed over the entire *Geschwader* to the Soviets. Soviet officers took charge of Graf. The man who had destroyed the equivalent of two Soviet air wings was now in their hands. His captivity was to last five years.

After Graf's return home there was much speculation as to why the highly-decorated officer had been released sooner than many of his comrades. He was accused of having conspired with the Soviets. But what had really happened? One day the camp commandant had asked Graf if he would like to attend an air display in Suchino, on the condition that he write an article about it for the camp newspaper. Graf agreed. His account was factual and non-political. But then, to his amazement and dismay, an article bearing his name appeared as a hymn of praise to the Soviet Air Force. It concluded with the words: "Long live the Red Air Force, the strongest air force in the world." Graf had never written that. The article's final sentence went on to say: "May the day not be far off when we too will again be allowed to participate in glorious aviation – in the service of peace."

Graf complained to the camp commandant, Lieutenant Colonel Martinov. The latter referred him to the "Antifa", a group of real and would-be communists who cooperated with the Soviet secret service and whose job it was to convert German prisoners of war to communism.

Thus compromised – thousands read and were angered by the article bearing Graf's signature – it was extremely difficult for him to rehabilitate himself, even though the ex-*Kommodore* had witnesses who had seen *his* article. Later, when Graf was taken to Moscow to be interrogated by Soviet Air Force officers, fellow POWs accused him of having declared himself ready to work with the Soviets. They also accused him of having done so in writing.

In reality Graf was asked by a high-ranking air force officer: "I want no secrets from you. We know them. But as a successful fighter pilot you can tell us what we did wrong for our air force to have suffered such high losses." Graf replied: "Your propaganda chief Ilya Ehrenburg claims that the 'Red Falcons' shot down 50,000 German aircraft. But we only had 25,000 in service during the entire war. You thus exceeded your quota by 100%." Annoyed, the Soviet officer jumped to his feet: "Ilya Ehrenburg lies as your propaganda Minister Goebbels lied. That is rubbish, we want to talk factually."

After a while the Russian called in an NKVD officer and asked him why Graf looked so poorly. The prisoner answered in place of the commissar: "Because I don't get enough food. I'm dying here slowly but surely." Afterward he was transferred to an engineering barracks, received a proper bed and was made chief cook. As long as he held this post there was no more stealing, the prisoners were fed regularly and well – compared to what they had been getting before – and there were no more deaths.

Graf was flown to Moscow several more times. He was put on trial for allegedly having killed Soviet pilots in their parachutes. Graf was able to prove that he and his *Geschwader* had been nowhere near the "scene of the crime" when the alleged incidents had taken place. The charge was withdrawn.

Even in a POW camp Graf was unable to dispense with his passion, soccer. He organized soccer matches to provide his comrades with a diversion and some exercise. On January 1, 1950 he was released in Berlin. Two days later he flew via Pan American Airlines to West Germany. At home he found that his apartment had been plundered. As the French were the occupying power in the area where he lived, Graf was once again arrested. He was released immediately, however, on the condition that he report daily. This went on for fourteen days and then he became a free man again. Hermann Graf spent more than two years recovering from the hardships of life as a POW. He was subsequently active in several fields in an attempt to earn a living – until Sepp Herberger came into the picture.

Struck down by illness, Graf refused to let it get the better of him. He could have applied for a pension, but here too Graf wanted to do his duty until age 65.

Answering the charges made against him, Hermann Graf wrote in *Bild am Sonntag* in 1971: "I took no 'other path' during the time of my captivity. The first part – after being handed over to the Russians by the Americans – I made together with Erich Hartmann. In the first Russian camp I too found myself in a rather miserable psychological and physical state. As an 'arch-enemy' of the Soviet Union I had no illusions as to my fate."

"In this desperate situation, still in shock over the manner in which the Americans had acted, I followed the suggestion of several other flying officers in the camp, to join the 'National Committee for a Free Germany'. I did this in the hope of assuring myself even a tiny chance of eventually surviving. I was not the only one to join this 'committee', for *Herr* Hartmann did the same, and surely for the same reasons as I. We attended a meeting and both felt disgusted. I was spared quitting the 'committee', for the association was disbanded soon afterward. Its place was taken by the ANTIFA. I did not belong to this until the time of my release."

"It is untrue and cannot be proved, that I 'decided for the Russians.' I do not feel like an 'outlaw', instead I see myself as the victim of a malicious legend concerning my behavior in Russian captivity, which was spread by 'good' comrades after the war."

Hermann Graf died on November 4, 1988.

CHAPTER VI

GENERALFELDMARSCHALL ERWIN ROMMEL

"There exists a real danger that our friend Rommel is becoming a kind of magician or bogey-man to our troops, who are talking far too much about him. He is by no means a superman, although he is undoubtedly very energetic and able. Even if he were a superman, it would still be highly undesirable that our men should credit him with supernatural powers."

"I wish you to dispel by all possible means the idea that Rommel represents something more than an ordinary German general. The important thing now is to see to it that we do not always talk of Rommel when we mean the enemy in Libya. We must refer to 'the Germans' or 'the Axis powers' or 'the enemy' and not always keep harping on Rommel."

"Please ensure that this order is put into immediate effect, and impress upon all Commanders that, from a psychological point of view, it is a matter of the highest importance."

(*Signed*) C.J. Auchinleck,
General
Commander-in-Chief, M.E.F.

"P.S. I am not jealous of Rommel."

This secret order to all British corps and division commanders in Africa fell into the hands of German troops. It said more about *Generalfeldmarschall* Erwin Rommel, commander of the German *Africa Korps* and later commander of an army and an army group, than the highest decoration could ever have done. What lay behind this order were great respect for Rommel and fear of his popularity, which he enjoyed among friend and foe.

"Rommel . . . !" The name frightened elite British divisions and caused their commanders to become nervous.

"We will fight our way through," was Rommel's solution, and this was a familiar quotation wherever the general appeared.

He was a genuine phenomenon among the soldiers of both warring parties, the Anglo-Americans and the Germans. The British called him the "Desert Fox." Germany's allies referred to him as "the Lion of Africa." To his own soldiers he was simply "Rommel."

Historians and military researchers are more factual and cooler in their assessment. They characterize Rommel as the "outstanding desert specialist." His bold operations in Cyrenaica, the impetuous drive to El Alamein, the daring plan to take Cairo and Alexandria and advance to the Caucasus in order to attack the Soviets in the rear, have long since become part of military history.

Rommel, who was sometimes characterized as a visionary, was in reality a sober calculator on the battlefield. He was a unit leader in the modern style and broke with tradition if it led to success. He thought and led in a revolutionary manner, and his bold plans were realized in large-scale and successful operations. It was one of the tragic chapters of the last war that Rommel's plans often foundered on the pigheadedness of the Italian command, on failures of senior Italian officers, and on the materiel superiority of the Allies. Moreover those in Führer Headquarters and in Rome took the setbacks in Africa all too lightly and placated themselves with the phrase: "Rommel will take care of it." Rommel's true stature was recognized by his British opponents Montgomery, Auchinleck and Wavell. A picture of Rommel hung in Montgomery's caravan.

Although the English feared him, the officers of the British Army finally became convinced that Rommel was only human after all. The British High Command knew of the "supply bottleneck" on the German side. Even the most skilled desert warrior must some day fall victim to the enemy's superiority in men and materiel. But they wanted to achieve their objective sooner than that and tried to eliminate the German *Feldmarschall*. A commando group led by Captain Stirling was sent against the headquarters of the *Africa Korps* in Beda Littoria, where it was thought Rommel was located, during the night of November 17/18, 1941. The British broke into the house but Rommel was not there. The *Feldmarschall* had given up these quarters and handed them over to the staff of the quartermaster. At the moment of the attack Rommel was in Rome. Had Rommel not changed headquarters who can say what his fate might have been . . .

Erwin Rommel was born in Heidenheim in Württemburg on November 15, 1891. The son of a professor, he joined the 124th Infantry Regiment (6th Württemburg) in Weingarten as an officer cadet. In 1912 he was commissioned as a *Leutnant*. He took part in World War One with his original unit, until in the autumn of 1915 he was transferred to a newly-formed Württemburg Mountain Infantry Battalion.

On October 25, 1917 the young company commander was awarded the Pour le Mérite after taking the 1,643-meter-high Monte Matajur in a daring raid and subsequently distinguishing himself in the fighting near Longarone in the Twelfth Battle of Isonzo. A year later he was promoted to the rank of *Hauptmann*.

After the war Rommel remained in Germany's 100,000-man Army, first as a company commander, then as an infantry instructor at the military school in Dresden. In the autumn of 1933 he was made the commander of a mountain infantry battalion in Goslar. Soon afterward he was assigned to the officer school in Potsdam as a course director and then Armed Forces High Command liaison officer on the staff of the Reich Youth Command. Finally he was made commander of the Wiener-Neustadt Military Academy. In 1938 Hitler named him commander of Führer Headquarters. At the same time he assumed command of the "Führer Escort Battalion", with which he took part in the march into Austria and Poland.

By now Rommel was fascinated by Hitler, even enthusiastic. On September 9, 1939, after a visit to Danzig, he wrote of Hitler in his diary: "He is extraordinarily friendly to me." On October 2 he related to Hitler after a visit with *Oberst* Schmundt in Warsaw: "The population breathed a sigh of relief when the Germans came and saved them."

Hitler saw in Rommel an officer capable of inspiring his troops and one who possessed a high level of leadership qualities. Prior to the beginning of the French Campaign he therefore gave him command of the 7th Panzer Division – a choice which was to prove to be a wise one and one of which Hitler spoke years later. He saw himself as the discoverer of the future field marshall.

Leading this division, in 1940 Rommel stormed across the Meuse, broke through the Maginot Line, and advanced to the La Basée Canal, where he was promoted to *Generalleutnant* and awarded the Knight's Cross on May 26. Without stopping he attacked Lille, turned, and crossed the Somme in order to crack the Weygand Line.

It was typical of Rommel that he was already leading his troops from the front, driving into cities immediately behind the advance patrols, capturing bridges and taking prisoners. Frequent changes of objective, lightning-quick advances with hastily-assembled battle groups, encirclements, and sudden appearances in the enemy's rear led his opponents to dub his panzer unit the "ghost division." Rommel always turned up where he was least expected, spreading fear and confusion. "The end soon followed . . ." said a French general.

The tactics and dash of the division commander caught the attention of *Generaloberst* Guderian, inspector of mobile forces and the initiator of modern tank warfare. He characterized Rommel as the prototype of the modern unit leader.

At the beginning of 1941 the Italian Army ran into difficulty against the British Army in Libya. Mussolini asked Hitler for help. On February 3 the latter tasked *Generalleutnant* Rommel with the formation of the *Africa Korps*, for he was of the opinion that only a tough man could handle this mission. "I consider Rommel an extremely tough commander," Hitler told his chief adjutant, *Oberst* Schmundt. Four days later Hitler personally briefed the newly-appointed Commander-in-Chief Africa and sent him to the new theater with *Oberst* Schmundt.

On February 9 Hitler received Mussolini's approval of the naming of Rommel, and three days later the first troops, of the 5th Light Division, disembarked in Tripoli. Following a 26-hour forced march they reached the front near El Agheila and the British forces under General Wavell. This feat was hailed enthusiastically by Hitler and Mussolini.

On March 20 Rommel reported to Hitler in Führer Headquarters. Hitler used the occasion to present Rommel with the Knight's Cross with Oak Leaves for the accomplishments of the 7th Panzer Division in France. Back in Africa, Rommel launched an offensive against the surprised British – contrary to the wishes of the OKH and without informing the Italian Commander-in-Chief, General Gariboldi. The German Africa Corps overran Marsa el Brega, took Ageolabia and secured important sources of fresh water. Mechilli fell, followed by Sollum.

Rommel's troops reached the Egyptian border before a lack of supplies forced them to halt. There was jubilation in Germany. In a few months Rommel had become Germany's most popular personality. His name became synonymous with bravery, daring, ability as a field commander, cunning and invincibility.

The German public never learned that the German and Italian forces had a daily requirement of 5,000 tonnes of food and materiel and that this norm was never achieved. In most cases this was the fault of Italian command centers, which betrayed the exact sailing times of the supply ships to the British. This soon became known to the Commander-in-Chief of the *Africa Korps*, Erwin Rommel.

Rommel received a surprise in his very first meeting with senior Italian officers: the carelessness with which they assessed the situation and their lack of regard for their troops caused him to become skeptical. When the poorly-led Italian soldiers became a burden on the German corps, Rommel came to despise his cowardly allies. He made no secret of his feelings. Encouraged to cooperate with the Italian headquarters, the "*Comando Supremo*", the result was conflict. Rommel had no intention of subordinating himself to the Italians and he drew his conclusions after his first discussions with Marshalls Cavallero and Bastico: "The German soldiers are led by me. See to it that your soldiers don't always run away and thus create situations which might become serious," he said to the Italians. Furious, they promptly complained to Mussolini about Rommel's behavior. Hitler let Rommel know that he should be more gentle in dealing with their sensitive allies. He approved all of the corps chief's operations, but he, Hitler, also had to consider Mussolini's feelings.

However the vigorous panzer commander did not concern himself with political considerations. He had other worries, and the longer he was in Africa the more he learned to despise the Italians. *Feldmarschall* Kesselring even maintained that Rommel hated the Italians because they were poor soldiers and their officer corps was totally corrupt. One thing was certain: Rommel, who had fought against the Italians in the First World War, spoke his mind loudly: "Better no allies at all than these. We will live to see them change sides." Rommel was to be proved right.

On November 19, 1941 the British attacked with strong armored forces and 100,000 men and overran the Italian positions. The weak German forces were also involved in heavy defensive fighting. But Rommel had recognized what was important in this theater of war. He shortened his supply lines, moved in reinforcements and bluffed the enemy. Mock tanks mounted on Volkswagens drove in circles. The resulting dust clouds were intended to simulate the approach of a large armored force. The British promptly fell for the ruse and broke off the attack.

On January 20, 1942 Rommel received the Oak Leaves with Swords. Two days later, without seeking the approval of the "*Comando Supremo*", he attacked the British again and drove them out of Cyrenaica.

Rommel's name will always be associated with the city and fortress of Tobruk. In a daring advance he cut off the British garrison from its army. The main body of his corps drove east, and it wasn't until June 19, 1942, when the enemy had been sufficiently weakened to prevent them from relieving the surrounded city, that he turned with part of his forces to attack Tobruk.

On June 22, 1942, 33,000 British troops, including five generals, began the march into captivity. Rommel was promoted to the rank of *Generalfeldmarschall*. he wrote to his wife: "I would rather have a fresh division than the field marshall's baton."

Near Bir el Gobi Rommel showed himself to be a strategist in the grand style. He joined battle against a numerically far superior force, and, employing the element of surprise and disregarding threats to his flanks, drove into the enemy's assembly areas. Rommel led the attack at the head of the 21st Panzer Division and directed the operation against the Halfaya Pass. That night, as he weaved between British tank and vehicle columns, he came close to being captured. Luckily he had "*Mammut*", a British command vehicle which had previously belonged to General Wavell. This deception saved him from being taken prisoner.

His daring attacks and breakthroughs repeatedly created the impression among the enemy that Rommel possessed far stronger forces than he actually did. The German commander knew that in the desert only a quick decision, courage and surprise attack could lead to success.

Often he found himself in close proximity to British troops and guns. Once he was forced to land his Fieseler *Storch*. When he approached the crew of the anti-aircraft gun he realized only at the last second that they were Tommies. Luckily a German Volkswagen appeared and snatched the field marshall and his party out from under the noses of the enemy.

During one of his vigorous attacks he was cut off from his command vehicle. Rommel recognized the danger and disappeared into a New Zealand Army hospital, which fortunately was located nearby. The hospital guards and the wounded were more than a little surprised to see the German field marshall – the famous Rommel – appear in their midst. He was led through the hospital tents by the doctor in charge. Rommel promised the New Zealanders good treatment as German prisoners and then disappeared the way he had come.

In June 1942 there existed a good chance of ending the African campaign quickly and victoriously. But whoever wished

to triumph in the desert first had to take possession of the island of Malta. Ceaseless air attacks against this British base
had been unable to convince the garrison to surrender. An
operation to capture Malta was conceived; Führer Headquarters dubbed it *Herkules*. The operation's leading proponents
were Mussolini and Kesselring. The Duce implored Rommel
to occupy fixed positions and wait until Operation *Herkules*
$s1tbegan. Then it would be only a matter of days, at most
weeks.

But Rommel had no intention of waiting. The British,
shocked by the loss of Tobruk, were showing signs of weakness and resignation. Rommel wanted to exploit this opportunity to smash the fleeing Eighth Army, following the maxim
which states that once the enemy starts running he should not
be allowed to stop.

On June 23 the *Africa Korps*, which by now had been en-
larged to a panzer army, drove across the Egyptian frontier
into the country. Rommel wanted to be in Cairo in a week. He
encircled four British divisions in Marsa Matruk. The British
Fleet evacuated Alexandria. Everywhere the British, Australians and New Zealanders were on the run. Victory was within
Rommel's grasp!

However *Feldmarschall* Kesselring and the "*Comando
Supremo*" were disappointed that Rommel had ignored them
and launched his offensive. Rommel's success was trumpeted
in Germany by Minister Goebbel's entire propaganda appara-
tus. Rommel on the advance! Rommel chases the British!
Rommel soon in Cairo! England driven out of Africa!

The headlines could not, however, gloss over what was
obvious in the German strategy and what had moved
Kesselring to warn against the attack. Rommel's desert supply lines were becoming ever longer, and he had only 70 tanks
and a worn-out, tired army. The *Africa Korps* lacked fuel, food,
munitions and vehicles.

But Rommel did not stop. He risked everything and walked
into a trap. The new commander of the British Eighth Army,
General Montgomery, had laid down a blocking line in the
desert narrows of El Alamein. Rommel got that far and no farther. All the effort expended in further attacks on the British

positions failed in the face of the superiority of the enemy's air force, which scarcely allowed Rommel's troops to move.

On October 1, while in Germany on sick leave, Rommel briefed an attentive Hitler on the situation in Africa. The bogging down of his offensive before El Alamein he blamed on the difficult supply situation, the allied superiority in the air and the cowardice of the Italians. Hitler promised tanks, fuel and fresh troops. Once again Rommel was swayed by Hitler's optimism and left convinced that the "Führer" would provide him with the necessary support.

On October 23, 1942, just before midnight, Montgomery's Eighth Army launched an attack with 150,000 men, taking the Germans completely by surprise. More than 1,000 tanks overran the Italians, who surrendered in the tens of thousands. The German positions, too, began to give way. The full weight of the British attack, which was supported by about 1,000 aircraft, struck an army which had not yet recovered from the strains of previous battles and which was awaiting fresh forces and supplies.

Rommel immediately hurried back to Africa. What he found there depressed him. The Italian units were in full disintegration, his own army was without tanks, its supplies at the bottom of the sea. But the German soldiers continued to hold before El Alamein. The extensive German minefields inflicted heavy losses on the British troops.

Montgomery gave the defenders no rest, however. He broke off the offensive, regrouped, and strengthened his artillery forces. Then, on November 2, he resumed the offensive with an artillery barrage greater than any seen before in Africa. The focal point: the German minefields. The artillery fired without pause; hundreds of aircraft attacked ceaselessly. When the necessary breaches had been smashed in the minefields the tanks attacked. With them came the infantry.

For the first time it seemed as if luck was about to abandon Rommel. He could not stop the enemy with an exhausted army and what remained of the Italians. Rommel saw through Montgomery's plan: he intended to catch the German army with a wide-ranging envelopment, then encircle and destroy it.

Rommel telegraphed Hitler:

"After ten days of the most difficult fighting against far superior British forces on land and in the air, the strength of the army is exhausted in spite of today's defensive success. The army is therefore not in a position to prevent the breakthrough attempt by strong enemy armored units expected tonight or tomorrow. Due to a shortage of vehicles, an orderly withdrawal of the six Italian and two German motorized divisions and brigades is not possible. A large proportion of these units will probably fall into the hands of the fully-motorized enemy. But the motorized troops, too, are so closely entangled in the battle that only a part of them will be able to disengage from the enemy. The remaining supplies of ammunition are in the area of the front, while no noteworthy amount is available in the rear area. The limited stocks of fuel are insufficient for a withdrawal over a long distance. The army will certainly be attacked by the British air force day and night on the one road available to it. In this situation we must reckon on the gradual destruction of the army in spite of the heroic resistance and exemplary spirit of the troops."

Rommel's words were a crushing blow to Hitler. The victorious Rommel, the heroic African army were both facing destruction. Only recently the papers had celebrated Rommel's success, and propaganda Minister Goebbels had ridiculed the British, predicting their total defeat. Now Rommel was almost finished.

The Italian *Comando Supremo* urged the *Feldmarschall* to persevere, to die on his feet as it were. There were already signs of extensive double dealing by Germany's allies. Germany's African Army was to be destroyed, thereby making things easy for the Allies. Then the Italian forces anticipated giving up.

Disappointed in Rommel, whom he intended to name Commander-in-Chief of the African Army – after Hube, whom he had originally chosen for the post, was killed in an accident – during the night Hitler sent him a telegram ordering him to hold on:

"Together with me, the German people are following the heroic defensive battle in Egypt, trusting faithfully in your leadership personality and in the bravery of the German-Italian troops under your command. In the situation in which you find yourself there can be no other thoughts but to persevere, not retreat a single step, and throw every weapon and every fighter who can be released into the battle. In spite of his superiority the enemy will also be at the end of his strength. It would not be the first time in history that the stronger will triumphed over the stronger battalions of the enemy. You can choose no other path for your troops but that which leads to victory or to death.

Adolf Hitler"

On November 3 the Africa Army had 24 tanks left. Half its personnel and artillery had been lost. The front had been shattered and a halt would only mean the encirclement of what was left of the army. Finally – responding to a telegram from Rommel – Hitler gave his authorization for a retreat.

On November 28, unannounced and without consulting the Italian *Comando Supremo*, Rommel flew to Führer Headquarters. Hitler received him immediately, but was very surprised to see the Feldmarschall in the "*Wolfsschanze*" and not with his troops. Rommel made it clear to Hitler that the visit was of the utmost importance, because he wanted to tell the Führer the plain truth. When Rommel then informed him that Africa would have to be abandoned in short order unless there was a decisive reversal of fortunes, Hitler forbade him to go on. Rommel refused to relent. He went on to describe the bitter struggle of the German soldiers, the terrible hardships they endured and the totally inadequate supplies they received. But Hitler wanted to hear nothing more of this. He even accused the *Africa Korps* of cowardice!

That was too much. When Rommel protested passionately against this accusation, Hitler relented and instructed Rommel to fly to Rome with Göring and from there undertake to supply the troops in Africa with the necessary goods.

But once again Rommel was disappointed. He was disheartened to learn that the Italians had no will to continue the war and that the Allies were preparing a major offensive in the rear of the German forces. Following his return to Africa an agent informed him that the Grand Mufti of Jerusalem had offered to mobilize all the muslims in North Africa against the Anglo-Americans and to wage a guerrilla war against them. In return he wanted assurances from Hitler and Mussolini that North Africa would be decolonialized after the war.

This offer was a factor in Rommel's strategy, but Hitler turned down the offer abruptly out of respect for Mussolini and Italy's colonial ambitions. Whereas only a few weeks earlier Rommel had been a great hero in Hitler's eyes, he was now often heard to speak disparagingly of him.

Hitler still thought of Rommel as a brave, skilled and clever leader, but within limits. He was certainly no stayer; that was Model and Schörner. The sympathy which Hitler had shown his *Feldmarschall* had sunk to the zero point. And nevertheless he did not want to and could not get rid of him. Rommel's standing with the German people was too great, propaganda had elevated him to too high a stature and had made him an invulnerable Siegfried. Hitler wouldn't have dared to let the *Feldmarschall* fall.

On March 4, 1943, Rommel was ordered to Führer Headquarters. The *Feldmarschall* reported on the situation and implored Hitler to shorten the front. But Hitler rejected the notion and ordered Rommel to attack Montgomery's Eighth Army on March 6. The German troops met an enemy who had been well-informed about their attack plans. After suffering heavy losses, the *Africa Korps* was forced to withdraw toward the Mareth Position. The same day Hitler summoned his former favorite from Africa, received him, sent him on sick leave, and on March 11 awarded him the Diamonds.

The German public was not allowed to learn that Rommel was no longer in command in Africa. The awarding of the Diamonds was also kept secret. Not until May 9, when Hitler had no one else to turn to for advice on how to stop the Allied invasion of Italy, did he summon Rommel. He intended to give him command of the Italian Front. On May 12 he had every radio station announce that Rommel had received the Diamonds in March.

On that same May 12 the last message from the *Africa Korps* was received in Führer Headquarters: "Ammunition expended. Weapons and equipment destroyed. As per orders, the DAK has fought until it is able to fight no more." An army of 120,000 men became prisoners of war.

Although *Generaloberst* Jodl had suggested finally giving overall command in Italy to Rommel, Hitler hesitated once again out of regard for Mussolini, whose generals rejected the German field marshall. Hitler thought he had reached a Solomon-like decision when he formed two army groups: Army Group B, under Rommel with its headquarters in Saloniki and responsibility for Crete, Greece and the Aegean, and Army Group E, under *Generaloberst* Löhr with its headquarters in Belgrade and responsibility for the Balkans.

This return to active service, even if he hadn't been given overall command in Italy, restored Rommel's optimism. He was often invited to eat with Hitler, took part in situation briefings and once again found himself becoming "fascinated" with the Führer. Rommel wrote: "What strength emanates from him. With what faith and confidence do his people cling to him."

Meanwhile Hitler had convinced himself that *Feldmarschall* Kesselring, who enjoyed Mussolini's trust, should be given overall command in Italy. Rommel, on the other hand, was placed in charge of the Atlantic Wall. Once again the name Rommel appeared in the headlines: the opinion of the unified German press was that if the field marshall had assumed responsibility for Germany's western bulwark then nothing could go wrong.

So Rommel awaited the invasion full of optimism. When the Allies landed on June 6, Rommel, Commander-in-Chief of the Normandy Front and of Army Group B, was in Germany. The commander of the Seventh Army, Dollmann, was taking part in a map exercise in Rennes, while the commander of I SS-Panzer Corps, Sepp Dietrich, was in Brussels.

Rommel was unable to prevent the collapse. He saw the end coming. Hitler meddled in the affairs of the Commander-in-Chief of the Western Front. *Feldmarschall* von Rundstedt and

Rommel defended themselves and asked hitler to come to the front to see the situation for himself.

Hitler didn't come until much later, on June 17, and refused to allow Rundstedt or Rommel influence his position. Finally he criticized the German generalship and expressed doubts as to the steadfastness of the troops. Rommel protested and proposed pulling the troops back beyond the Orne and concluding a cease-fire. Hitler snapped back: "You worry about the invasion front and not about the outcome of the war."

After this conversation the band that bound Rommel to Hitler was severed. Von Rundstedt was relieved and *Feldmarschall* von Kluge was placed in overall command. Rommel saw the senselessness of the war and urged von Kluge to do all that he could to save the lives of the German soldiers. Von Kluge rejected Rommel's request. "We will fight to the last round . . ." But Rommel did not give up. He asked the field marshall to go to the front and see things for himself. Von Kluge went to the front, examined the situation and came back depressed. He apologized to Rommel.

Rommel now sought further allies in order to make clear to Hitler that the fight against the allies in the west was a crime against the German people. He made contact with the commander of I SS-Panzer Corps (later Commander-in-Chief, Fifth SS-Panzer Army), Sepp Dietrich. The two men knew and respected one another. Dietrich shared Rommel's opinion, having drawn similar conclusions of his own. Together they tried to get *Generalfeldmarschall* von Kluge, the Commander-in-Chief West, on their side. They met like conspirators. But von Kluge hesitated, unwilling to commit a breach of faith, and said: "Gentlemen, I realize that things do not look good, but I cannot break my oath!" Rommel and Dietrich admitted that they were faced with a similar situation, but declared that, as unit leaders, they must place their responsibility to their men above all else. Von Kluge replied: "The Führer will have you shot."

Rommel and Dietrich didn't give up hope of winning over von Kluge. In the meantime, the commander of II SS-Panzer Corps, *Obergruppenführer* Wilhelm Bittrich, wearer of the Oak Leaves with Swords, had declared himself ready to join Rommel.

Rommel explained to von Kluge that all that was required was a letter or a conversation with Hitler – nothing else. If three popular and respected generals approached Hitler with their concerns he would have no option but to act as they suggested. After an hour von Kluge promised to think everything over once again and to inform the others of his decision.

Finally, on July 13, von Kluge gave *Feldmarschall* Rommel permission to draft a memo to Hitler. With von Kluge's approval he described the situation on the Western Front, stressing the bravery of the troops and the materiel superiority of the Allies, and ended with: "I must ask you to immediately draw the conclusions from this situation. I feel it is my duty, as Commander-in-Chief of the army group, to state this clearly." Rommel's objective was – and he once again reassured himself of Sepp Dietrich's loyalty – to conclude a cease-fire in the west.

But the cup had to be emptied to the bitter dregs. July 17 was the fateful day on the Western Front. Rommel visited the command posts and spoke with Sepp Dietrich by telephone. The two were united in their decision. While driving between Livarot and Vimoutiers, Rommel's car was attacked by enemy fighter-bombers. The vehicle skidded, Rommel fell out and lay on the road with serious head injuries. He barely escaped death. The doctors diagnosed a multiple skull fracture. Rommel was no longer able to lead. He gave up command of the army group. The dream of a cease-fire had died.

The *Feldmarschall*'s condition was grave and he was moved to Ulm Hospital.

On July 20 Graf Stauffenburg's bomb exploded in "*Wolfsschanze*" Führer Headquarters, however Hitler escaped with minor injuries. The revolt which began in Paris also failed quickly; the resistance movement collapsed.

General von Stulpnagel, one of the co-conspirators, shot himself in the head, but his aim was poor. Blinded, he was taken to hospital. *Feldmarschall* von Kluge suffered the consequences in his own way. He drove to the battlefields of Verdun, where he had fought as a young officer in the First World War, and poisoned himself.

In his delirium *General* von Stulpnagel several times spoke the name Rommel. Once he said, "Rommel is our last hope." The two Gestapo men who watched him day and night noted every word spoken by the delirious general. Himmler was shocked when he learned that Rommel, the folk hero, might also be one of the conspirators. He knew Hitler's state of mind after the coup. And now Rommel! This would be a hard blow for Hitler. "Rommel was there too," he said casually to Hitler. "What?" he snapped at the *Reichsführer SS*, "What are you saying?" Himmler hesitated a moment and reconsidered. If the report was inaccurate, if it was all a fantasy from the brain of *General* Stulpnagel, if Rommel had nothing to do with the affair . . . he calculated the consequences he might have to face. But then he drew himself up and said, "Several times von Stulpnagel has mentioned the name Rommel in connection with your betrayal, *mein Führer*."

Rommel recovered from his serious injuries at his house in Herrlingen. In September he received a visit from his former Chief-of-Staff and friend, *General* Speidel. Rommel asked him to drive to Führer Headquarters and speak with *Generaloberst* Guderian, the newly-appointed Chief-of-Staff. He was to tell him that he must conclude a cease-fire in the west, even if Hitler was against it. Rommel was against killing Hitler, in order to try him later. But Hitler reacted more quickly. He ordered an immediate investigation into the "Rommel case." When he believed he had found evidence of cooperation between Rommel and the conspirators he called together the "Wehrmacht Court of Honor", a so-called honor court to which only generals belonged. The chair was held by *Feldmarschall* von Rundstedt.

What had happened? The imprisoned *Oberstleutnant* Dr. Cäsar von Hofacker, co-conspirator, intimate and cousin of Graf Stauffenberg, signed a confession before he was executed, stating that *Feldmarschall* Rommel had been involved in the conspiracy against Hitler. Rommel had promised the most important member of the resistance movement, the former chief mayor of Leipzig, Dr. Gördeler, that he would take part and would accept the office of Reich President if it were offered him.

This piece of evidence was Rommel's death sentence. It will never be known what might have led von Hofacker, who had already been sentenced, to implicate the field marshall.

Rommel was requested to travel to Führer Headquarters on October 7. The *Feldmarschall* remarked that he would probably not return alive. He therefore declined, referring to his poor health, and stayed at home. Eight days later, on October 14, at twelve noon, Generals Burgdorf (successor to Chief Adjutant and Head of the Army Personnel Office *General* Schmundt, who had been killed during the coup attempt) and Maisel, as well as *Major* Ehrensperger and SS-driver Dose arrived in Herrlingen. Present were Frau Rommel, son Manfred, who as a flak auxiliary had just gone on leave, and *Hauptmann* Aldinger, Rommel's friend and adjutant.

Generals Burgdorf and Maisel asked to speak with Rommel. In the office they informed him that the "Honor Court" had discharged the Field Marshall from the Wehrmacht and that the Führer was going to bring him before a peoples court on charges of conspiracy and treason. The generals went on to say that because of his record he was being given an opportunity to avoid the consequences by committing suicide. They had brought poison with them and after his death his family would be cared for.

First Maisel left the room, then Burgdorf. Rommel spoke to his wife. "I'll be dead in fifteen minutes . . ." he whispered. He revealed what the generals had told him. "The poison will take effect in three seconds . . ." The field marshall said goodbye to his wife, his son and his friend Aldinger. Then he got into the car. Somewhere on the country road it stopped. The others got out and left Rommel alone. Three seconds later he was dead.

Rommel was given a state funeral. The people were not to know what had really happened. Almost no one suspected when Hitler sent the widow a telegram with the text: "I express my deepest sympathy over the death of your husband. The name of the field marshall will be associated with the heroism of the *Africa Korps* for all time. Adolf Hitler"

The funeral service in Ulm's city hall was a farce. Rommel's widow and son remained silent, condemned to silence, as *Feldmarschall* von Rundstedt delivered the eulogy, the same *Feldmarschall* von Rundstedt who had presided over the "Honor Court" which had expelled Rommel from the Wehrmacht.

CHAPTER VII

KAPITÄN ZUR SEE WOLFGANG LÜTH

U-181 slid smoothly through the water. It was finally back in Bordeaux harbor. The crew had been assembled on the quarterdeck in their light tropical uniforms. Before them stood their commander, a little pale, but smiling, as the boat docked and the flotilla commander came on board. A band played as the German war flag was run up the mast.

Then the ship's commander made his report: "U-181 back from its second sortie in the South African and Indian Ocean area of operations. 103,712 tonnes sunk."

The flotilla commander nodded to the brave men and congratulated the ship's commander on the Diamonds, which had been awarded him on August 11, 1943.

The commander of U-181 was *Korvettenkapitän* Wolfgang Lüth, thirty years of age. In the period from September 1942 to October 1943 he sortied twice with U-181, logging a total of 333 days at sea. One of these was the second longest sortie of the Second World War, lasting 205 days. (First sortie from September 12, 1942 to January 18, 1943. 58,381 tonnes of shipping sunk. Second sortie from March 23, 1943 to October 14, 1943. 103,712 tonnes of shipping sunk.) Lüth's totals were 17 operations lasting 609 days at sea (U-9/U-138/U-43/U-181, sunk: 43 ships totalling 215,147 tonnes and one submarine. The Wehrmacht High Command mistakenly reported 264,567 tonnes of shipping sunk).

The submarine had plowed through the mountainous waves of the earth's oceans for more than six and a half months. Thousands of miles from base, totally on their own, the men of U-181 had sailed the endless vastness of the seas. The ordeal was visible in their faces. Often they had been forced to remain under water for days, only surfacing for a few hours each night. But with temperatures of 55 degrees Celsius the nights were stifling. The air was heavy as lead and breathing became an ordeal.

Now they stood on the deck, the men of U-181, and celebrated the beginning of their well-earned and much longed for leave. Their commander was proud of them. For he knew that their success had been possible only because they had held together for better or worse. They had been together for 205 days, and yet it seemed to the men as if it had only been yesterday . . .

Silently the slender shadow pulled away from the pier. The night was dark, the only light a few twinkling stars in the heavens. Submarine U-181 was beginning a lengthy combat sortie. There was no marching music, no handshakes, no waving, no tossing of flowers. U-181 stole noiselessly out to sea. It was March 23, 1943. In command of the vessel was Wolfgang Lüth. He stood on the bridge and gazed back at the berth where the submarine had been only minutes ago. Now there was only a dark, gaping hole.

Several weeks earlier he had received orders to sail to the coast of Africa and the Indian Ocean. Lüth knew that it would be more difficult this time. For the Allies had learned from the losses inflicted upon them by the German submarines.

Lüth also knew that he would not be alone this time. Several boats, some commanded by officers of rank and name, had volunteered for the operation against the enemy's shipping. Nevertheless in the vastness of the sea a submarine was like a needle in a haystack. Preparations were made with care. Ship and crew had to be in order. The condition of the machinery and the health of the crew were checked closely.

Lüth was a submarine commander possessed with great experience and personal bravery. It was said of him that he had no nerves and that he understood how to command men like scarcely anyone else. On November 17, 1942 he had received the Oak Leaves for his most recent operation off Africa.

This U-Boat commander knew what awaited him and his men. Iron discipline was a prerequisite for the success of such an operation. Comradeship and a feeling of belonging were the invisible band which had often made the seemingly impossible possible. And because Lüth knew this he made the necessary provisions. He had the submarine loaded, not just with torpedoes and food, but with a generous supply of records, magazines and books as well.

Lüth wanted to give the men something to do in their off hours besides doze. Nothing is more detrimental to fighting morale than for the crew not to know what they should do with their free time.

The captain and one of his officers worked out a recreation program: skat and chess tournaments, singing contests and plays. Luth: "Gentlemen, on this sortie we'll probably see nothing but water for weeks. Water and not another ship . . ."

The officers looked at one another suggestively. "And to which corner of this lovely world are you taking us . . .?" they asked. Lüth smiled. He didn't know that himself. All he knew was that they were to sortie into the Indian Ocean.

When U-181 cast off on March 23, 1943, Lüth was at the top of the list of Germany's active submarine commanders. Only one, the unsurpassed Otto Kretschmer, had sunk more ships. However, Kretschmer's submarine had been sunk on March 17, 1941, and since then Kretschmer was in a British POW camp.

The sortie began well. U-181 had orders to attack a convoy which had been reported west of the Bay of Biscay. Lüth lost the convoy but soon afterward sunk the 5,983-tonne *Empire Whimbrel*. It was followed exactly one month later by the 5,232-tonne *Tinhow*.

The cruise became a tiresome pursuit of lone ships and "old tubs". Nothing was more dangerous to crew morale than a boring mission without attacks and success. Lüth was aware of this; he scanned the sea for steamers but rarely found one. Now and then a few small, old ships appeared, on which under normal circumstances Lüth wouldn't have wasted a torpedo. But here in the Indian Ocean he had to take whatever was offered him. The crew's feeling of sailing in a successful submarine was reinforced, especially after Wolfgang Lüth was awarded the Oak Leaves on April 15, 1943.

The search patterns and lying in wait for fat ships cost fuel. Lüth received information that the German tanker *Charlotte Schliemann* was waiting near the island of Mauritius. The "milk cow" supplied German U-Boats operating in the Indian Ocean with fuel, munitions and food.

On June 21, 1943 Lüth rendezvoused with the submarines U-177, U-178, U-196, U-197 and U-198. The meeting with his fellow captains Hartmann, Gysae, Kentrat, Bartels and Domme took place on the *Charlotte Schliemann*. The captains exchanged experiences. A common puzzle was the cause of the numerous failures of torpedoes to function.

The first to leave the tanker was U-181. Lüth had received orders from the BDU (Commander of Submarines) to operate near the island of Mauritius. American and British control of the seas was becoming more noticeable, not just on the water, but in the air as well. German submarines were no longer safe in the vast oceans, for the Allies had formed so-called "killer groups", specialized anti-submarine units using camouflaged ships. The true nature of these vessels did not become apparent until they had located the German submarine on radar (if the U-Boat was surfaced) or sonar (if the U-Boat was submerged).

The occasions when Lüth's submarine was forced under water by destroyers and aircraft became more frequent. The ship's crew had to endure hours of depth charge attacks. Often they were very lucky, as in the case when the commander of an American submarine trap, which had located U-181, called off the attack in the belief that he had sunk the U-Boat. Finally, after hours of waiting, with the crew clenching potassium tablets between their teeth to save air and at the end of their strength, Lüth gave the command to surface. They had escaped once again.

Iron discipline was necessary to endure life aboard a submarine in such climatic conditions. But Wolfgang Lüth was an outstanding leader of men. His strength was as great as his fairness and concern. The story was often told aboard U-181 of how it had been on U-9, when Lüth's submarine had been shaken by depth charges and no one believed they would ever survive – it was early 1940 . . .

"Report damage," ordered Lüth as the emergency lighting flickered to life. At the same moment a fresh series of depth charges came down. One-two-three . . . The men stopped counting at seven. This time they were significantly closer. The boat was tossed about like a rubber ball. The next series must be a direct hit.

"What's happening?" asked Lüth in the silence.

"Engine room reporting: pressure gauge has burst."

If nothing else is broken we can carry on, thought Lüth. The next series of seven depth charges shook the submarine mightily.

"Go to eighty meters."

The submarine sank more quickly than usual.

"Eighty meters," reported the chief engineer.

"Try to get us to one hundred meters . . . !"

Depth charges!

"I have one-hundred-and-twenty, *Herr Oberleutnant*," reported the chief engineer.

"Perhaps we'll be lucky and survive this mess," Lüth murmured to himself.

"Depth charges in the water!"

The radio operator kept silent. He sat at his position, not allowed to move from it, to take cover. More depth charges! The emergency lighting went out.

"Everyone listen to me," Lüth shouted into the darkness. The men listened. "Stay absolutely quiet. This business will pass," he said with a calm voice. A fresh series of depth charges forced the boat even deeper. Stools rolled about the compartment, men fell to the floor. Cries! A number of men were cut when they struck their heads on angular metal structures. The captain clung grimly to the periscope. He too stared upward in fear. He cursed himself once again for having disregarded the second destroyer. In the meantime the chief engineer had restored the lights. When light once again filled the compartment the men were noticeably green in the face. Then another explosion extinguished the lights again. Suddenly there was water in the compartment. Someone shouted: "A valve has burst in the bilge line. Fire!"

There – everyone could see – the instrument panel in the central control console was burning. The fire spread very quickly. The men seemed paralyzed. Before Lüth could say anything, someone came out of the darkness and plunged into the flames, oblivious to the danger. The man – no one yet knew who it was – extinguished the flames with a blanket and his bare hands.

The fire was out, the danger over. No one had taken any notice of the two additional depth charge attacks. The bilge pump was soon back in order and the leak stopped.

Lüth heard someone say, "We've put a dressing on Malik, *Herr Oberleutnant.*" So that's who had saved the boat. Malik? He remembered: that was the sailor he had been forced to take on board to prove himself.

"Bring him here," ordered Lüth, wiping his forehead and mouth with the back of his hand. The air was thick enough to cut, and to add to their misery the sound locator operator continued to report screw noises nearby. That could only be the destroyers.

Seaman Malik stood before the captain with bandaged hands. The emergency lighting cast bizarre shadows on the faces of both men. The others listened with one ear for screw noises, which they could no longer hear, and with the other in vain for a speech.

However nothing happened. There was absolute silence in the submarine. The only sounds were the breathing of the men and the light swishing of water against the ship's hull. Then Lüth broke the silence. No one could and would say what he might be feeling. Even later he said nothing of it. Only in his eyes was there a light, which was always visible when he was extraordinarily happy about something and when he was grateful.

"Thank you," he said in a soft but firm voice and offered his hand to the seaman. Only then did Lüth see the thick bandages covering the man's fingers. He did not squeeze hard, but he felt how the sailor's fingers closed around his hand and he stood erect. "As you were . . . You saved the ship."

They had all heard it. The sailor started back to his post but Lüth held him back once again. The *Oberleutnant* stood before the man and said, this time in a louder voice: "I am going to recommend you for the Iron Cross, First Class for fearless acts in the face of the enemy." Then a thunderous hurray went through the ship, something Lüth had not expected.

"Everyone to their stations," ordered Lüth, interrupting the outburst of joy which the men had so badly needed and which acted as a valve through which their depressed mood and fear was blown away . . .

That was then on U-9. Now Lüth led a new crew into the Indian Ocean. This was his second voyage aboard U-181, and the men who had taken part in the first knew that the rules were the same as in the Atlantic.

Then they sank the *Empire Lake*, a modern British vessel, even if only of 2,852 tonnes. When the two torpedoes bored through the side of the ship's hull the crew roared "hit" in unison. Then *Obergefreiter* Krüger put on the record with the victory march – that was Lüth's custom. But the commander gestured to him to wait:

"Just a moment! Pappy wants to have a look!" Peering through the periscope Lüth saw the effects of the torpedoes. The ship had been hit in the stern and amidships. The *Empire Lake* sent an SOS: "Torpedoed by enemy submarine!" Then it broke apart with a terrible din.

The ships crew tried to escape the maelstrom in the lifeboats. It was a horrible scene.

"Blow tanks, surface," Lüth ordered a short time later. U-181 surfaced in the midst of the survivors. Slowly Lüth moved toward the nearest lifeboat. "Is the captain on board?" he asked. The men shook their heads. "Any officers?"

One officer identified himself. Lüth ordered him on board. He asked him why they hadn't detected the submarine.

"The range of our detection equipment was inadequate," replied the Australian. The ship had been carrying a cargo of vegetable oil and frozen meat for England. "I can't assist you," said Lüth. "There's no room for your men on board. You'll surely be picked up soon by a rescue vessel."

The officer smiled skeptically. "No one will look for us here and no one will find us. If we're lucky we might by chance cross the route of a freighter."

And softly he added, "I know what's left – thirst and the sharks."

Lüth's men tossed the survivors rope and rolls of wire, so that they could tie their lifeboats together and at least be safe from the sharks. "Anyone who has to swim here won't live long," whispered someone behind the commander.

Lüth turned slowly and looked at the man. "Then we'll just have to make sure that we don't get into a situation where we have to go swimming. That depends on each individual . . ."

Lüth's men had a great deal of luck in all their operations. The list of enemy ships sunk grew. The last on this operation was the 10,528-tonne *Clan MacArthur*, a fully-laden refrigerator ship bound for Mauritius. With only one torpedo left on board Lüth set course for home, ignoring an order from Dönitz to search for the damaged U-197. The reason for his decision: as fuel was running low he would not be able to find or assist U-197 and his own ship and crew would be endangered, especially since enemy anti-submarine aircraft were becoming more active. Nothing more was said of the incident. U-181 arrived in Bordeaux on October 14 after 203 days at sea and a total of 45,331 tonnes of enemy shipping sunk.

Wolfgang Lüth was thirty years old when he received the Diamonds on August 11, 1943. Barely a year later he was promoted to the rank of *Kapitän zur See*. This extremely capable and courageous submarine commander was destined for a great career. *Grossadmiral* Dönitz wanted to name him commander of submarines.

Born in Riga on October 15, 1913, Lüth completed his schooling there and studied law for three semesters at the Herda Institute. But he wanted to go to sea. On April 1, 1933 he joined the German navy as an officer cadet.

After basic training he was assigned to the training sailing ship Gorch Fock. There he was promoted to sea cadet. Lüth sailed around the world aboard the cruiser *Karlsruhe*. He passed his final naval officer examinations at Flensburg-Murwik Naval Academy. On October 1, 1936 Wolfgang Lüth was promoted to the rank of *Leutnant zur See*. A year later he joined the submarine service. On June 1, 1938 he was promoted to the rank of *Oberleutnant zur See*.

Lüth sailed aboard various submarines as 1st Watch Officer and Deputy Commander until, in December 1939, he was given his first command. With U-9 he sank 16,669 tonnes of enemy shipping in five sorties. In one special operation he was supposed to guard German ships sailing to Norway against submarine attack. He succeeded in damaging an enemy destroyer and sinking a submarine. Following this operation he took command of U-138, with which he was active in the North Atlantic until September 25, 1940. On two sorties totalling 27 days at sea he sank 39,971 tonnes of enemy shipping. Lüth was awarded the Knight's Cross on October 24, 1940 in recognition of his success. As commander of U-43, Lüth made six sorties into the North Atlantic in the period November 1940 to February 1942, and in 192 days at sea sank nine enemy ships totalling 54,795 tonnes.

On May 9, 1942 he took charge of U-181. The BDU and its Chief of the Operations Section, Admiral Godt, had come up with a special route for the fearless commander: to South Africa and the Indian Ocean. Lüth knew the stresses and difficulties this voyage would involve: unusual climate, thousands of miles from home port and support bases, no hope of assistance if they were disabled. He could only rendezvous with the submarine tanker at specified times. All in all it was an operation which should contain many surprises for the commander and his crew.

Four and a half months is a long time. Four and a half months of water, attacks, torpedoes, bombs, diving, surfacing for air, chasing and being chased. Lüth and his men survived 128 days at sea and during this first sortie sank twelve enemy ships totalling 58,381 tonnes. On November 17, 1942 he received the Oak Leaves.

The second cruise into the Indian Ocean lasted from March 23 to October 14, 1943. In the course of this sortie Lüth achieved a unique record. He and his men were 205 days at sea. Nothing but sky and water, ships, depth charges and torpedoes.

During this sortie he sank 103,712 tonnes of enemy shipping. On April 1, 1943 Lüth was promoted to *Korvettenkapitän*, then received the Swords on April 15 and the Diamonds on August 11, 1943.

On January 15, 1944 Wolfgang Lüth was placed in command of the 22nd Submarine Flotilla in Gotenhafen. On August 1 he was promoted to *Fregattenkapitän* and transferred to Flensburg-Murwik Naval Academy, where he became commander of 1 Division. Lüth was promoted to *Kapitän zur See* on September 1. With the help of his friend Klaus Korth he wrote a book about his experiences in submarines.

Lüth became a sought-after and popular advisor on submarine questions. He spoke before officers and officer cadets, before generals and admirals. What he said was simple and clear. During this time he worked on a "Guide Book for Future Naval Officers", which went on to become a standard text for young cadets.

On September 18, 1944 *Kapitän zur See* Lüth received a surprise appointment as commander of the Naval Academy (at 31 years of age!). In the past this position had always been held by an admiral. This unusual choice made clear Dönitz's intentions to ease Lüth's path to the highest command positions in the German Navy.

Lüth commanded with a firm hand, for he knew that the officers of tomorrow would face far greater challenges than in the past. As it turned out there was little he could do – the end of the war was at hand.

May 1945. The last president of the Reich, which had meanwhile been occupied by the Allies, was *Grossadmiral* Dönitz. The government transferred its headquarters from Plön to the Flensburg-Murwik Naval Academy. The academy's commanding officer, Wolfgang Lüth, moved out of the building which housed his headquarters. He was responsible for the safety of the government. On the academy grounds Oak Leaves wearer Ali Cremer, last captain of the U-2519, commanded the "Dönitz Guard Battalion", the last fighting force – 400 men strong – of the last Reich President. On May 5 the English occupied Flensburg, but in the naval academy nothing changed. German soldiers and sailors were allowed to carry arms, their commander Lüth was even empowered to defend the academy against anyone who dared attack it. The English had learned that freed foreign workers intended to carry out a surprise attack on the Naval Academy.

Lüth issued orders to place placards at the outer boundaries of the facility which bore the words: "Warning! This area is off limits to civilians. Anyone who enters without passing through the main gate will be fired on without warning."

That was the general warning.

But Lüth was concerned about security. He issued several memos to the guards, one of which stated: "The guards are to issue one challenge. If this is not answered they are to fire immediately."

The commanding officer ensured that Ali Cremer's guard battalion was made aware of this order.

On May 13, 1945 the password was "Tannenberg". The watch officer, *Maschinenmaat* Karl Franz, checked the sentries. Seaman Mathias Gottlob, eighteen years old, prepared for a twenty-hour watch. Outside it was warm. The watch was changed "without incident". At midnight it was Gottlob's turn to stand guard again. The warm spring evening had become a stormy night. The wind howled, and one could scarcely hear himself speak. *Maschinenmaat* Karl Franz checked the sentries, for he knew that Lüth could turn up unannounced to check on the alertness of his soldiers. The CO has said, "Anyone sleeping here will be court-martialled. The sentry is responsible for the safety of his comrades and the government."

Franz asked the sentries, who made their rounds on the road and around the sports school, if they had seen anything out of the ordinary. "Nothing new!"

"Stay alert. Lüth is coming any minute," he admonished them.

Lüth came several minutes later. He had just participated in a conference in the government building. His collars turned up, he pressed on into the storm. *Maschinenmaat* Franz came toward him and reported. Tired and a little apathetic, Lüth raised his hand to his cap and walked on.

Franz watched the captain go, turned round and walked toward the next sentry. Then he heard someone shout "halt!"

Franz stopped and listened into the night. Again the same shout, "Halt!"

Then he thought he heard it again, somewhat softer this time. Right away there was a shot, muffled as if fired with a silencer. Franz ran toward the sound. "What's going on?" he shouted from a distance.

"I fired," answered the sentry.

"Yes, man, but at whom . . . ?"

Seaman Mathias Gottlob pointed with one hand. "There .. ." The machinists mate ran, stopped, bent down. He saw an officer's cap. He picked it up and an icy chill went through him. He was holding *Kapitän* Wolfgang Lüth's cap in his hand.

Then he saw the figure on the ground. He kneeled down and tried to recognize the face. Fingers shaking, he felt along the leather coat, touched the face and felt something wet between his fingers. Blood!

The other two sentries came hurrying up to the scene. When Franz turned round he saw Gottlob, still with the rifle in his hands, staring at the form lying on the ground. "I didn't even aim," he said softly. "My God, my God . . ."

A few minutes later the medical officer determined that *Kapitän zur See* Wolfgang Lüth was dead, killed by a bullet in the head.

When *Grossadmiral* Dönitz' adjutant, Lüdde-Neurath, learned by telephone what had happened, he thought someone was playing a terrible joke on him. But the voice of the watch officer suggested it was true. Lüdde-Neurath woke Lüth's brother Joachim, who was sleeping in the *Kapitän's* office, and told him what he had just learned. At first Joachim Lüth didn't comprehend what was being said. What, shot five days after the surrender? Now, after Wolfgang had survived all of his combat sorties? How was he supposed to tell Lüth's wife, who was living in the same building with their four children?

The officer of the watch interrogated Seaman Gottlob and watch officer Franz. He listened to what both had to say and he believed them. He was shaken by the tragedy. An officer had been shot because a sentry had followed his orders to the letter.

"I didn't want to shoot him. I didn't recognize him," Gottlob assured his interrogator. "But when I challenged him three times and received no answer, I was suddenly afraid that it might be a foreigner. Then I pressed the trigger – I was holding the rifle at my hip and didn't even aim . . ."

Gottlob had told the truth. Later, when Dönitz demanded a preliminary examination to determine whether a court-martial was warranted – even though the German Armed Forces had surrendered and no longer existed – it proved Gottlob's innocence. Four officers and the local navy legal officer listened once again to the account of the tragic incident. Then Dönitz interviewed Gottlob. All reached the same conclusion and after twenty minutes announced: "Seaman Mathias Gottlob carried out the standing order and followed this correctly. He did his duty as a soldier and fired after issuing three challenges and receiving no response. He bears no guilt in the death of *Kapitän zur See* Wolfgang Lüth."

Services for Wolfgang Lüth took place on May 16. The British city commandant, Colonel Roberts, authorized a state funeral.

The coffin containing the body of *Kapitän zur See* Wolfgang Lüth was laid out in the auditorium of the naval academy. Six of his comrades, all recipients of the Knight's Cross, formed the guard of honor, in full dress uniform with drawn swords. *Grossadmiral* Dönitz delivered the eulogy. Then officer cadets bore the coffin from the auditorium to the Adelby Church cemetery. Ali Cremer commanded the honor party. For the last time a firing party fired the final salute to a German officer.

Thirty years later, in May 1975, a new generation was growing up and once again young men were called upon to defend the freedom of the nation. The *Bundesmarine*, the new German navy, dedicated a memorial to *Kapitän zur See* Wolfgang Lüth. This irreproachable officer is an example to every young man who is ready to risk his life for the maintenance of parliamentary democracy. "His memory remains alive today," said an article in the newspaper *Die Bundesmarine*. Lüth would have said: "You're fine lads."

CHAPTER VIII

MAJOR
WALTER NOWOTNY

Vilna, October 19, 1943, shortly before midnight. In the Ria Bar the telephone rang. The office clerk, a German *Oberfeldwebel*, picked up the receiver. He covered his left ear with his free hand, for the noise from the cheerful throng inside reached into the telephone booth next to the bar.

"*Herr Hauptmann* Nowotny to the telephone . . ."

A young officer got up from a stool. With uncertain steps, a cigarette in his hand, he walked toward the corner where the telephone was. "Yes, Nowotny here."

There was a crackling in the line. Then a voice squeaked: "*Hauptmann* Nowotny?"

"Yes, speaking."

"One moment please, I'll connect you with the Führer."

Shocked and surprised, Nowotny let the cigarette drop to the floor and raised his right hand to his throat. Now, and here of all places! But perhaps a comrade was playing a joke. That wasn't out of the question. After all everyone knew that today he had shot down his 250th enemy aircraft and that he was celebrating with a few old friends in the bar.

Seconds later he received congratulations for the Diamonds which Hitler had just awarded him – in the Ria Bar in Vilna, surrounded by pretty girls and laughing friends. The surroundings suddenly seemed less comfortable to Nowotny.

The next day Nowotny flew to Führer Headquarters to receive Germany's highest decoration for bravery.

It had been more than two years earlier, on July 23, 1941, when he shot down his first enemy aircraft, a Russian I-18. Three months earlier, on April 1, he had been promoted to *Leutnant*. Then two days later, after shooting three Soviet machines out of the sky, he almost became a victim himself. The third enemy aircraft went down in flames and Nowotny headed for home. But over the Baltic near the island of Oesel he ran out of fuel. Forced landing? No! He would bail out. Nowotny spent three days in his inflatable raft, exhausted, under the blazing sun all day long and in bitter cold by night. He lost consciousness and on awaking found himself in a farmer's bed. Latvians had spotted his life raft, pulled him ashore and saved the young flier's life.

In August Nowotny received the Iron Cross, First Class for his tenth victory. This was followed on September 14, 1942 by the Knight's Cross after 56 kills. Flying near Leningrad, Nowotny shot down seven Soviet fighters in one day. Later he was on patrol with other aircraft when they were attacked by 60 enemy fighters. Three I-18s fell to Nowotny's guns before his own aircraft was hit. His Messerschmitt was on fire, but the young pilot nevertheless landed successfully.

The youthful *Oberleutnant* embarked on a tremendous run of success. By now he was the leader of a *Staffel* in the *Gruppe* commanded by *Major* Philipp. With 203 kills, Philipp led the field of German fighter pilots.

Nowotny never missed an opportunity to dogfight nor did he hesitate to attack superior numbers of enemy aircraft. He shot down the first Spitfire and one of the first American fighters which the Russians had received from the western allies under lend-lease. The aircraft were flown by Russian pilots. On one occasion he tackled 14 enemy aircraft alone in his Focke Wulf, shooting down three and returning with a shot-up machine.

On July 17, 1943 he reported his 100th kill, and on July 24 his 124th. On August 18 he shot down his 150th and 151st enemy aircraft and three days later his 161st.

Nowotny's successes were reported almost daily by German radio: the young *Oberleutnant* now commanded a *Gruppe* and by September 1 had 183 kills to his credit. He shot down ten enemy aircraft in one day. Two days later, on September 3, 1943, after his 191st kill, he received the Oak Leaves, and on September 22 the Swords for his 220th victory. After this run of success Walter Nowotny was Germany's most successful fighter pilot. Behind him were *Major* Philipp with 203, *Major* Graf with 202 and *Hauptmann* Rall with 200.

Nowotny was promoted to *Hauptmann* following his 225th kill. When he became the first pilot in the world to shoot down 250 enemy aircraft – a tremendous feat in only 442 missions – the airfield flak fired a salute and the men of the *Geschwader* created a fireworks display with signal flares. Germany's most successful fighter pilot was receiving the Diamonds!

That was Walter Nowotny's path from his first victory to the amazing telephone conversation in the Ria Bar in Vilna.

Walter Nowotny was a modest man. His father was a railway official, his two brothers officers. One was posted missing in Stalingrad.

When the mayor of Vienna, Dipl.-Ing. Hannes Blaschke, awarded the young *Major* Walter Nowotny the city's ring of honor, the twenty-two-year-old officer didn't want to accept it out of modesty. He suggested that he hadn't earned such an honor. But the city administration and the mayor insisted.

Nowotny had never dreamed that he would become such a public figure. He had been born in the small city of Gmünd on December 7, 1920. The young man became a singer in the Cistercian convent in Zwettl. When his father was transferred the family moved to Waidhofen where he attended high school. Nowotny passed his final examinations with a mark of "very good." From the labor service he joined the Luftwaffe as an officer cadet and on October 1, 1939 was called up at Breslau-Schögarten. At first he flew fighter cover for the Leuna works, then he was transferred to *Jagdgeschwader* 54 under *Major* Trautloft.

Nowotny was a gifted pilot, a tough fighter and a man who loved the social life. He was not happy when, in February 1944, he had to give up his *Gruppe* and leave his *Geschwader* to take command of Fighter Training School 1 in Paux in the French Pyrenees. The orders came from on high. In Paux he simultaneously took command of *Jagdgeschwader* 101 as *Kommodore*.

Nowotny wanted only to fly, for flying was his passion. But in Berlin, in the headquarters of the *General der Jagdflieger*, they had come up with a new mission for him: Nowotny was to lead the first Me 262 unit. The first *Staffel* or *Gruppe*, perhaps even a *Geschwader*, would be equipped with the world's first turbojet-powered fighter! This assignment excited Nowotny, even though he knew little about the Me 262. All that he knew was that aviation and the air war was about to enter a new phase. The first time he saw the "miracle aircraft" he was amazed. The Messerschmitt design had a nosewheel under-carriage, a wingspan of 12.65 meters and was 10.60 meters long. Two jet engines, each of which produced 1,980 pounds of thrust, were said to propel the machine as if shot from a catapult. With a speed of 850 to 900 kph, it was then the fastest aircraft in the world. The fuel consumption of 2,500 liters per hour caused no headaches, as the turbines were very simple and could achieve peak performance using low-grade fuel. The fast fighter's armament was extraordinarily heavy. Four 30mm cannon with a total of 360 rounds of ammunition made the aircraft a deadly attacker. Later it was to be equipped with 16 or 24 R4M air-to-air rockets beneath each wing, each of which was sufficient to bring down an enemy aircraft.

Nowotny was enthusiastic. Granted, the aircraft required a takeoff and landing surface two kilometers long, and land-ing this new "bird" was very difficult. As well, aerobatics were impossible with the aircraft. But dogfighting was no longer necessary. The future program for Messerschmitt jet pilots con-sisted of sweeping turns and shallow dives. The aircraft climbed so rapidly that other maneuvers were unnecessary to approach the enemy. This miraculous machine flew like a bul-let, enabling deadly surprise attacks to be made.

Nowotny was to command a unit of these "heavy fight-ers", which it was hoped would bring about a change in the way aerial warfare was conducted. That this did not come to pass was due to errors committed by higher authorities.

Nowotny test flew the Me 262 at Rechlin. He gathered about him several of his former *Geschwader* comrades, all successful fighter pilots. For only first-class pilots could survive against the English and Americans, who were now escorting the bomber units with long-range P-47 Thunderbolt and P-51 Mustang fighters, which circled their charges tirelessly like watchdogs.

Nowotny's greatest worry related to production of the Me 262. Only 564 machines had been built, while at the time of the invasion the other side possessed 12,387 aircraft, 5,600 of which were fighters.

In addition to difficulties in the production program there were material and technical problems. Good pilots crashed for reasons other than enemy action. The jet engines failed and the aircraft fell to earth like a stone. Only a few pilots succeeded in escaping by parachute.

The responsibilities of his new position weighed heavily on Nowotny. He held lengthy discussions with his pilots in an effort to eliminate shortcomings and identify new problems. The aircraft was so good and so effective that it made all the effort – and the sacrifices – worthwhile.

The Allies were surprised and shocked at the performance of the Me 262. "If the Germans manufacture this aircraft in quantity quickly, our losses will become so great that we will be unable to risk sending any aircraft over German territory," England's bomber leader Harris said to Churchill. His prognosis was correct. Had the Me 262 been accepted into the large-scale fighter program and produced exclusively, Harris' fears would have become reality. But Hitler had other ideas. On his order the Me 262 was to be used as a fighter-bomber. The decision was contrary to the advice of the experts and went against all strategic reason. The pilots who had tested the aircraft were speechless when *Reichsmarschall* Göring, jumping on Hitler's bandwagon, stated that the Me 262 was much too fast and that pilots wouldn't be able to hit anything with it.

The initial teething troubles in the test program were soon overcome. Under Nowotny's command the first successes were achieved while the jet unit's losses were low.

Although Nowotny himself had been forbidden to fly, one day he climbed into an aircraft and took off after a bomber formation. In a matter of a few minutes he shot down a four-engined bomber with a single burst from his cannon. Afterward he asked *General der Jagdflieger* Adolf Galland and the

Reichsmarschall to lift the flying ban. Both said no. The senior Luftwaffe commanders didn't want to lose an officer like Nowotny, who possessed special command and organizational talents. They saw in him one of the leading men of the new Luftwaffe. However things were to turn out very differently.

Achmer, November 8, 1944

The telephone rang in *Kommando* Nowotny's command post. The *Kommodore* was on the airfield. Moments later he had the receiver in his hand and learned that the previous evening's visitor was coming back. Nowotny said, "*Jawohl Herr General. . .* I'll be waiting", and hung up. But he was not enthusiastic.

Since the day before, the *General der Jagdflieger* and *Generaloberst* Keller, Göring's representative, had been in the young jet commander's area of command. The general said what Göring had told him to say: the aces of past years had become cowards, the Luftwaffe had lost its spirit. The *Reichsmarschall* insisted that he would man the new jet fighters with young men who had been trained as glider pilots.

Nowotny couldn't believe what he was hearing. He protested vigorously against the notion that the older aces, of whom he was one, were cowards. He brazenly spoke his mind and asked how it was that experienced pilots were being sent to the infantry instead of being used as instructors. Perhaps Nowotny would still be alive if the sentence about "cowardly fighter aces" had never been spoken.

The *Major* looked at the clock. The general and his party arrived. The reception was frosty. Nowotny felt offended. They discussed the situation in the air and possible countermeasures. *General* Galland expressly declared that Nowotny was not to fly as he was needed in a command role.

Immediately afterward the signals officer reported the approach of large numbers of enemy aircraft. Nowotny gave the order to take off. Moments later the jet fighters made contact with the enemy, shot down several aircraft and began a second attack.

Then radio contact was lost with *Leutnant* Schall. His Messerschmitt crashed near Bramsche. Another aircraft made a forced landing, while a third was caught in a hail of bullets from two Mustangs and a Flying Fortress and fell to earth.

When Nowotny heard the bad news there was no keeping him in the command post. His best friends were being killed while he sat idly by. He recalled the general's words: "The older fighter pilots have become cowards." Dismayed, he stared at the generals. Had one of them really said that the older fighter pilots had become cowards? Good, he had said it – and he, *Major* Nowotny, would convince him otherwise. Before *General* Galland could stop him, the major had left the building and was sitting behind the wheel of his car. He turned in the seat and called back: "I'm sorry *Herr General* that I cannot obey your order. But I am going to fly now and will prove that we can still achieve something." Then he drove off. Galland shouted after him, ordered him to come back, but Nowotny did not hear.

Seconds later he dove on an enemy bomber formation flying in the vicinity of the airfield. Like an arrow he shot toward a Boeing and blew off a wing with his first burst.

The Flying Fortress went into a spin, flames shot from the machine. It raced toward the earth like a stone. Nowotny now turned to attack one of the escorting Mustangs. But suddenly his aircraft sagged. Those in the ground control station heard Nowotny's desperate call; the jet engines were no longer functioning. The machine was loosing altitude. Nowotny jettisoned the canopy. His parachute billowed open, but as it had opened too soon it became caught on the tail surfaces. The Messerschmitt crashed on the airfield. Beside it lay the shattered body of Walter Nowotny.

The state funeral took place in Vienna. He was buried in a grave of honor in the central cemetery next to the Lueger Chapel. Nowotny found his last resting place among scientists, statesmen and poets. Vienna wanted to give its brave soldier a worthy burial site.

A few months later, after the Red Army had taken the city, communists destroyed the mound under which Nowotny was buried. The Soviets turned the cemetery into a cow pasture, and the city administration refused to care for burial sites. Family members made repeated requests to be allowed to erect a headstone, but were refused.

Not until later, in 1950, were Nowotny's parents and brother Adolf permitted to mark the grave of the successful flier. On a small, inconspicuous tablet was the name Walter Nowotny. Until then no one knew who lay buried there. The authorities declared that it was an "unknown soldier."

But the Soviets and communists could not prevent the populace from placing flowers, wreaths and candles at the grave mound of Walter Nowotny. And then all at once the young began coming. No one organized them, they came on their own. Their parents had told them who it was who lay in the central cemetery, and the Soviets were in the process of withdrawing. These young people transformed the grave into a sea of flowers and mounted a death watch on All Soul's Day. They did it not as a demonstration, but rather to pay thanks to someone who had accomplished much in the course of his heroic life.

However the police showed little understanding. They carried out lengthy investigations and sought the "ring leader." The Viennese shook their heads. They had not forgotten Walter Nowotny. They venerated him, the brave pilot who had proved that the "old aces" were not cowards.

Walter Nowotny was also held in high esteem by the fighter pilot fraternity in the enemy camp. The highly-decorated French pilot Pierre Closterman, who flew with the RAF, wrote in his book *The Big Show*:

> "Walter Nowotny was dead. Our adversary over Normandy and in the German skies was killed the day before yesterday. The Luftwaffe, whose declared hero he was, would not long survive his death, which was as it were the turning point of the air war.
>
> That evening in the mess his name was often on our lips. We spoke of him without hatred and without rancor. Each one of us recalled his memories of him, with respect, almost with affection. It was the first time I had heard this note in a conversation in the RAF, and it was also the first time that I heard, openly expressed, that curious solidarity among fighter pilots which is above all tragedies and all prejudices.

This war has witnessed appalling massacres, towns crushed by bombs, the butchery of Oradour, the ruins of Hamburg. We ourselves have been sickened when our shells exploded in a peaceful village street, mowing down women and children round the German tank we were attacking. In comparison our tussles with Nowotny and his Messerschmitts were something clean, above the fighting on the ground, in the mud and the blood, in the deafening din of the crawling, stinking tanks.

Dogfights in the sky: silver midges dancing in graceful arabesques – the diaphanous tracery of milky condensation trails skimming like toys in the infinite sky.

We too, of course, were involved in less noble fighting: that strafing of trains in the grey dawn of winter mornings when you tried not to think of the shrieks of terror, not to see your shells smashing through the wood, the windows shivering in fragments, the engine drivers writhing in the burning jets of steam, all those human beings trapped in the coaches, panic-stricken by the roar of our engines and the barking of the flak; all those inhuman, immoral jobs we had to do because we were soldiers and because war is war.

We could rise above all this today by saluting a brave enemy who had just died, by saying that Nowotny belonged to us, that he was part of our world, where there were no ideologies, no hatred and no frontiers. This sense of comradeship had nothing to do with patriotism, democracy, Nazism or humanity. All those chaps that evening felt this instinctively, and as for those who shrug their shoulders, they just can't know – they aren't fighter pilots. The conversation had ceased, the beer mugs were empty, the wireless was silent as it was past midnight. Bruce Cole, who was neither poet nor philosopher, let fall these words: 'Whoever first dared paint markings on an aircraft was a swine!'"

CHAPTER IX

GENERALMAJOR ADELBERT SCHULZ

The Soviets were attempting to break through near Kiev. Their artillery pounded the German positions cease lessly. None of the German grenadiers believed they would come out of this hell alive.

Somewhere near the German front line, heavy tanks sat behind the small, straw-covered houses of a village. Looked upon as "corset stays" for the front, their job was to relieve the pressure where it was greatest.

The tanks were under the command of a young *Oberst*. His men called him "Panzer-Schulz." He was Adalbert Schulz, and most of his tank drivers knew him simply as the commander who always had a cigar in his mouth.

The Soviet offensive was aimed at the northern wing of the German infantry division, which had been under barrage fire for hours. Then the whistling and howling stopped and, with loud shouts of "Urray," the Soviet soldiers stormed out of their trenches.

"Mount up!" the *Oberst* called to the infantry who were to accompany the counterattack.

The 1st Battalion drove into the enemy's flank and drove him back to his jumping-off positions; the Soviet attack formations were smashed. Then, suddenly, Soviet tanks attacked. From his position in a village Schulz watched them approach; he estimated sixty T 34s and KV 85s. They could not be allowed to reach the German infantry positions. If they broke through they would be in a position to roll up the entire front.

The consequences of this would have been unforeseeable.

The 2nd Battalion, with which Schulz carried out the attack, lay in wait for the enemy in a shattered village. The heavy tanks took the Soviets in the flank as they drove past to the left and blasted the attack spearhead. By the time the following T 34s realized what was going on "up front," they were already being fired upon by the German tanks.

Of the sixty enemy tanks not a single one returned to its starting position. Now Schulz wanted to exploit this success. He drove past the burnt-out and shattered wrecks, overran the Soviet trenches and broke through to the artillery positions, where his tanks destroyed heavy guns and "Stalin Organ" rocket launchers. Then he linked up with his 1st Battalion and expanded the attack.

Schulz didn't have long to celebrate this success, however. The Soviets moved up fresh forces and attempted to encircle the German tanks. They were aware that only a small force had broken through. Fighting hard, the panzers withdrew to their own starting position. The Soviet attempt to encircle and destroy them failed. Along the way Schulz's tank crews destroyed more than 150 T 34s.

As a result of this action the enemy called off his planned attack and regrouped his forces, giving the German command time to establish a stable main line of resistance.

For this and other decisive acts, the energetic, clever and aggressive *Oberst*, who commanded the 7th Panzer Division's 25th Panzer Regiment, was awarded the Diamonds.

Adalbert Schulz was a native of Berlin. He was known for his readiness to strike and his unshakable calmness. Even when strong enemy forces attacked with the element of surprise and stood, as it were, "at the front door", Schulz refused to let this unnerve him or force him to act in haste.

In the Western Campaign Schulz took part in the armored advance as a battalion commander in the same regiment, overrunning Belgian, French and British positions and helping enable the breakthrough to Cherbourg. The division to which he belonged earned great honors in France. On September 29, 1940 Schulz received the Knight's Cross. The division went into the history of armored warfare as the "Ghost Division" and was skillfully led by a man who became the terror of the enemy: Erwin Rommel.

Schulz's enthusiastic flexibility, combined with the elan of a modern unit leader, set the tone for the success of his men, who were always victorious over the enemy. His concern for his troops knew no bounds – he was a friend and father in one.

Schulz originally wanted to become a bank employee. He graduated from a Berlin scientific secondary school, after which he became active in the banking field. From 1923 to 1924 he attended business school, but then gave up his chosen career and a year later joined the police. In 1934 he became a *Leutnant* and in 1935 transferred to the Wehrmacht as an *Oberleutnant*. Schulz participated in the marches into Austria and the Sudetenland. He took part in the campaign against France as a *Hauptmann*. Schulz distinguished himself in the early weeks of the war against the Soviet Union. He broke into the retreating mass of enemy soldiers, completed minor encirclements, and led the way for the following troops.

Schulz gave a spectacular demonstration of his skill as a tank commander in the area around Klin, in Army Group Center's sector. The energetic commander attacked a Soviet force eight times larger than his own and destroyed it. In the ice and snow of winter, with temperatures of forty below zero, he mounted such vigorous resistance with his few tanks that the Soviets had to withdraw troops from other sectors to dislodge Schulz from his position. But the German commander lured the Soviets into a trap, allowed them to roll past and attacked from behind. Soon afterward he broke into the flank of a Siberian guards regiment, rolled it up and destroyed the fresh, well-equipped unit. In the same series of attacks he covered the retreat of German troops and a field hospital with more than 4,000 wounded. For these feats Schulz was awarded the Oak Leaves on December 31, 1941.

Meanwhile promoted to *Oberstleutnant*, in 1943 Adalbert Schulz assumed command of the 25th Panzer Regiment, later the 7th Panzer Regiment, with which he achieved such great success. Schulz and his unit repeatedly distinguished themselves, whether acting as the focal point of the defence or leading an attack.

On August 6 of that same year Adalbert Schulz received the Swords. In November he was promoted to *Oberst* and on December 14 received a radio message informing him that he was being awarded the Diamonds. Schulz was supposed to drive to Führer Headquarters to receive the decoration from Hitler. Instead he advised: "I can't leave, the devil's loose here!"

During the winter months of 1943 a heavy defensive battle broke out in the southern sector of the Eastern Front. The 7th Panzer Division was employed as a mobile fire-brigade, closing gaps in the front, eliminating enemy penetrations, conducting counterattacks and fighting off enemy assaults. The veteran panzer division was employed wherever the situation was in doubt. At the outset of the battle the division commander, *Generalmajor* Hasso von Manteuffel, received orders from Führer Headquarters to leave the 7th Panzer Division and take command of the *Großdeutschland* Division. Von Manteuffel asked that the implementation of the order be delayed until the 7th Panzer Division's defensive success was assured. Afterward he would hand over the division to Adalbert Schulz, whom he proposed as his successor. Hitler agreed, and after Schulz had the opportunity to receive the Diamonds in Führer Headquarters on January 9, 1944, he was promoted on the spot to the rank of *Generalmajor* and named division commander.

Schulz, who had "grown up" in the division and earned the highest decorations for bravery, was now allowed to command the division which Rommel had once led. His objective was to lead the troops just as well and with the same success as his predecessor. But fate held something else in store.

Following a brief leave at home with his family Schulz returned to the front. His division had meanwhile been deployed in the Shepetovka area and was supposed to carry out a counterattack. The enemy defended grimly and showed no signs of willingness to abandon his positions.

The attack got under way and several local penetrations were made, however the desired breakthrough could not be achieved. Schulz was about to outflank the enemy when he learned by radio that the attack had bogged down along the entire line. The division commander drove in his armored car to the battalions and ordered their commanders to attend a conference. But then a shell fell nearby. A shell fragment struck Schulz in the head and the general collapsed, unconscious. Although he was taken immediately to hospital, it was too late. Adalbert Schulz died on the way to hospital without regaining consciousness.

The Wehrmacht communique of January 28, 1944 ended with the words: "The fate and conduct of this man are a shining and obligating example."

CHAPTER X

OBERST HANS-ULRICH RUDEL

"You are the greatest and bravest soldier that the German people have ever had," said Adolf Hitler to the minister's son on January 1, 1945.

In October 1976 German Defence Minister Georg Leber forced two air force generals, Karl Heinz Franke and Walter Krupinski, into retirement because they dared compare the national-socialist past of this soldier from a Christian family with the communist past of the social democrat Herbert Wehner.

Three decades after the Third Reich sank in rubble and ashes the single recipient of that state's highest decoration for bravery had once again gained the attention of the entire nation: Hans-Ulrich Rudel, 60, wearer of the Golden Oak Leaves with Swords and Diamonds and holder of a Paraguayan passport.

Rudel's name had once again become a symbol. Once it had been synonymous with courage. Now his person was a symbolic figure of the past. For members of the left and liberals his name was like a red flag to a bull.

The minister's son from Konradswaldau in Silesia had in fact belonged to a National-Socialist organization: he was a troop leader (*Scharführer*) in the Hitler Youth. But Rudel had never been a member of the National-Socialist Party. For after completing his schooling in Schweidnitz and Görlitz he had joined the Luftwaffe as an officer candidate at the age of 20.

Those who had known him as a child were amazed at his choice of careers. His mother recalled that her son had been "delicate and shy." His sister observed that he had been afraid to go into the cellar alone. And the assessment of his teacher: "He was a lovely child but a terrible student." And yet in the decade which the young Rudel spent in the Luftwaffe he was to fulfil his destiny. Rudel participated in the Polish Campaign as an officer and observer in a reconnaissance *Gruppe*. In September 1940, at his own request, he was transferred to a dive-bomber unit. Rudel became a Stuka pilot, one of those who dove his machine at the target like a hawk and dropped his bombs just before pulling up. In contrast to conventional bombers, whose carpet-bombing tactics caused damage over a wide area, a Stuka attack always concentrated on a single object.

"If one can have a clear conscience at all in war, it is most likely as a Stuka pilot," Rudel observed later.

In one of his most successful attacks, Rudel dove from the sky at an angle of 90 degrees in his Ju 87 and pulled out only four meters above the surface of the water. That was on September 23, 1941, when he destroyed the Soviet battleship *Marat* (23,600 tonnes) with a 1,000-kilogram bomb as it lay at anchor in Kronstadt harbor.

Rudel later said of this difficult mission:

"It was horrible. There were flashes all around me. The air seemed to be filled with brimstone. The clouds shone yellow. The roar of exploding munitions even penetrated the thick panelling of the machine. I was nearly sick and the flight was pure torture. We had flown a mission to the harbor area the day before. But today the flak was so massive that I had to have doubts about our success. *Gruppe* leader *Hauptmann* Steen had positioned himself right in front of me. I could see him clearly. The dive, at an angle of 70 to 80 degrees, took my breath away. I hung almost on the tail of Steen's aircraft. Our high speed ruled out the use of dive brakes. I had the *Marat* in my sight. She came toward me faster and faster. The ship became ever larger. I saw the open mouths of the anti-aircraft guns pointing threateningly at me. If someone was sitting there and pressed the trigger! But I had to dive even steeper! I saw the horrified face of *Hauptmann* Steen's gunner. His eyes were wide with terror, for he feared that I would cut off his tail surfaces with my propeller. I summoned all my strength. There was no time to worry that a direct hit by flak might tear me apart. I just flitted past Steen. The *Marat* was square in my sight. Sailors ran about on the deck. Some carried ammunition, others took cover. They must see me! A flak turret turned in my direction. If it opened fire now! Then I pressed the bomb release button on the stick. I pulled back with all my strength, attempting to bring the machine out of its dive, for my altitude was only 300 meters. The 1,000-kilogram bomb I had just released wasn't supposed to be dropped from a height of less than 1,000 meters due to the threat of self-destruction by bomb fragments. But I didn't worry about that. I wanted to hit the *Marat*! Nothing else. Although I pulled back on the stick like a madman, I had the feeling that the aircraft wasn't coming out of its dive. All at once I felt myself beginning to faint. It was a feeling I had never known before. Had the effort in fact been too great? I knew of no other way but to abruptly pull back with all my strength. There was a terrible feeling in my stomach and head, when I heard the excited voice of my gunner Scharnowski: 'Herr *Oberleutnant*, the ship has just exploded!' Slowly I turned around. There lay the *Marat*, behind an almost impenetrable, 400-meter-high cloud of smoke. Then I discovered to my horror that I was flying only three or four meters above the glassy surface of Kronstadt Harbor, but I realized that I was still alive!"

This feat earned Rudel a decoration, but he did not receive it. *Hauptmann* Steen would have liked to recommend him for the Knight's Cross – but he didn't. "I'm sure you will all understand that I can't single out one man after this courageous mission in which the entire *Gruppe* participated, even though that man sank the *Marat*. Please try to understand, but I consider the value of a close-knit team, such as we are, greater and more important than recommending Oberleutnant Rudel as the only one for the Knight's Cross."

In addition to the *Marat*, Rudel and his Ju 87 sank a cruiser, a destroyer and 70 landing craft and as well severely damaged the battleship "October Revolution." He destroyed bridges, took out bunkers, smashed supply columns. Rudel's growing fame spread far and wide and decorations were showered upon him.

He destroyed 150 anti-aircraft and anti-tank gun positions, shot down nine enemy aircraft in aerial combat and six times landed behind Soviet lines to rescue downed crews.

Rudel established a record which remains untouched to this day: 2,530 combat missions, in the course of which he was himself shot down 30 times by flak and infantry ground fire.

And yet all these numbers pale in comparison to one of his totals: flying his dive-bomber, Rudel single-handedly destroyed 519 Soviet tanks – five complete tank corps. A prayer often spoken by Eastern Front soldiers when the Red Army's T 34s advanced toward the German lines was: "Dear God, let Rudel come." And he came often. Never has a single man inflicted such damage on an enemy – at an age when most students are taking their exams today! It was no wonder that the Soviets put a price of 100,000 rubles on his head! There were days when he destroyed as many as 17 enemy tanks. He alone! "For me this was no sporting contest," Rudel said later. "Rather it was a battle of existence for life and death. It all came down to one thing: you or me. That is why one becomes a soldier, to fight."

The young *Kommodore* of the Stuka *Geschwader* nevertheless stood out from his officer comrades: he neither drank nor smoke, and when the others gathered in the mess he preferred to take up the javelin and the shot and train. On any day when the operational schedule allowed, the small (1.74 meters) Spartan ran 10,000 meters cross country. His passion for sports was rewarded. During a mission over the southern sector of the Eastern Front on March 21, 1944 – an attack on a bridge over the Dnestr near Yampol – the then *Hauptmann* Rudel's wingman was forced to land behind enemy lines. Rudel set his machine down beside the crippled aircraft to pick up the crew. However the ground was soft, making takeoff impossible. Soviet soldiers appeared. The four Germans fled toward the west. Soon a broad stream, the Dnestr, barred the way. They had to swim the river. Rudel's gunner, wearer of the Knight's Cross *Oberfeldwebel* Hentschel, faltered and sank in the icy flood. Rudel, who had already crossed, swam back to help him. But his efforts were in vain. The other two had meanwhile reached the other shore, where they collapsed. They were so totally exhausted that they fell easy prey to the Soviet soldiers who suddenly appeared. Rudel continued his flight. With a bullet in his shoulder and pursued by dogs and mounted soldiers, he walked barefoot about 50 kilometers to his own lines.

A few days later he undertook his 1,800th combat mission. A week later Rudel was decorated again, becoming the tenth soldier of the German armed forces to be presented the Oak Leaves with Swords and Diamonds by Hitler. The young officer had ultimately entered into the intimate circle of his leader. Rudel was enchanted by Hitler, and was, as he later admitted, "fascinated" by him.

On January 1, 1945 Hitler created "a new supreme decoration for bravery" for his faithful soldier: the Golden Oak Leaves with Swords and Diamonds. (This decoration was created by Hitler for the most worthy soldiers who had carried out individual feats of skill and bravery. It was to be the supreme German decoration for bravery and the intention was that it be awarded only twelve times.) Rudel received the decoration and was promoted to the rank of *Oberst* – at the age of 28.

Rudel's first thoughts however concerned the flying ban of which Hitler and Göring had spoken. Both were of the opinion that such outstanding officers and fliers should not be allowed to risk their lives. Instead they should serve as an inspiration to the youth of Germany and pass on their experiences.

Rudel was one of those pilots who either secretly ignored such a ban or who bombarded Hitler and Göring with requests that it be lifted. Rudel's tactics usually worked. In each previous case Hitler allowed himself to "yield" and the flying ban was lifted. But not this time. Hitler was insistent that Rudel be banned from further flying. He knew of the officer's daring actions and he was of the opinion that he had done enough. Rudel was later to take on another, greater mission. The just-promoted *Oberst* had this to say: "*Mein Führer*, I will not accept the decoration and the promotion if I am not allowed to continue flying with my Geschwader!" Later *Oberst* von Below told Rudel that he and the other Wehrmacht notables had been "struck dumb" when they heard him say this. This young and highly-decorated officer, just promoted to *Oberst*, had dared to contradict his supreme commander and even issue him a sort of ultimatum! Such a thing had never happened before!

Hitler looked at Rudel for a long time. "Very well. If you absolutely must fly . . . go ahead then," he said softly. "But look out for yourself. I need you. The German people need you."

Five weeks later Rudel's luck ran out. On February 9, 1945 he once again took to the air against Soviet armor. A forty-millimeter anti-aircraft shell shattered his lower, right leg. The limb was almost torn off. Rudel managed to crash-land his stricken aircraft and it was only the efforts of his gunner, *Stabsarzt* Dr. Gadermann, which saved him from bleeding to death. The wounded pilot was taken to a dressing station in Seelow where his lower leg was amputated.

But after only a few days in hospital, his stump bandaged and fitted with a primitive prosthesis, Rudel climbed back into the cockpit of a Ju 87. By the end of the war the one-legged pilot had destroyed 13 more enemy tanks.

It was openly recognized that Rudel was a phenomenon, a type of soldier who had crossed the boundary between courage and fatalism and who put himself to the breaking test. The minister's son from Konradswaldau fought on all fronts. On the Volga, on the Danube and on the Oder. He was the sole foreigner to wear Hungary's highest medal for bravery. As well he owned high Rumanian and Italian decorations. Once, on learning that Rudel was to be removed from his area of command on Himmler's orders, *Generalfeldmarschall* Schörner said of him: "Rudel is worth a division."

The commander of the *Immelmann Geschwader* spent the evening before Hitler's last birthday in the bunker beneath the Reich Chancellery: that day Marshall Zhukov had crossed the Oder and had launched the Soviet assault on Berlin. Why, Rudel asked his leader, do you not negotiate a cease-fire in the west in order to achieve a victory in the east? Hitler smiled wearily, indulging his hero: "It is easy to talk about such a thing . . ."

Hitler's biographer John Toland described the scene: "It was late, after midnight, when Rudel was dismissed. And when he hobbled through the ante-room he saw that it was already filled with people who were eager to be among the first to congratulate the Führer on his fifty-sixth birthday."

A few days after Hitler's suicide Rudel and his *Geschwader* flew out of Czechoslovakia to Kitzingen, near Würzburg, and surrendered there to the Americans on May 8. He was soon released on account of his injuries (Rudel had been wounded a total of five times). The wrecked Germany of de-nazification and reeducation had nothing to offer him. He crossed the Austrian border illegally, on foot, and walked through the Zillertal to Italy, finally arriving in Rome. There he obtained a forged passport under the name of Emilio Meier. Soon afterward this Emilio Meier arrived in distant Buenos Aires.

Argentina's head of state, Juan Peron, welcomed the war heroes of the Third Reich warmly. Rudel went to work for the Argentine Air Ministry. In the aviation works of Cordoba he was assigned to the design group, where work was under way on the "Pulqui 2" jet fighter.

Emilio Meier was not the only prominent figure from the defeated Germany in Cordoba. Also active there were the former Focke-Wulf designer Kurt Tank and the all-wing aircraft specialist Dr. Horten. Also working in the Air Ministry were the former General Galland and the famous German bomber pilot $t2Ober*st* Werner Baumbach, along with test pilots Henrici, Behrens and Steinkamp.

After emigrating to Argentina Rudel wrote his memoirs. Entitled *Trotzdem*, the book was first published in Argentina. Since then it has been translated into eight languages (English, French, Spanish, Portuguese, Italian, Japanese, Finnish and Arabic) and has reached a total publication of over three million – almost a million in the United States alone.

After at least one illegal visit to the Federal Republic, in the early 1950s Rudel returned to Germany for good and became active in politics. But his political clock seemed to be stuck at 1945, and his views were viewed as having a strongly nationalist tinge.

Rudel, however, had a completely different view of things: he had fought for Germany, not for Hitler. Now he wished to dedicate his efforts exclusively to the welfare of the German soldiers who had fought in World War Two. As he put it, he was no totalitarian, rather "a one-hundred percent democrat."

Rudel: "I believe that our democracy has not yet reached the level of that in the USA. There one can state his views openly, something which we apparently still cannot always do. Only one political direction is welcome. When I express my opinions I am immediately slandered and characterized as a nazi colonel. Since the war I have dared speak openly against the people who have slandered us soldiers. Consequently I was classed as a radical rightist."

Rudel won no laurels as a politician. Nevertheless, the strength of will exhibited by this man in peacetime was just as impressive as that which he had shown during the war.

In spite of his prosthesis he became the first man to climb the highest volcano in the world, the 6,902-meter-high Llullay-Yacu in Argentina. As a skier Rudel won prizes and victory goblets wherever he competed. On one occasion, at the skiing center of Bariloche on Monte Catedral, he raced down the course, crouched low. Suddenly, to the horror of the onlookers, he lost a ski and with it half a leg. A cry went up from the crowd – Mamá mia! – the skier skillfully maintained his balance on one leg. Rudel's prosthesis had come loose and carried on solo! Rudel's fame spread throughout the land following this incident. Afterward he was known as "the crazy German with one leg."

But once again fate struck Rudel a hard blow: in 1970 he suffered a stroke while ski training. He was treated in America's Mayo Clinic. Rudel's right arm was left paralyzed.

Hans-Ulrich Rudel never gave up on himself. The close-shorn hair had become white, but there was still a gleam in his brown eyes. In spite of his disability he became relatively prosperous through his book and his activities in South America on behalf of German companies such as Siemens. Always on the move, he commuted between Europe and the four South American countries of Argentina, Chile, Bolivia and Paraguay, travelling on a German and a Paraguayan passport.

Several times a year Rudel flew to the USA. He was a guest of the Air Force and consulted with four-star generals over a machine designated the Type A-10, which the Americans had designed on the example of the old Ju 87 Stuka. Rudel: "I was asked my opinion on it and was supposed to speak about my experiences in combatting tanks from the air." Everywhere in the West Rudel was welcomed as a respected guest. He remained true to his motto: "Only he who gives up on himself is lost."

The most highly-decorated soldier of the former Wehrmacht died on December 18, 1982.

CHAPTER XI

GENERAL HYAZINTH GRAF STRACHWITZ

He was a master of deception – daring, crafty and brave, wounded fourteen times. He operated 150 kilometers behind the Soviet front and returned to his point of departure with no losses. In the north of the Eastern Front he took Tukkum, a city of great importance to the further operations of the army group. It had been considered unconquerable. Strachwitz deceived the enemy, outflanked the city, struck quickly and rolled through the city. There were fifty Soviet tanks in Tukkum, T 34s and KV 85s, all with their guns facing west. They intended to overrun the German positions. Within a matter of minutes they were ablaze. When several generals asked Strachwitz how he had done it, he said, "You see, gentlemen, I am Karl May himself." He was without a doubt the most imaginative commander of armored forces there was. Strachwitz was a master of small unit tactics, achieving unbelievable success with only a handful of tanks.

The Strachwitz clan is an old Upper Silesian noble family. Like every first-born of the Strachwitz family for the past 700 years, Hyazinth, born on July 30, 1893 in Grosstein, was named after a Silesian saint. In honor of the saints the Counts Strachwitz built a chapel in the courtyard of Grosstein Castle.

The family of Count Hyazinth Strachwitz von Grossgaucha-Gammnitz were among the most wealthy of Silesia's land and estate owners. However the outcome of the last war resulted in them joining the great army of refugees and homeless. The count, who had been wounded fourteen times, owned noth-

ing but a torn uniform. Behind him lay a brilliant career as a
soldier.

Hyazinth Graf Strachwitz became a *Leutnant* in the Garde
du Corps Regiment in Potsdam. Among his comrades during
his period as a cadet in Lichterfelde were Manfred von
Richthofen and Hans von Aulok. Following the shots in
Sarajevo which ignited the First World War, the young count
rode into France with his regiment. The German High Command decided to send a mounted long-range patrol to determine where the enemy's main force was. Far exceeding the
aims of his mission, *Leutnant* Graf Strachwitz advanced deep
into the enemy's rear, terrifying the French by appearing at
the gates of Paris.

Panic broke out in the city when the news spread that German troops had been sighted. In reality it was no more than a
handful of daring soldiers riding between the French Army
columns, who recognized a great opportunity to end the war
through quick action and the seizing of Paris.

Strachwitz was taken prisoner in this operation. He and
his fellow prisoners were dragged from prison to prison and
finally sentenced to death. Then, at the last second, the order
was withdrawn. On October 14, 1914 Strachwitz was sentenced
to forced labor at Cayenne, thus losing his status as a prisoner
of war. Luckily the transfer to Cayenne did not take place. His
path took him through Lyon and Montpelier to the peniten-
tiary on the island of Rè, which served as the last stop before
Cayenne. Other penitentiaries – and escape attempts – followed.

Finally a Swiss medical commission from the International
Red Cross found him in Carcassonne prison, apathetic, in rags
and reduced to a skeleton by starvation. Strachwitz was moved
to Switzerland in their care. When Strachwitz was released
from Switzerland to return to Germany in 1918 he was a very
sick man. A dangerous neuritis almost made him unfit for service. In 1920 he went on recovery leave. A year later the
Reichswehrministerium informed him that he had been promoted to the rank of *Oberleutnant*, back-dated to 1916.

When in 1921/22 Poland tried to separate Upper Silesia
from the German Reich, Graf Strachwitz was one of the tire-

less men who organized the self-defence of the area and drove the enemy from the territory.

Serving under the command of Generals von Hülsen and Höfer, Strachwitz performed so magnificently that the headquarters of the Polish irregulars put a price on his head. The decisive toss of the dice was made when the Poles dug in on the Annaberg, the symbol of Upper Silesia, which had changed hands several times. The German *Freikorps* launched the final assault. Graf Strachwitz and his men outflanked the Polish positions and overran part of them in bitter hand-to-hand fighting. In the course of the battle Strachwitz became the first German to reach the summit of the Annaberg. Since those days the count's name has been linked with the fight for the freedom and existence of his Upper Silesian homeland.

Following the defeat of the Polish uprising the young officer took off his uniform and took charge of his family's affairs. Not until 1935 did he have the opportunity to take part in a military exercise, with the 7th Cavalry in Breslau. Strachwitz was promoted to the rank of *Rittmeister*. He soon realized that the tank arm had taken the place of the cavalry in a modern army. Strachwitz asked for a transfer to the panzer troops, which were being formed by Generals Lutz and Guderian. From then on he took part in reserve operations with the 2nd Panzer Regiment in Eisenach.

Reserve officer Graf Strachwitz made a name for himself in the campaigns against Poland and France, charging into the middle of battles in his Kübelwagen and carrying out one-man attacks. His escapades contributed to the creation of the legend of the "bold count."

Guderian's "blitz" operations conformed to Strachwitz's notions of the modern command of armored forces. During the advance in France he came to the realization which was later elevated to the maxim of all modern-thinking armored commanders: "Tanks must be led from the front!" Even when Strachwitz temporarily had no panzers to command, he applied this maxim to the position of supply officer of a panzer division. He led "from the front." In recognition of his individual undertakings he became the first officer of his regiment to be awarded the Bar to the Iron Cross, First Class.

In the course of one of these "solo runs", as his operations were designated by his superiors, Strachwitz stumbled into an enemy-occupied barracks. "We can't turn around, or they'll get us for sure," he said to his driver. "But I think we can get them." The French soldier in front of the sentry box was wide-eyed with astonishment when he saw the German officer in his black panzer uniform.

Where did he come from?, the sentry must have asked himself. The latest reports indicated that the front was still thirty kilometers away, so there hadn't been a breakthrough. But there was a stranger before him in a uniform like those worn by the Germans, German panzer troops. Black cloth, death's heads on the collar tabs. They had been told about these in briefings: panzers! the damned German panzers. The German said something in French.

"Fetch the duty officer."

"Yes sir."

The sentry saluted and disappeared. Strachwitz calmly lit a cigarette and waited. Would the sentry sound the alarm? Or would he fetch the duty officer?

Meanwhile the Frenchman had flung open the door of the duty officer's office. Annoyed, the captain looked up from his desk. "What the devil are you bothering me for? Don't you know how to knock?"

Pardon me *mon Capitaine*, but there's a German panzer officer outside and he wishes to speak to you."

"A German panzer officer! You must be seeing ghosts in the twilight. There can't be one. Or are you drunk?" The captain put on his cap and stood up: "Alright." With long strides he walked to the barracks door, where he almost ran into Strachwitz. The German smiled at him as if he were about to take him to the mess for a drink.

"Have your unit assemble without weapons! You are prisoners!" declared the count, betraying no emotion whatsoever.

The Frenchman looked at him in amazement. "But . . ."

Strachwitz shook his head. "No buts captain. Do as I order. Resistance is pointless."

Stunned and confused, the officer stared at his fingernails. Was it to end like this? Over? He couldn't even report to his superiors that it was all over, that he and his men had been taken prisoner.

What is the Frenchman thinking about for so long? thought the count, and then said energetically: "Hurry up! Have your men fall out! I can't give you any more time."

After all Strachwitz had only one officer and his driver with him, and the situation was becoming more precarious from minute to minute.

The Frenchman nodded. "*Clairon!*" The bugler reported and blew the specified signal. French soldiers streamed in from all sides, without weapons as ordered. They formed up as if for roll call. On the right wing stood the officers, who eyed the three Germans in astonishment.

The captain positioned himself in front of the open square which his men had formed. His voice wavered as he reported to Strachwitz: "Six-hundred French soldiers surrender as prisoners of war."

Walking slowly, Strachwitz reviewed the French formation with the French captain. Twelve-hundred eyes followed him. On reaching the end of the formation the count turned to the French officer and saluted.

"*Merci.*"

Then he pointed to the long row of brand-new special vehicles belonging to the signals unit, parked behind the assembled troops. "Have your men get aboard their vehicles. You can accompany me in my car." Strachwitz gave the accompanying *Leutnant* a wink. "I'll drive. You take over the last vehicle in the column so that no one strays off."

"As ordered, *Herr Graf.*"

The column pulled away. Leading the way, Count Strachwitz and the commander of the captured French unit drove toward the German panzer division.

Operations of this sort were not rare for the count. Repeatedly he distinguished himself through his personal courage, inventive planning and the ability to react quickly. Surprise was his most potent weapon. The element of surprise was enough to overcome even a numerically-superior enemy.

One of the count's maxims was: "One can achieve enormous success with only a few, but good people," He held to this belief, even long after he had become a unit commander and leader of larger formations.

After the war against France in 1940 Count Strachwitz, who had meanwhile been promoted to Major of the Reserve, devoted himself to his duties. He was transferred to the 16th Panzer Division, commanded by *General* Hube. The unit was stationed in Romania, where it was serving as an instructional unit for a Romanian army.

During the campaign against Yugoslavia in 1941, Strachwitz was given a special assignment within the 16th Panzer Division, which he fulfilled splendidly.

On June 22, 1941, the day chosen by Hitler for the attack against the Soviet Union, *Major* Count Strachwitz attacked Soviet forces beyond the demarcation line. Exploiting the ensuing confusion, he drove deep into enemy territory, clearing a path for the infantry. But the Soviets had recovered from the shock of the surprise German attack more quickly than expected. In the Ivka sector they attacked the advancing German spearhead with superior infantry forces. Strachwitz suddenly found himself surrounded and ordered his forces to go over to the defensive. In the course of the battle he was struck by a bullet. After a temporary dressing was placed on the wound he led the next attack at the head of his battalion. Near Werba his unit destroyed enemy tanks which had broken through, before they could reach the supply train positions of the German units. He continued pursuing the fleeing Soviets into the night, encircled the enemy, then broke contact with them and operated in their rear.In this way he destroyed several batteries and smashed open a breach for the advancing German divisions. In recognition of these heroic actions Count Strachwitz was awarded the Knight's Cross on August 25, 1941. One year later, on November 17, 1942, he received the Oak Leaves.

The surprise attack was Count Strachwitz's strong suit. In this way he took the tough Soviet strongpoint of Pervomaysk. Leading the attack in his battalion's first tank, he crossed the Bug bridge, attacked a column of 300 vehicles and destroyed anti-tank guns and artillery pieces. Near Uman, far behind enemy lines, he smashed assembled reserves and tanks, spreading panic and terror.

Strachwitz was an *Oberstleutnant* by the time the battle for Stalingrad began. He and his tanks raced ahead of the other units and were the first German troops to enter the streets of the city. There Strachwitz was wounded again but remained with his unit. Fighting in the rear of the grimly-defending Soviets, he and his battalion destroyed 100 T 34 tanks. The *Oberstleutnant* was wounded again. Following his convalescence he assumed command of the *Großdeutschland* Panzer Regiment, which had grown from the battalion of the same name, and led it with great success.

Count Strachwitz maintained that he actually possessed a "sixth sense." The regimental commander, who had meanwhile been promoted to *Oberst*, was a capable and successful diviner, and he spent every free hour cultivating his gift. There was in fact a history of this in his family; one of his relatives was the famous Count Matuschka, well-known for his clairvoyant abilities.

His friends maintained that magical powers emanated from the hands of the count. In addition he was said to possess an unusually strong ability to sense future happenings. Strachwitz himself said, "I feel it when an enemy tank is looking at me."

Once, when he led four tanks deep into enemy territory to scout the enemy's position, he spotted a long, seemingly endless column of slow-moving enemy vehicles silhouetted against the horizon. Tanks! The German panzers waited for the Soviets in a carefully-camouflaged ambush position. The unsuspecting enemy approached the trap. The count's optimism sank quickly when he counted the enemy tanks. "No one fire until I do," he ordered. "The outer tanks take the center, I'll knock out the leader, my neighbor may select targets at will."

Thirty minutes later 105 burnt-out and shattered Soviet tanks littered the countryside. Not a single one of Strachwitz's men and tanks had been hit.

Strachwitz constantly pondered how to inflict the maximum losses on the enemy with his few panzers. In this way he became a unique, almost independent tank commander, who preferred the small-scale battle. He attacked the Soviets where they least expected it.

Legendary cold-bloodedness and tremendous boldness were the marks of this dashing cavalry officer, for whom the attack, in particular the surprise attack, were the alpha and omega of his military mission. "There's nothing I hate more than tanks which stand about. Tanks must roll!" When he couldn't fire he charged toward or after the enemy at maximum speed. Asked why he always drove so fast, he answered: "Because we're afraid. Tanks are only in danger when they drive slowly or stand still."

Reserve *Oberst* Strachwitz became the first regimental commander to receive a Tiger battalion for front-line testing. Weapons experts swore by the super-heavy panzer, which was said to be far superior to the fast and deadly T 34. The tank's 88mm gun, capable of accurate shooting at ranges of four kilometers, were far superior to anything which had come before. When the count received this "heavy artillery" in 1943 the Battle of Belgorod was already in full swing.

Kharkov was in the focal point of the battle. The Germans were forced out of the city, the pivotal point on the southern front for both warring parties. Kharkov would have to be retaken. A report that the Soviets were attempting to break through the weakly-manned German front with 80 fast-moving tanks was received calmly by the count. He assembled his forces, keeping the Tigers close by him. Strachwitz wanted to see if the heavy tanks would prove themselves in action. Suddenly eighteen T 34s appeared. "Range four kilometers," reported the radio operator. "No one fire. I want to see what the Russians have behind the hill," declared the count. And in fact a few minutes later a further eighteen T 34s and KV 85s approached.

Strachwitz and his panzers waited for the approaching enemy behind the wooden houses of a village. The German defensive front was in the shape of a horseshoe. He wanted to lure the Soviets into the center of the village. Before him several T 34s moved about on the hill. They were attempting to draw the fire of the German guns in order to reveal their positions. Strachwitz was familiar with this tactic and did not fall for it. Instead he said, "We must trick the Soviets into feeling safe and convince them that we're not strong enough to repulse their attack."

At about two in the morning the Soviets began preparations to engage the German forces. Strachwitz's tanks were under orders not to fire. "Not until dawn. We'll fire at first light," he ordered. The men heard the enemy tanks, which now and then drove into the village and fired on and set fire to a house. But Strachwitz and his tanks did not move. Not an unnecessary step was taken, not a shot was fired.

Emboldened, the Soviets moved toward the village on a broad front, suspecting only weak German forces to be there. Like Strachwitz and his men, they too were waiting for first light. The leading Soviet tanks slowly approached the outer houses of the village. Their command tank was only 35 meters from Strachwitz's Tiger. A biting crack shattered the grey morning and the turret of a stricken T 34 flew high into the air.

That was the signal for Strachwitz's men to attack. Instantly eight enemy tanks were ablaze. Minutes later ten more had been put out of action. Several tried to escape, but the Tigers pursued and knocked out another eighteen.

For his tremendous daring near Belgorod, Count Strachwitz was awarded the Swords on March 28, 1943.

Back in 1941 Strachwitz had come up with the idea of mounting loud-speakers on his tanks for the purpose of urging the surrender of masses of Soviet infantry which had fled into the forest, thus clearing the way for the German troops. Many Soviet soldiers responded to these requests. As instructed by Strachwitz they brought their weapons with them. The count was generous and allowed the enemy to march to the reception camps in the rear with their rifles. "In this way the Russians don't feel naked," he observed, and added: "That's the right thing to do psychologically, for they throw down their weapons on their own."

Early one morning a ragged deserter asked to speak to the German commander. The Russian introduced himself: "Colonel Berger, commander of the 190th Infantry Division, which is opposing you."

The count was surprised. It turned out that the Soviet colonel had a German father and was a Soviet citizen. "Go back and fetch your division. I won't take you prisoner without your division," replied Strachwitz.

The Soviet colonel blanched. "I can't go back dressed like this, without rank badges and barefoot. I slipped through our lines unrecognized. If I go back I'll be shot at once."

Strachwitz maintained his hard stance. "Put shoes on and come back with your division." He turned away and left the colonel standing. A few hours later Colonel Berger returned and surrendered to Count Strachwitz along with his entire division.

Speaking of his actions, Count Strachwitz said, "I had more luck then brains." Two head wounds, nine serious and several minor wounds and an automobile accident were the price he paid for his daring. But in each case Strachwitz returned to lead his regiment after a brief convalescence.

On April 1, 1944 Reserve *Oberst* Count Strachwitz was promoted to *Generalmajor*. Since the rank of General of the Reserve did not exist in the German Army, he had to have himself reactivated. Strachwitz became commander of the 1st Panzer Division and then senior panzer commander of Army Group North, with three panzer divisions and an anti-tank brigade.

On the northern front Strachwitz was as feared by the Soviets as he had once been by the Poles at the Annaberg in 1922. The general possessed so much nonchalance that he informed the Soviets of his arrival by radio and revealed that he intended to attack in a certain sector. The Soviets were surprised, for they believed that Strachwitz was still in hospital in Germany recovering from wounds. They radioed the units of their army group: "Attention, Strachwitz is here, he will attack!"

In fact the count deceived the Soviets as to the time of the attack in the sector in question. They had withdrawn their troops from that sector and regrouped. It was their intention to allow Strachwitz to advance, then encircle and destroy him. Strachwitz counted on this and attacked the Soviets where he saw a road sign with the legend "490 kilometers to Moscow." His forces drove into the Soviet rear, scattering the enemy and spreading confusion.

When Riga was encircled by the Soviets, Strachwitz's battle group was outside the city. Wanting to see the situation for himself, he set out with a group of tanks and broke through the ring of Soviet forces around the city. On seeing or hearing about the arrival of German tanks, the wounded and the German nurses thought they had been saved. But suddenly Strachwitz's tank was stopped by three generals. Oil-smeared and wearing no rank badges, Strachwitz stuck his head out of the turret hatch. One of the generals waved to him cordially: "Bravo, Leutnant, well done!" The count climbed slowly out of the tank and went over to the generals. "Gentlemen, you are speaking not to a lieutenant, but to a real general," he said, and left the disconcerted officers standing.

News that Strachwitz had been awarded the Diamonds arrived in the middle of the night on April 15, 1944. The count was sleeping and looked up in astonishment when he was awakened by his "maid of all work", *Unteroffizier* Rosenstock. The NCO was waving a teletype message and stated, "*Herr Graf, we* have received the Diamonds . . ."

During a visit to a division command post Strachwitz was badly injured in an automobile accident. The vehicle rolled over several times and his survival was in doubt for some time. Those with him were killed on the spot, while he escaped with a fractured skull and broken ribs, legs, arms and hands. The doctors held out little hope for the officer who had been wounded thirteen times before. But Strachwitz wanted to live. As soon as he began showing signs that he would survive, Strachwitz, in a tremendous display of will power, began attempts to walk. He worked out his own therapy:

"Morning of the first day: practice sitting up and sitting down until I can do it unassisted.
Second Day: hang legs over side of bed.
Third Day: walk to wash basin on crutches.
Fourth Day: take a bath with assistance.
Fifth Day: go to the door on crutches by myself.
Sixth Day: take steps.
Seventh Day: leave!"

Although no one believed it, that is exactly what happened. Strachwitz kept to his program day by day, including his departure, which took place in spite of protests and warnings from the doctors. He reported himself "fit for duty" to *Generalfeldmarschall* Schörner and, walking on crutches, formed an anti-tank brigade in Bad Kudova. He had under his command 8,000 magnificently-trained soldiers whose specialty was destroying tanks in any situation. The unit did not see large-scale action, however. Instead it operated in small formations in cooperation with the Stuka *Oberst* Hans-Ulrich Rudel.

After the surrender Strachwitz released his troops and ordered them to withdraw toward the west. He himself travelled through the Sudetenland, which had been made unsafe by Czech partisans, with his adjutant to Felgen in Bavaria, where he was taken prisoner by the Americans.

Strachwitz summed things up: his young daughter Lisalex was somewhere in Germany after she and 36 other German girls, armed with rifles, had travelled from Brindisi to Rome through partisan territory and reported for duty to a German commander. His oldest son had been wounded and was confined to bed, gravely ill, after having been mistakenly declared dead. His youngest son, who had been severely wounded and lost a leg at eighteen, had nevertheless reported for duty. He was killed in the final days of the war. A year later, on May 8, 1946, Count Strachwitz received news that his wife Alda had been struck and killed by an American army vehicle. His request to be present at the funeral was turned down by the camp commandant.

When Strachwitz returned to his chosen home in Bavaria he had nothing but a torn uniform, a body battered by his numerous wounds and the will to go on living. When his distress was greatest he accepted an offer from the Syrian government to serve as a general advisor in agriculture and forestry to the president, but also to help build up the country's army. The count was enthusiastic about Syria. There were all sorts of possibilities there. He and his German staff set up a program which enthused the Syrians.

Soon, however, when the question of cost was brought up, their enthusiasm sank by several degrees. The only heavy weapons possessed by the Syrian Army were two old 75mm guns. Deficiencies in the agricultural sector seemed to have no bounds. But when the president was overthrown by Colonel Husni Seim, Strachwitz's days in Syria were numbered. In the middle of the night the count and his young second wife left for Lebanon, with not a penny to their name. In June 1949 he arrived in Italy where he ran a wine estate near Livorno.

In the autumn of 1951, a red cross passport in his hand, Strachwitz stepped back onto German soil.

Count Strachwitz, who founded the "Upper Silesian Relief Organization", survived on a minuscule pension. But he remained the old "spark plug" who could not avoid physical pain and severe mental suffering, a man who refused to surrender to fate. Within the circle of his family – two boys and two girls from his second marriage – the "count", as he was known by his friends, spent the next quiet years on a small property on the Chiemsee which his wife had gained through an inheritance. Hyazinth Graf Strachwitz died on April 25, 1968. Officers of the *Bundeswehr* provided the honor guard.

CHAPTER XII

GENERAL DER WAFFEN-SS HERBERT OTTO GILLE

T he mousetrap called Cherkassy snapped shut on January 28, 1944. Trapped inside the pocket were divisions of the army, the SS unit *Wiking* and the Assault Brigade *Wallonie*. Every one of the trapped men knew the situation: the Soviets hoped to inflict a second Stalingrad on the Wehrmacht. The enemy attacked without pause with tanks and infantry, supported by artillery fire. Bombs, "Stalin Organs" and gunfire from low-flying close-support aircraft forced the surrounded troops to go to ground.

Only five days later British and Soviet radio announced, "The imminent destruction of several German armies near Cherkassy." The surrounded troops responded to this propaganda: they held out for three weeks against everything the enemy could throw at them.

When the bombers and tanks failed to achieve the desired success the Soviets pulled out all the stops. Each day loudspeaker trucks drove up to the German lines. Deserters encouraged the men to surrender. When this request was answered with furious defensive fire, captured German officers, members of the National Committee for a Free Germany, stepped in front of the microphones and called upon the surrounded soldiers to lay down their weapons and surrender.

When all these appeals proved ineffectual, *General* von Seydlitz, a prisoner of war and president of the "League of German Officers", dispatched a hand-written note to *General* Gille, commander of the SS-Division *Wiking*. Von Seydlitz promised good treatment for the soldiers and an early release from captivity after the war.

The Soviets had counted on success, not on the failure of their loud-speaker attacks, which proved to be a miscalculation. The men in the Cherkassy Pocket were haunted by the specter of captivity in the hands of the Soviets. The name Stalingrad haunted the foxholes – no one wanted to set out on the path to uncertainty. No, they didn't want to die on some road of hunger, thirst, cold or at the hands of their captors. For the surrounded men there was only one solution: hold out! They believed that the opportunity would come for a break-out or that the pocket would be cracked from the outside.

Fighting in the Cherkassy Pocket were volunteers from almost every European nation. Men from many nations manned a front against the Soviet Army, something unique in recent history. They lay in muddy holes, some filled with icy water, clutching their rifles with cold-numbed hands. They smoked what little tobacco they had left and shared what was left of their bread: Germans and Dutch, Swedes and Belgians, Finns and Swiss, Danes and Flemings, Walloons and Norwegians. They rose to meet each fresh attack, defended themselves in close-quarters fighting, repulsed the enemy and held their positions.

The thoughts of the men were lost in the crashing of shells, the nerve-shattering howls of "Katushka" rocket salvoes, the explosion of bombs and the shouts of "Urray" from the attacking Soviets. They spoke different languages but they fought the same fight. During the night of February 16/17, at about midnight, the men of the first assault wave prepared for the attack. The tension ate at the nerves. The mood was oppressive. The artillery had been forbidden to fire to avoid tipping off the Soviets that a break-out attempt was imminent. They must succeed in taking the enemy by surprise; the men inside the pocket had staked everything on the element of surprise. Minutes became an eternity. Then the first close-assault battalions leapt into the Soviet trenches. Fighting with edged weapons only, they smashed open the way for the following units. The lane through the enemy lines was narrow. The heavy weapons and all the vehicles had to be left behind in the pocket. The swampy terrain, which was traversed by numerous streams, left no other alternative. The Soviets found themselves facing an opponent who was resolute to the last man. Hungry and tired, but with a boundless will to live, the SS units smashed their way through thirty kilometers of enemy-held territory. The break-out had succeeded, they could link up with their comrades who had supported the attack from "outside."

Among the last troops to leave the hard-won corridor were a platoon of courageous Walloons. The grey, mud-encrusted figures carried the body of their battalion commander on a litter. How strong must the bond of comradeship have been for these Walloons to carry their officer out of the pocket under enemy fire!

The procession had a magnetic effect on all the German soldiers it passed. All the weariness, hunger and deprivation were banished for a few seconds. They stood in salute to the men from the foreign land and their dead.

On February 20, 1944 the commander of these brave fighting men, *SS-Obergruppenführer* Gille, was awarded the Oak Leaves with Swords after the conclusion of this hard-won, but successful break-out.

The road from officer cadet at Gross-Lichterfeld to this high point in his military career was a hard one for Herbert Otto Gille, born in Gandersheim in the Harz Mountains on March 8, 1897.

The 1914-18 world war was lost for Germany and *Oberleutnant* Gille, who had been discharged from military service, was left "lying by the side of the road." He had never learned a civilian career, so he returned to school and prepared for his future career as the administrator and inspector of an estate. Even when he later took up this career his predisposition toward the military remained alive.

Gille worked at his civilian occupation for fifteen years until, in 1934, he was presented with the opportunity to once again become a soldier. Gille had himself reactivated in the *SS-Verfügungstruppe*. He became a platoon and company commander in Ellwangen, then commander of a battalion of the *Germania* SS-Regiment in Arolsen. Finally he was entrusted with the formation of an artillery unit for the new service in

Jüterbog. It was May 1939, and within a short time the first Waffen-SS artillery regiment had been formed from men drawn from every branch of the armed forces. Gille took part in the Polish and French campaigns as a battalion commander in this regiment and in 1940 took command of the artillery regiment of the SS-Division *Wiking*, led by *SS-Obergruppenführer* Felix Steiner. The two SS officers had much in common. Both had been unit officers in the First World War, and both were "soldiers only", rejecting any ideological and political influencing of soldiers. Small wonder, then, that both, as Heinz Höhne wrote in his book *Der Orden unter dem Totenkopf*, struck *Reichsführer-SS* Heinrich Himmler as unpleasant.

Apart from the fact that Gille despised the military dilettante Himmler and denounced his brutal methods whenever the opportunity arose, he mistrusted him. The man struck him as sinister. Gille also did not hesitate to express his opinions to his superiors, and when he became aware of a spy in his regiment he immediately warned all the other officers who thought as he did.

In the war against the Soviet Union, which Gille considered unavoidable, he distinguished himself through his outstanding tactical skill combined with personal bravery. His motto was: "Always stay on top of the enemy." The advance battalion of the SS-Division *Wiking*, which he led, drove into the main body of the retreating enemy. Wherever the enemy showed himself he was attacked and not for a moment left in peace. Far ahead of their own forces, the men of the *Wiking* Division attacked, ignoring the danger of encirclement, and drove elements of a Soviet army from Yegorslikaya. The prisoners wore the numbers of ten divisions. Advancing relentlessly, the division reached the Kuban River, opening the way for further wide-ranging operations by the German armies. Following these battles, on October 8, 1942 Herbert Otto Gille was awarded the Knight's Cross for his actions while leading the *Wiking* Division's advance battalion.

Soon afterward Gille became commanding officer of the *Wiking* Division, a unit which had earned an enviable reputation on the Eastern Front. Army commanders unselfishly lauded the bravery of the "*Wikinger*" and confidence spread among army soldiers when they learned that they had the Waffen-SS as neighbors. In the autumn of 1941 the Soviet Major General Artemenko, commander of the 27th Army Corps, was captured by the Germans. He openly admitted that he was fascinated by the bravery of the men of the *Wiking* Division and praised their striking power, which exceeded anything he had experienced, their aggressiveness and the tactical skill of their officers. Those on the Soviet side had been happy one day when the "Vikings" were withdrawn, for they finally got a little peace. However this quiet did not last long. When the SS soldiers reappeared and attacked three days later, "All hell was let loose," as Artemenko put it. "You see the result . . . my corps smashed, destroyed, my staff and I captured."

Near Klenovoye 400 men of the *Wiking* Division held a 32-kilometer section of front against every Soviet attack. The men of the division distinguished themselves, especially at Valki-Olchany and Kharkov, through their will to persevere, but with Cherkassy and Kovel they and their commander went into military history. They held the East Prussian frontier, together with an *SS-Totenkopf* unit, against a 21-fold superiority and in the autumn of 1944 prevented a planned Soviet breakthrough to Berlin. Gille's men also performed in superhuman fashion in the energetic operations in Hungary – Budapest, Lake Balaton and during the fighting withdrawal.

The circumspect unit leader Gille had noticed that signals and important reports directed to Chief of Staff Guderian via the Waffen-SS liaison officer in Führer Headquarters only very rarely reached the addressee. It was also determined that signals which passed through the hands of *SS-Brigadeführer* Fegelein (later *Generalleutnant der Waffen-SS*, shot following a summary court martial on Hitler's order, whose brother-in-law he was) were often completely garbled or altered before being passed on.

Gille was mistrustful and spoke with Hitler very clearly about the situation at the front. "*Mein Führer*, come and visit us again, then you can study the conditions on the spot."

Hitler refused to listen. "I think you see everything too negatively. According to the latest reports the situation has long since been stabilized."

Gille thought he must have heard incorrectly. He came from the area in question and he knew how things really looked. "*Mein Führer*, you're being lied to," he replied, "X has been in Soviet hands since yesterday morning."

The year 1944 began ominously for the Eastern Front. While during the early winter months the Soviets completed a huge, but very well camouflaged build-up of armored, artillery and infantry forces opposite Army Group Center under *General-feldmarschall* Busch, farther to the south the surrounded First Panzer Army under *Generaloberst* Hube made its way westward. But this "wandering pocket" wasn't the only worry of Führer Headquarters and of the Commander-in-Chief of Army Group Northern Ukraine, *Generaldeldmarschall* Model. He was under instructions from Führer Headquarters to keep the approaches to the Carpathians open at all costs and not to give up the Kolomea – Ternopol –Kovel line. But in the meantime the Soviets had encircled the city of Kovel. Hitler declared it a "fortified place." This important position at the boundary between Army Groups Center and North Ukraine had to be held at all costs.

At this time *SS-Brigadeführer* Fegelein telephoned General Gille from Führer Headquarters. "*Herr General*, on orders of the Führer you are to assemble a battle group at once, march to Kovel and hold the city."

Without hesitation Gille responded: "Fegelein, tell the Führer that I refuse to form a battle group. Furthermore I wish to speak to the Führer personally."

"The Führer is in a conference."

"Then I will fly to the headquarters at once."

Gille flew to Führer Headquarters, however Hitler refused to see him. Finally he succeeded in reaching the current Chief of Staff, *Generaloberst* Guderian.

Gille protested against this "Führer Order." "What do you want? There is no longer a *Wiking* Division! We are just a bunch of men who are finished!" he raged.

Guderian was visibly impressed by Gille's unvarnished assessment of the situation, and he promised weapons, munitions and personnel replacements. But he also asked Gille to march to Kovel with the men he had left.

"Herr Generaloberst! I can't burden my men with that, they simply can't do any more. But I can see from my assessment of the overall situation that Kovel must be held. I will fly to Kovel alone and organize resistance in the city."

In encircled Kovel there was a mood of panic. Police General Bach-Zelewski, commander of the armed forces in the city, was not equal to the situation. He had lost his nerve and reported himself sick. Gille explored the situation and took stock of what was on hand. What he found was depressing: a small cavalry unit, a few police companies and a thrown-together group of regional defense personnel. The men had absolutely no combat experience, but they knew that they must fight, as that was the only possible way of avoiding capture by the Soviets.

After Gille had held the city with the limited forces available for ten days, preparations were made outside the Soviet ring around the city to relieve the defenders. From the pocket Gille radioed: "We're holding!" even though the situation looked almost hopeless. For the houses had no cellars, the terrain offered no natural cover and losses were mounting. Nevertheless Gille promised to hold.

How much longer? The general knew that he and his weak force could not defend Kovel much longer. He had not a single tank in the city. On the other hand the Soviet T 34s rolled up to the weakly-manned positions and blazed away with all guns. The situation became ever more threatening for the defenders. A battle group commanded by *Generalleutnant* von Saucken did succeed in establishing contact with the defenders on April 4/5, but it was too weak to drive through to the city or clear the way for a breakout. The Soviets exploited the situation and tried to separate Army Group Center from its neighbor. They hoped to drive a wedge between the German forces with the 11th Guards Army and two guards cavalry corps.

While, on April 5, *Generaloberst* Hube and his "wandering pocket" succeeded in establishing contact with the Fourth Panzer Army and clearing the pocket, the fate of the "fortified place" Kovel remained uncertain. On the Obersalzberg *Feldmarschall* Model and Hitler argued about the significance of the city. As was always the case in such situations Hitler wanted to "hold to the last man." Model suggested that they either abandon the city or incorporate it into a new defensive line, which would necessitate an offensive.

Hitler was enthused by Model's plan. However when the field marshall discussed the situation with his advisors back at his headquarters he was forced to admit that his plan wasn't feasible. After considering the situation briefly he called Hitler and proposed that they surrender the "fortified place" Kovel.

"That won't do . . . I forbid it . . ." said Hitler, betraying little emotion. But Model interrupted. "I must see to it that I seal the boundary, otherwise everything here will collapse."

Finally Hitler agreed to Model's plan. Kovel would be abandoned.

In Kovel *Gruppenführer* and *General der Waffen-SS* Gille knew nothing of this. He had been instructed to hold the city. He had neither the time nor inclination for higher strategy. He had to keep a firm grip on his weak defensive forces.

Gille received information by radio that outside Kovel *SS-Standartenführer* Richter was forming a battle group to relieve the city. A daring plan had been conceived, which on the fourteenth day of the encirclement would be translated into fact.

It was early in the morning when eight Panther tanks of the SS-Division *Wiking* under the command of a *Leutnant* and eighty men of the 131st Infantry Division under the command of an army *Hauptmann* advanced along the railway embankment toward Kovel. It was a desperate gamble but it succeeded. His forces bolstered by the arrival of the panzers, Gille held the city for another eight days, until the 131st Infantry Division, the 4th and 5th Panzer Divisions and the *Wiking* battle group opened the pocket. Within 48 hours Gille evacuated 2,000 wounded and all the tracked vehicles through a narrow corridor. Four Soviet armies had failed to dislodge a handful of men. For this exemplary act, on April 19, 1944 Gille, who had meanwhile been promoted to the rank of *SS-Obergruppenführer*, was awarded the Diamonds.

Six weeks later Gille was tasked with the formation of IV SS-Panzer Corps. Its area of operations was in the Narew position as part of Army Group Center. In a surprise move, in midwinter the corps was transferred to the Budapest area. This mistake by Hitler was to have grave consequences for Army Group Center, which was anticipating a major Soviet offensive. Hitler ordered the attack to relieve the Hungarian capital of Budapest on December 24, purely for reasons of prestige. Gille wanted to attack, but once again he was frustrated by baffling orders from above, which forced him to withdraw. In the course of subsequent operations in Hungary the corps fought at Lake balaton as part of the Sixth SS-Panzer Army.

The defeat of Germany was now a foregone conclusion. For Gille there was only one decision: not to surrender to the Soviets. As the Americans were in the rear of his corps, he marched toward them and surrendered in Radstadt in Austria. It was a coincidence that its name was similar to that of a city which played a significant role in Gille's life. He had become a recruit and an officer in Rastatt in Baden, and in the Austrian Radstadt he carried out the final act in his military career.

For weeks the corps camped in the fields near Wagrein with all its weapons and vehicles. One day a jeep carrying several American staff officers pulled up near Gille. "The Commander-in-Chief of American forces in Salzburg would like to speak to you and your Chief-of-Staff. You are guaranteed an honor guard and may travel in your own vehicles if you like."

Gille and his Chief-of-Staff agreed and drove with the Americans officers to Salzburg. There they were detained and placed under arrest by American soldiers. The general sat in a cell for two hours. Then he was taken out and led into a room. There, with his legs stretched out on the desk, sat a young US Army Lieutenant, who every few seconds tapped the desk with a riding crop.

"That's the Diamonds you're wearing, is it not?" was his first question.

Fourteen days later Gille was transferred to Augsburg. There his decorations were taken from him.

The Americans handled SS prisoners of war differently from those of the other German armed services. This was because they did not consider members of SS formations regular soldiers, rather saw them as members of a political organization. Later they declared the SS a "criminal organization."

Thus it was that Gille, too, was treated not as a member of the armed forces, but wrongly as a member of a political organization. He was sentenced to one and a half years in prison, however because of his time as an internee he was judged to have already served his sentence.

The crimes committed in the concentration camps by special detachments of the SS, which had nothing to do with the Waffen-SS, also cast their shadow over the civilian life of the former *SS-Obergruppenführer*. Gille had to live through some difficult years. His wife was forced to work as a domestic in order for them to survive, for Gille received only a minuscule salary as a worker in Hannover. Later he opened a mail-order book business together with his family. He founded the newsletter of the HIAG, the Assistance Association of Former members of the Waffen-SS, serving as editor and publisher until 1958.

Herbert Otto Gille died unexpectedly of a heart attack on December 26, 1966.

Oberst Mölders conducts a situation briefing before a mission by his Jagdgeschwader.

Previous Page
Above:
The best-known German fighter aces (from left): Generaloberst Ernst Udet, one of the most successful fighter pilots of WW I and later world-famous as a stunt pilot, who committed suicide on November 17, 1941, in conversation with Oberst Werner Mölders and Oberst Adolf Galland.

Below:
Werner Mölders, the first German soldier to receive his country's highest decoration for valor, was the idol of the nation's youth. He scored a total of 115 air victories and died in an airplane crash on November 22, 1941.

Galland never dispensed with his cigar, even just before takeoff.

Adolf Galland receives a warm welcome from the ground personnel after returning from a combat mission.

Oberstleutnant Galland uses graphic hand movements to describe to his host, Generalmajor Osterkamp, and Oberstleutnant Mölders how he obtained his 59th and 60th victories.

Galland as the guest of honor of the Norwich Military Academy in Northfield, Vermont. The cadets presented Galland with a plaque bearing the emblems of those units in which the university's served.

Major Gollob inspects combat damage sustained by his Bf 109 of the Geschwaderstab of JG 52.

This highly-decorated pilot ("Hero of the Soviet Union), a Major and the commander of a fighter unit, was shot down over Gonshatovka airfield and taken prisoner. Second from the right in the photo is Hauptmann Dickfeld, and beside him Major Gollob.

The past is not forgotten. Gordon M. Gollob with a book he wrote.

Hauptmann Joachim Marseille received the Diamonds at the age of twenty-two; in total he shot down 158 British aircraft. He died on September 30, 1942, when forced to abandon his aircraft due to engine trouble. Marseille's parachute failed to open.

This RAF Hurricane was Marseille's 48th kill.

Marseille (center) shot down seventeen aircraft in a single day over the African desert.

"Here Hans-Joachim Marseille died undefeated." Members of his Staffel erected this stone pyramid on the spot where he fell to his death.

The designer of the Bf 109, Professor Messerschmitt, was a frequent guest of Kommodore Graf, who related his experiences in this famous machine.

Coffee break between sorties at Pitomnik airfield, situated at the edge of Stalingrad.

His passion was soccer. During the war Hermann Graf put together an outstanding team, the "Red Fighters." Other members included Fritz Walter, Franz Hahnreiter, Moog and Klingler. Graf was himself an excellent goalkeeper. here he is seen with national player Fritz Walter, the legendary captain of Germany's post-war national team.

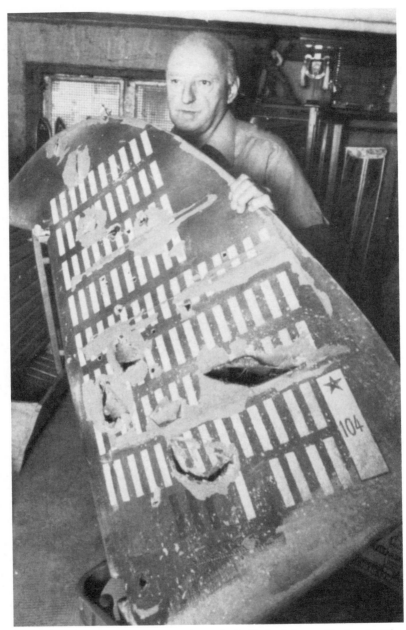

Memories remain. In the basement of his home: Graf with the shot-up rudder from his Bf 109.

Rommel and General Gariboldi with the Italian colonial minister Tericzi during a briefing.

Rommel and his command post outside Tobruk, June 1941.

Outside Tobruk, June 1942.

Stuck in the desert sand.

Field Marshalls Rommel and Kesselring met in this command post, whose construction was augmented through the use of wooden boards, in early 1942.

Nothing could stop Rommel. Here he walks through the Eighth Army's barbed wire near El Alamein.

Rommel during the Battle of Normandy.

Rommel's death mask.

Kapitän zur See Wolfgang Lüth sank 215,147 tonnes of enemy shipping and one submarine in the course of 14 sorties lasting 609 days at sea. He achieved his greatest success in the Indian Ocean and off the coast of South Africa. Lüth was the Kriegsmarine's first recipient of the Diamonds and was slated to become commander of submarines.

Forty-eight victory pennants on U-181. Korvettenkapitän Wolfgang Lüth returns from a combat patrol. Here he is seen directing the docking maneuver.

For Lüth and his crew a few days to recover after the long sortie.

State funeral for Wolfgang Lüth, authorized by the British city commandant after the end of the war. Lüth died when shot in error by a sentry.

Afterward things don't look quite so serious as during the life-and-death struggle: Major Nowotny describes a successful dogfight.

Walter Nowotny as a guest of the navy, which received valuable support from his unit.

Nowotny often came home with battle damage such as this.

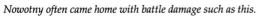

Situation briefing in the Shepetovka area: the commander of the 7th Panzer Division, Generalleutnant von Manteuffel and Oberst Schulz (center).

Adalbert Schulz, photographed after receiving the Diamonds in Führer Headquarters.

Two friends: Oberst Rudel and his gunner Hauptmann Dr. Gadermann, who saved his life in February 1945.

Over the front in Hungary, December 1944. In this cannon-armed anti-tank aircraft were Oberstleutnant Rudel and gunner Dr. Gadermann. Visible beneath the aircraft's wings are the "long rods," two 37mm cannon.

The Soviet battleship "Marat" explodes after a direct hit by Oberleutnant Rudel.

An historic moment in the life of Hans Ulrich Rudel. On January 1, 1945 he became the sole German soldier to receive the Golden Oak Leaves. Present were GenOb Jodl, FM Keitel (3rd and 4th from left), Reichsmarschall Göring (extreme right) and Grossadmiral Dönitz (not in photo).

Graf Strachwitz as commander of a panzer regiment of the Grossdeutschland Panzer-Grenadier Division with GenLt Hoernlein (right).

"Panzers must not be allowed to sit, they must always be in motion." This was the motto which Strachwitz employed in command.

The final words before an attack. Hyazinth Graf Strachwitz, an outstanding tank commander who inflicted heavy losses on the Soviets through his unorthodox tactics.

Kovel. SS-General Herbert Gille discusses the situation in the front lines with a wounded soldier.

June 1944. Situation briefing in Heidelager, near Debica.

At a regimental command post Gille listens to a description of the course of the battle for Budapest.

"Sicilian General" Hans Hube. He left the island with his soldiers on the last ferry.

As Commander-in-Chief of the Southern Front, FM Kesselring was also responsible for operations in Africa. Even Kesselring was unable to improve the strained relations with Germany's Italian allies in the Comando Supremo.

GenLt. Heidrich briefs Kesselring on the situation during the Battle of Cassino at the headquarters of a parachute unit.

CHAPTER XIII

GENERAL HANS HUBE

Among the most outstanding personalities of the German Armed Forces was *Generaloberst* Hans Hube. As an infantry officer in the First World War and a member of the 100,000-man army, from whose ranks came so many outstanding officers, he came to know the top class of soldiers. As the crowning achievement of his career and the last command before his death, Hube, who had never been trained in the general staff, commanded an army and was in line for the post of Commander-in-Chief of the Army. Hitler could not get over Hube's death. To officers and party leaders he described Hube as a shining example and wished, as he said, that there were more generals cut from the same wood. The same opinion was expressed by *Generalfeldmarschall* von Manstein, who was Hube's superior for a time.

Hans Hube stood out, not just on account of his circumspection as a commander, but through his personal bravery and comradeship as well. He was a soldier's officer, one who lived with his men, trained them and led them in two world wars.

Spiritually Hube was a complete soldier. He was hard on himself, strong and tough, correct and kind to subordinates, skillful and personally courageous, always an example to his soldiers. He demanded nothing that he could or would not do himself. He was imbued with the Frederican spirit, but his training methods and his views may not always have met with the full understanding of his superiors – yet in the end his measures were for the good of his troops. During an inspection in the time of the 100,000-man army, the then Chief of the Army Command, *Generaloberst* von Seeckt, said of Hube's company: "It was a pleasure to review this company. It reminded me vividly of my service with the Guards, whose best company would be rivalled by your men!"

Born on October 29, 1890, Hube distinguished himself as an officer cadet in the Fürst Leopold von Anhalt-Dessau Infantry Regiment No. 26 in Magdeburg, where on August 22, 1910 he was promoted to the rank of *Leutnant* after only 18 months in the service. Together with the other recruits of his age class, some of whom he had trained, in 1914 Hube was drawn into World War One. He became battalion adjutant and on September 20, 1914, near Fontenay, he was badly wounded, necessitating the amputation of his left arm. Hube returned to the front in December 1915 as an *Oberleutnant* and company commander. In 1916 he received the Iron Cross, First Class on the Somme, and a year and a half later, in 1917, he was promoted to *Hauptmann* and awarded the Knight's Cross of the House Order of Hohenzollern.

As a battalion commander Hube repulsed the first British tank attack with heavy losses to the enemy. Soon afterwards he was badly gassed and had to be evacuated to hospital. Hube was recommended for the Pour le Mérite for his exemplary bravery, however he did not receive the award as the war ended in November 1918.

This one-armed officer had an unbending will to live. He played a part in the defeat of the communist uprising in central Germany and after the demobilization of his unit was one of the first to report for service in the 100,000-man army. But although the young *Hauptmann*'s bravery was well-known, he was rejected because it was thought that an amputee could not be in the front rank. Hube was of a different opinion. He later recounted how he, a man who during the First World War had returned to the front before his wounds had completely healed and successfully led companies and battalions, jumped into the water from the ten-meter tower wearing full uniform with pack and rifle before a group of invited officers. After he had climbed out of the water, the one-armed man declared to the officers present: "If they won't take me, then I will demand that each officer who is taken ahead of me must first make this jump."

This attitude best characterizes the man and the soldier Hans Hube: unshakable, tough, fighting his way through with an iron will and always master of himself. His motto was: It is the spirit which is decisive, not the letter.

Hube was finally accepted as a company commander, and his 11th was the best company in the regiment. He was known for employing very strict standards in selecting his NCOs and officer candidates. He placed physical training before the theoretical: in difficult cross-country rides he led all others on his mare Riekchen, he skied icy slopes, dove from the ten-meter tower and distinguished himself in track and field.

Hube's superiors soon took notice; he received early promotion. At this time he wrote a book, *Der Infanterist*, which soon became the standard guide for every soldier and officer of the *Reichswehr* and later the *Wehrmacht*. In it Hube characterized concern for the welfare of subordinates as the greatest asset of the soldier. He considered field training the alpha and omega of soldierly upbringing and pushed for the training of assault teams. His attention was already directed at anti-tank defense and the combatting of tanks at close range.

Because of his extraordinary achievements and knowledge, in 1928 Hube was sent on an official trip to the United States and later was transferred to the war college in Dresden. In 1932, now with the rank of *Major*, he assumed command of I Battalion of the 3rd Infantry Regiment in East Prussia. This was followed two years later by a promotion to *Oberstleutnant*. With his transfer to Döberitz on May 1, 1935, as commander of the infantry school there, the second phase of Hube's military career came to an end.

Hube did not receive a front-line command until after the Polish Campaign. Happily for him it was his old unit, the 3rd Regiment. In the area of the Westwall he prepared his men for the coming confrontation with the French and British.

During an exercise in attacking enemy bunkers, in which live ammunition was used, I Battalion's 7th Company was ordered to attack suspected enemy positions under the covering fire of the artillery. The company was in cover in a wood when suddenly the heavy batteries opened fire. The first salvo fell very near the troops, the second landed in the company's midst. A number of men were killed or wounded. Hube immediately called off the exercise, but asked *Hauptmann* Arning, who went on to become a *Generalmajor* and commander of the 75th Infantry Division, that the exercise be repeated the following day, and by the same company.

The men hadn't got over the shock of the previous day when they were forced to begin the same attack exercise all over again. But Hube led the attack and walked under the fire of the German artillery.

This attitude on the part of the regimental commander left a deep impression on every soldier; not only had he provided them with an example in personal courage, he had reinforced their self-confidence as well. Nevertheless, superior officers firmly rejected such "suicide actions", as they termed those conducted by Hube. Veteran front-line soldiers also considered them crazy and overdone, the outpouring of a ruthless drive for action, in which men counted only as "materiel."

On May 14, 1940 Hube took command of the 16th Motorized Infantry Division. Weeks later he was promoted to *Generalmajor*. As part of *Panzergruppe* Kleist he fought his way to the Channel Coast, then drove into Lorraine as far as Vaudemont, near Mirecourt, where he took the surrender of General Flavigny's 21st Corps two days before the cease-fire negotiations.

Following the western campaign Hube was ordered to reorganize the 16th Infantry Division as a panzer unit and transfer it to Transylvania to serve as an instructional unit for Germany's ally Romania. From there it was transported to Poland, where it once again joined *Panzergruppe* Kleist, which was preparing to spearhead the attack on the Soviet Union. Everywhere the division was committed it distinguished itself through its will to fight, extreme offensive spirit and enormous discipline. In the early summer of 1941 it smashed through the Stalin Line in its first attempt, for which *Generalmajor* Hube received the Knight's Cross on August 1, 1941. Later the division destroyed two Soviet armies near

Nikolayev and Kiev, in recognition of which Hube became the 62nd German soldier to be awarded the Oak Leaves.

Wherever things were hot, Hans Hube was there. He led his soldiers with success at the front. When he received the news that his only son, a twenty-year-old *Leutnant*, had been killed leading his platoon, he left the command post and drove to the front to be with his men. On September 16, 1942 he was promoted to *Generalleutnant* and made commanding general of XIV Panzer Corps, which was deployed in Stalingrad. Then, on December 28, he received Hitler's order to fly out of the pocket to report on the situation and receive the Swords, which had been awarded him on the 21st. The command corps of the Sixth Army were in agreement that holding Stalingrad meant the destruction of the army. Hube expressed these concerns to Hitler and requested approval for a breakout. Hitler turned down the request as he had before.

When Hube flew back into the pocket on January 8, 1943, the fate awaiting the surrounded troops was even more obvious. The Soviets had delivered an ultimatum to Paulus, and as Hube described the mood which prevailed in Führer Headquarters he could read the disappointment in the faces of the commanding generals.

Two days later the enemy launched a major offensive. For Hube there was only one thing to do: go to the front and there fight and die with his soldiers in the icy snowstorm. At that time *Oberst* Bernd von Pezold led a battle group of volunteers which was employed as a "fire-brigade." *General der Panzertruppe* Hube confided in him that he did not wish to survive the end. The battle group commander was not a little shocked and tried to change Hube's mind. But the general stuck to his plans. Dismayed, Hube told the *Oberst* of his unsuccessful visit to Führer Headquarters and of the frivolous manner in which those there assessed the situation in Stalingrad.

Then, completely unexpectedly, an order arrived from Hitler: *General* Hube is to fly out of the pocket immediately. At first the general refused. But then, believing that he could yet change Hitler's mind about allowing what was left of the Sixth Army to leave the pocket, Hube once again made his way to Führer Headquarters. Hube left the pocket on January 18, 1943.

He dropped in on the Commander-in-Chief of Army Group South, *Generalfeldmarschall* von Manstein, and proposed that they persuade Hitler to appoint a "Commander-in-Chief East", who alone would be responsible for operations in that theater. Von Manstein encouraged Hube to pursue this idea. Soon afterward he met with Hitler and implored him to allow the Sixth Army to break out and to appoint a Commander-in-Chief East. Hitler refused. When Hube then expressed a wish to be flown back into the pocket at once, Hitler blew up. He ordered the general to immediately take charge of the effort to supply of the defenders of Stalingrad from outside. The catastrophic conditions – Hube served as a liaison officer with *Generalfeldmarschall* Milch, who was with *Generaloberst* von Richthofen's supply headquarters in Mariupol – prevented any effective help from reaching the Sixth Army. Göring's exaggerated statement that he would supply the Sixth Army from the air settled the fate of 225,000 soldiers.

Afterward Hube sent a memorandum to *Generaloberst* Jodl concerning the purpose of fortresses in a war of movement. Like so many other proposals from front-line officers it was paid scant attention.

In February 1943 the OKH tasked *General der Panzertruppe* Hube with the formation of a new XIV Panzer Corps, which was to be moved to Sicily. The situation there had grown very serious in the meantime. The Allies had landed on the European mainland and had overrun the Italian positions. Intrigue and betrayal on the one hand and personal and internal conflicts within the Italian officer corps on the other prevented clear decisions and operations. In this situation Hitler decided to leave the defense of Sicily to German troops. He appointed a "German Commandant Strait of Messina" without informing the Italian command, for it had been learned that the Italian Marshall Ambrosio was conspiring with the Allies. It was odd that Ambrosio, a member of the "Comando Supremo", demanded more German troops for Sicily. Suspicious, Hitler and *Generaloberst* Jodl refused. They feared a trap: Ambrosio wanted to tie up German troops and deliver them to the Allies when a suitable opportunity arose. Much later it turned out that their suspicions were correct.

Hitler's decision stood firm. He needed a capable, experienced and above all uncompromising commanding officer in Sicily. For him there was no other choice but *General der Panzertruppe* Hans Hube. He appointed him Commander-in-Chief of all army and flak units in Sicily. *Reichsmarschall* Göring objected. For reasons of prestige he wanted a Luftwaffe officer as commander and proposed *General* Stahel. However *Feldmarschall* Rommel and Hitler refused. Hube could command. Rommel wrote in his diary: "Göring proposed Stahel as Commander-in-Chief. I won through with Hube and *General* Bayerlein as Chief-of-Staff. Führer is in agreement."

The Allies had committed 5,000 aircraft and massed naval guns. More than 2,000 transports spewed infantry and masses of tanks by the hour. Hube was supposed to hold the island against this unimaginable superiority with four divisions. After bitter resistance he and his corps were forced to pull back in a fighting withdrawal. After 38 combat-filled days he crossed the Strait of Messina on August 17, the last German soldier to do so.

Hube's veteran 16th Panzer Division bore the brunt of the attack. Two American divisions were destroyed and Hube nearly succeeded in driving the entire Fifth Army into the sea near Salerno. The Luftwaffe, the anti-aircraft guns and *Nebelwerfer* rocket battalions inflicted heavy losses on the American invasion army and sowed great confusion in its ranks. But as bravely as Hube's divisions fought, they were denied any decisive success. The counterattack bogged down under heavy naval gunfire and now the German losses mounted. Nevertheless Hitler spoke of *General der Panzertruppe* Hube as "the victor of Salerno."

In November 1943 Hans Hube assumed command of the First Panzer Army. He had mixed feelings about this as the army's previous commander, *Generaloberst* von Mackensen, had been relieved by Hitler, who went over the head of the army group Commander-in-Chief, *Feldmarschall* von Manstein. This was the first time Hube had commanded a large formation, but it was soon demonstrated that he was capable of fulfilling the task which had been set him. South of Pogobitche his army smashed five Soviet armies and three tank corps.

However in spite of their severe losses the Soviets attacked without letup. On March 8 the enemy broke through the German front near Berdichev, while in the north equally strong enemy infantry forces prepared to attack. It began during the night of March 9.

The danger existed that the main body of the First Panzer Army would be surrounded. *General* Hube's headquarters were located between Vinnitsa and Kalinovka in the former headquarters of Hermann Göring. The soldiers joked about it. For it was known that Göring only visited his headquarters when he felt the urge to hunt. This was to be the last visit by a German unit. The wooden structure was abandoned after a few hours. Engineers burned it down with flamethrowers.

General Hube considered holding Vinnitsa absurd. But Hitler's orders were to make it a "fortified place", whereby the sole artillery division in the German armed forces, the 18th Artillery Division, was to assume responsibility for its defense. With its 132 guns the division would have been welcome reinforcement to any other army. But Hitler refused to listen to any objections.

While the columns of the withdrawing units stalled in Vinnitsa, Soviet infantry in trucks was approaching fast. This time the Russians had done something different: the first wave consisted not of T 34s, but of infantry in trucks, in an effort to make contact with the enemy more quickly.

The enemy stormed Vinnitsa three sides. Hube's troops realized that they were trapped. Panic threatened to break out. Military police maintained order. However most of the soldiers knew what was at stake. They waited soberly and took their places in the withdrawal. Endless columns waited to cross the lone bridge over the Bug; the Soviets were already firing into the city with mortars.

But Hitler was determined to hold and the army command under *General* Hube followed his order. But then *General* Nehring, the commander of a panzer corps, raised an objection: "Holding Vinnitsa would be sheer madness! We need every man and here we'll all be sacrificed senselessly." He was to be proved right.

Miraculously all the vehicles crossed the Bug within 24 hours. Immediately afterward the engineers hastened to blow up the bridge. The first enemy assault squads were already in the streets of Vinnitsa.

The Soviets aim was to destroy the First Panzer Army. Meanwhile the leading elements of Hube's forces had reached the Dnestr. But the Soviets were even quicker. They had overtaken the Germans and were waiting for them on the opposite bank. There they destroyed the spearhead of the German army.

Things looked bad for the First Panzer Army. The enemy had created a huge pocket around it. Five Soviet armies were trying to compress, split and then destroy it. The front which Army Group South was supposed to hold had collapsed. Kamenets-Podol'skiy was already in enemy hands. The situation was desperate; the spring muddy period, which had begun several weeks before, made movement difficult. *General* Hube proposed to army group that his army break out to the south. But *Feldmarschall* von Manstein rejected this and ordered Hube to prepare to break out to the west to link up with the Fourth Panzer Army under *Generaloberst* Raus. Meanwhile the 7th and 16th Panzer Divisions, the 20th Motorized Infantry Division and the 29th Infantry Division were approaching the pocket from the outside. Hube ordered *Oberst* Mauss, the commander of the 7th Panzer Division, to establish contact with these divisions and burst the pocket from outside. Further he was to launch a joint attack across the Zbruch and establish a bridgehead.

The troops were exhausted, but Hube, who was well aware of this, had no choice but to ask the nearly impossible if his army was to escape destruction. He appealed to his soldiers: "The Russians have broken through on both sides of the First Panzer Army and have cut us off from our lines of supply. The army will fight its way through the enemy and smash him wherever it encounters him. Hard battles, exertions and deprivations face us in the coming days. Only if every single man attacks or defends with determined energy using the absolute minimum of ammunition required, wherever he is committed by command, can the great objective be reached by us all: breakthrough and safety at home. The fate of one of our most glorious armies is at stake!"

Far to the west, ahead of the First Army, Soviet armies had streamed into the land. Normally an escape, a withdrawal and breakout from the pocket, would not have been possible. The enemy had completely wiped out and destroyed Hungarian and German units which were supposed to hold south of the Dnestr. If the First Army crossed the Zbruch it would immediately meet heavy resistance. The enemy was everywhere, all around!

The Mauss group, which had now been joined by the *SS-Leibstandarte*, was given the task of covering First Panzer Army's flank in the north and crossing the Zbruch. Mauss received further reinforcement in the shape of the "Chevallerie Corps Group." Hube knew that he could depend on Mauss and his 7th Panzer Division. It was one of the very few units still intact and with full striking power. Hube had a special mission for the division, which, as it turned out, was not practicable. Mauss was to turn south, take the crossing near Husytyn and wait for the rearguard. Corps Group Breith launched a surprise attack on the enemy near Kamenets-Podol'skiy and established a bridgehead near Okopi. Where was the help? On March 28 *Oberst* Mauss received the following radio message from Hube: "Who's winning, Breith or Mauss? Whoever wins gets three weeks at home."

Mauss answered quickly: "No one can keep up with Mauss if he has enough fuel!"

Gallows humor? Optimism? How can one say today what was going through the minds of these men, upon whose shoulders so much responsibility lay?

Surprisingly, the weather turned and it became cold. Mauss could roll again. His advance detachment drove to Borcow, overran the enemy and reached the Seret, crossed the river and established a bridgehead. Mauss now bet everything on one card. He knew that if it trumped he had won, if not then any further effort was futile. Not one surplus man was to stay behind with the train. Everyone who could walk and shoot was put into the line. Even those with minor wounds had to get down from the vehicles and fight. And they did so willingly, for their lives were at stake. "The enemy is to be attacked and destroyed wherever he is, employing every member of the division present at that location."

Movement was suspended by day. Air superiority had long since been in the hands of the enemy. His patrols were not to discern the army's direction of advance prematurely. All movement was by night, following the compass and the North Star as *General* Hube ordered.

On April 1, 1944 the Soviet forces were sixty kilometers west of the pocket containing First Panzer Army. There was practically no hope of escape for Hube's soldiers. Who would or who could fight his way through sixty kilometers of enemy-held territory thick with troops? When one considered that the forces which formed the pocket would intervene in any battle, it looked as if a breakthrough was impossible.

The Soviets were visibly nervous about having such a relatively strong group of enemy forces in its rear. Obviously they tied down a number of capable units which the front's high command would gladly have had for the attack. Based on this consideration, the Soviet Marshall Zhukov sent a request for surrender to the officers and men of the First Panzer Army which was worded as follows:

"In order to avoid further sacrifice I propose that you cease your senseless resistance and surrender with all the units under your command. There is no hope of help from the outside. It is impossible for you to get out of the encirclement, as a solid ring has closed around you. I propose:

1. Surrender by April 2, 1944,
2. Officers and soldiers retain their rifles, decorations and means of transportation,
3. If you do not surrender you will be shot.

Front High Command of the Soviet Union

Zhukov
Marshall of the Soviet Union."

But they did not surrender. They fought on. Hitler's intention, to allow the First Panzer Army to operate as a moving pocket in the Soviets' rear, a thorn in their flesh, came to nothing due to the weakened state of the Luftwaffe. It was no longer capable of supplying the army from the air.

General Hube decided to break through the enemy lines, using the 7th Panzer Division as a battering ram, and drive toward the northwest, where he expected to find German units. Intercepted radio messages confirmed that the Fourth Panzer Army commanded by *Generaloberst* Raus was involved in heavy fighting with the Soviets.

After several bleak hours he succeeded in establishing contact with Raus. The Commander-in-Chief radioed: "We're coming!"

Now Hube could put into action his plan to use the 7th Panzer Division as a battering ram. But the Fourth Panzer Army also knew that the freeing of their comrades in the pocket was at stake. When the army assaulted the Soviet positions it broke through. The 16th Panzer Division broke out of the pocket, drove to Buchach, smashed the enemy and linked up with the Fourth Panzer Army.

Farther to the north the 7th Panzer Division overran the enemy positions, destroying 53 tanks and a number of guns and taking several hundred prisoners.

The same day Hube released an order of the day, which said: "The encircling ring of strong enemy forces has been pierced. On March 23 the Russians stood poised to successfully conclude a battle of destruction the equal of Cannae, Sedan and Tannenberg. Following successful breakthroughs from the east and west against our neighbors, they had completed a double outflanking of the First Panzer Army north and south of the Dnestr and were attacking the army's eastern and northern fronts with their masses of infantry without letup. But First Panzer Army, its lines of communication cut, surrounded on all sides, a broad river with only a single crossing at its back, stood firm like a rock. And when the order was given to do so the army attacked, initially with inadequate supplies, under extremely difficult terrain and weather conditions. The encircling enemy was himself encircled, smashed, driven back and his lines of communication cut. Our panzer and infantry forces poured into the startled enemy like a storm flood and smashed his forces and plan of operations. The accomplishments of the troops and commanders are unprecedented."

The enemy was flabbergasted. His losses were extraordinarily high. 358 tanks, 190 artillery pieces, 20 assault guns and more than 200 armored personnel carriers and self-propelled guns were destroyed. Personnel losses were especially high during the phase of the final attack by Fourth Panzer Army and the tremendous exertions by First Panzer Army prior to the link-up. The enemy suddenly found himself under attack from two sides, surrounded in small pockets. In the end the Soviets suffered the fate they had been preparing for the First Panzer Army.

In recognition of this superlative feat of command *General* Hube was awarded the Diamonds on April 20, 1944. Simultaneously he was promoted to *Generaloberst*.

The next day his aircraft crashed near the Obersalzberg on its way to Berlin. Hube's injuries proved fatal.

The remains of the outstanding commander Hans Hube were buried at the Invaliden Cemetery in Berlin in a state funeral attended by Hitler and his entire cabinet. The eulogy was delivered by *Generaloberst* Guderian.

CHAPTER XIV

GENERALFELDMARSCHALL ALBERT KESSELRING

May 6, 1946 had taken a special place in the life of the *Generalfeldmarschall*. It was a day like any other. And yet it was to become one of the blackest in the history of British military justice. It was in Venedig, when, in the gloomy hall of the Military Central Tribunal, the president of the highest British military court delivered the following sentence: "The former *Generalfeldmarschall* of the German Air Force, Albert Kesselring, is sentenced to death by firing squad for war crimes."

Generalfeldmarschall Albert Kesselring listened calmly to the reading of the sentence, in the same way he had lived and fought. He was not allowed to make a final statement. But the field marshall didn't wish to plead or beg for mercy. He merely wished to make a statement, which is repeated here:

"Shortly before the beginning of the trial I stood before the graves of 6,000 of my brave soldiers at the German military cemetery at Cervia-Rimini. In silent reflection I thought of their heroic fight and sacrifice, and in doing so I felt that I had to intervene on behalf of the honor of my soldiers and the German command, at a time when almost every German was looked upon as a criminal. This reinforced my decision to defend myself and to accept the weight of the long and not always easy court proceedings in addition to the burden of often unbearable months in captivity.

"As a senior commander of the German Armed Forces, it was my duty to show in this trial that a high moral ethos also resided in the German officers and soldiers, which might allow the grieving mothers and children to make sense of the sacrificial deaths of their loved ones and perhaps also facilitate an understanding between peoples.

"I alone bear the responsibility for my orders. If I have erred as a commander and as a man, then I must bear the consequences. But I will never accept penal laws which were enacted one-sidedly only against Germans and which are applied retroactively contrary to accepted law. I will never acknowledge that two kinds of law are still law and that gaps in international criminal law can be made liable to prosecution. I believe that every right-thinking person will agree with me.

"On the other hand I can appreciate the difficulties facing these international legal proceedings. I know from my own experience how difficult it is to appreciate the atmosphere surrounding events which took place years before, even those which one has experienced personally. I know how difficult it is for a court to go deeply into another national character and to understand the unique, incomparable command structure of National-Socialist Germany. I know that high politics can place restraints even on the administration of justice.

"I must resign myself to these facts. I would, however, like to conclude with the following:

"Very many Germans and foreigners refuse me their respect as a man, a person and an officer.

"I can leave the judgement of my military measures to historical research with a clear conscience.

"And with my conscience I will stand before my God. My house is in order.

"Your decision, honored judges, will go beyond my person to the most senior military leaders of the world, who were and will be in the same situation.

"Unbowed, I, as a front-line soldier, await your judgement as front-line soldiers. No matter how it turns out I will be able to bear it. I have learned in long periods of deepest degradation to tread on my misery in order to stand taller."

The field marshall was not alone in the world. Voices which could not be ignored intervened on Kesselring's behalf, and on August 4, 1947 his sentence was reduced to life imprisonment. But with this began what, for the soldier Kesselring, was the bitter degradation of captivity. Rubbing elbows with career criminals. Locked up with murderers, pimps and swindlers. Execution of the death sentence would often have come as a relief. To a soldier like Kesselring, who fought and thought chivalrously, this unworthy treatment by the enemy was impossible to understand.

The officer candidate, who was born on November 13, 1885 in Marksteft (Lower Franconia) and joined the 2nd Bavarian Foot Regiment in 1904, had at that time a special love for the "upper regions." He trained as a balloon observer. The first step to the later air fleet commander had been taken.

Kesselring took part in the 1914 to 1918 World War with the troops and as a general staff officer and brigade adjutant. After demobilization he came to know the communists, who stormed the headquarters of the 3rd Bavarian Army Corps in Nuremberg. The measures taken by the communists, who wished to change Germany's political system, made Kesselring their implacable enemy. He received a foretaste of what it meant to be a prisoner, something he was to experience again in Oberursel and Dachau almost thirty years later.

In 1919 Kesselring joined the *Reichswehr*. After three years of service he was summoned to join the general staff. In the capacity of a "Savings and Simplification Commissar" he gained insight into the multifarious administration branch of the armed forces. In 1930 he was made a battalion commander in the 4th Artillery Regiment and the same year was promoted to the rank of *Oberst*. Three years later he was transferred to the newly-emerging Luftwaffe, where he held the positions of Chief-of-Staff in the Luftwaffe Administration Office (LVA) and the Luftwaffe Command Office (LKA).

On the basis of his qualifications Kesselring received rapid promotion: in 1935 to *Generalmajor*, in 1936 to *Generalleutnant*, and in 1937 to *General der Flieger*. He took command of *Luftkreis* (Air District) 3 Dresden; a year later he became commander of Luftwaffe Group I Berlin, which soon afterward became

Luftflotte (Air Fleet) 1. At that time he was in command of all German airspace east of Berlin and central Germany.

Kesselring's units provided air cover for the marches into the Sudetenland and Czechoslovakia from the north. The issue became serious when an attack against Poland was ordered. It was in part due to Kesselring that army operations in *Generaloberst* von Bock's sector of the front were so successfully and contributed to a rapid German victory. For his outstanding command achievements Kesselring was awarded the Knight's Cross on September 30, 1939.

During the *Reichstag* sitting of July 19, 1940 – after the French Campaign – Kesselring was promoted to the rank of *Generalfeldmarschall*, skipping *Generaloberst*. This was in recognition of the outstanding performance of the armed forces and at the same time his command of *Luftflotte* 2, which carried out the first large-scale airborne landing, against Holland. The participation of the Luftwaffe was one of the keys to the rapid defeat of Holland, Belgium and France.

In these operations, as in Poland, Kesselring once again worked closely with the Commander-in-Chief of Army Group von Bock, who had also been promoted to *Generalfeldmarschall*. Kesselring's years as a general staff officer stood him in good stead. Nothing could keep him from flying himself. But his request to occasionally fly missions against England was rejected by *Reichsmarschall* Göring, who issued a flying ban for the field marshal.

The Battle of Britain was a difficult and costly affair for the aircrews and commanders; it ended as an entr'acte to the Russian Campaign, but without the desired success. Kesselring was in favor of an invasion of England. For him the period after the defeat of France – with Germany possessing air superiority, its armies victorious and confident, and the enemy demoralized to a certain extent – was the obvious time to strike and destroy the enemy. In his opinion the invasion of England would have brought the war on the western side of Europe to a conclusion.

The war against the Soviet Union saw Kesselring and his *Luftflotte* 2 once again in *Feldmarschall* von Bock's area of operations. His units took part in the rapid advance and victorious battles of encirclement in the summer of 1941, flying constantly and effectively supporting the hard-fighting ground forces.

Kesselring did not stay long in the East. Toward the end of 1941 Hitler appointed him "Commander-in-Chief South" and handed him control of the air forces in the Mediterranean area and Africa. At that time Kesselring spoke out in favor of a change of emphasis, and with it a strengthening of the fighter arm. He could see that the initiative would soon pass to the enemy and that the Allies would try to attack the mainland with their superior air forces and smash Germany. His efforts were unsuccessful, for those in high places still believed in the decisive effect of bombers.

As "Commander-in-Chief South" the field marshall demonstrated his skill in combined operations with other branches of the armed forces, which was acknowledged by friend and foe alike. Whether it was the invasion of Malta, which Kesselring supported but which was cancelled on instructions from above, the costly convoy escort operations over water, or the supporting of the Africa Corps in its offensive and defensive operations from El Gaza to Tobruk and El Alamein, all the threads ran through the hands of the field marshall.

Further recognition of the accomplishments of his forces and of his personal efforts and command skill were not long in coming: on February 25, 1942 Kesselring received the Oak Leaves and half a year later, on July 18, 1942, the Swords.

When the battles in Tunisia began, he became Commander-in-Chief of all Wehrmacht elements in the area of operations, which, in spite of their numerical inferiority, fought an exemplary defensive battle for some months.

The allied landings in Sicily were a prelude to a large-scale invasion of Italy. As Commander-in-Chief of Army Group C, Kesselring destroyed the enemy's optimistic view that they could sweep the Germans out of Italy in one go. He skillfully defended against an enemy far superior in numbers and materiel and conducted the German withdrawal with minimal losses in spite of the enemy's constant superiority in the air and on the sea.

In recognition of his extraordinary services to the Reich he was awarded the Diamonds on July 19, 1944 – one day before his fortieth service anniversary.

The high esteem in which Kesselring's accomplishments were held abroad is evident in a 1944 article from the Swedish newspaper *Dagens Nyheter*:

> "Churchill, as well as all the other allied experts, should concede that the German strategy and tactics in Italy are nothing short of brilliant. Generalfeldmarschall Kesselring has carried out his withdrawal movements to the Arno with unparalleled skill."

The British *Manchester Guardian* also attested to the field marshall's great military skill that same month:

> "The German defense in Italy will surely one day be written of with praise and recognition by war historians. In spite of all the traps which were laid south of Rome, in each case Field Marshall Kesselring has been able to withdraw his forces. He has done so repeatedly, cleverly exploiting every opportunity, never adopting a too-rigid defensive stance which might have catastrophic consequences, until finally his forces reach a new defensive line, which appears to be better than any other, in order to once again offer the most bitter resistance, so that new outflanking maneuvers through landings in the rear become necessary."

At the end of 1943 the growing seriousness of the situation made it appear advisable to Führer Headquarters to create a unified high command over forces and operations in the Mediterranean area. Hitler proposed to Mussolini that overall command – including over Italian forces – be handed to Kesselring, in order to eliminate the bifurcated nature of military command in the immediate area of operations.

Mussolini concurred with Hitler's assessment, but he feared that it might create discord in the Italian command. Wanting to prevent this he requested instead a carefully-coordinated joint command by the *"Comando Supremo"* and the Commander-in-Chief South. This arrangement was adopted and ensured smooth cooperation between the highest levels of command in the Italian Theater until Italy's cease-fire on September 8, 1943. The field marshall enjoyed a high standing with Germany's Italian allies; this allowed him to exert considerable influence on the Italian commanders. Mussolini supported him in every way possible. Italy's departure simplified Kesselring's command tasks. This was of great significance in the increasingly hard and heavy fighting. During the last two years of the war Germany's troops and commanders alike were taxed to the extreme limits of their ability to carry on and keep fighting.

In October 1944, toward the end of one of the heaviest defensive battles in Italy, on the north slope of the Apennines, Kesselring was seriously wounded in the course of one of his daily visits with the troops. A cranial injury kept the field marshall away from the front for almost three months. The accident occurred when Kesselring's car collided with a long-barrelled gun backing out of a side road.

At the beginning of 1945 Kesselring assumed supreme command in Italy, even though he had not yet completely recuperated from his injuries. On March 9, 1945, with the collapse imminent and Soviet troops deep in German territory, Kesselring was given overall command of the western theater. In April this was expanded to include the entire southern area. It was there that Kesselring experienced the end of the war.

Kesselring's association with the events in the Italian theater were best described in Mussolini's parting letter:

"Dear Marshall Kesselring. The news of your departure from Italy to take command of the Western Front is a painful surprise for me. However I think that in doing so the Führer has shown proof that he places the greatest trust in you, which you thoroughly deserve.

"Dear Field Marshall, we have worked together for almost three years, in Africa and on Italian soil, which you have defended step by step to the Apennines at the head of your wonderful soldiers. Your name will always be associated with this segment of Italy's history, and your achievements as army commander and field marshall will be acknowledged everywhere as an example of generalship.

"I thank you for everything that you have done in Italy, and I ask you to accept my most heartfelt wishes at your entrance into the highest field of duty, which has been entrusted to you.

Your Mussolini"

In fact, not only did Kesselring enjoy great popularity among his officers and men, but he was well thought of far beyond that. He especially demonstrated his vision in the final phase of the war, when the most difficult and responsible period of his life began. His objective was to hold up the allied advance through delaying actions, in order to enable the maximum possible number of troops who had fought against the Soviets to surrender to the western allies. Kesselring's efforts enabled hundreds of thousands of German soldiers to avoid the fate of Soviet captivity.

As his record would suggest, Kesselring was never bound to his desk. He flew over the front more than 200 times, especially in the Mediterranean area and in Africa, in order to be with his units. He received the Golden Operational Flying Clasp in 1942. Regard for his own life was something he did not know. For this reason the end struck him all the harder.

Kesselring's British interrogation officer indisputably made a significant contribution to his release in 1952, which followed several hospital visits and operations. The officer was Lieutenant Colonel Alexander Scotland, and he treated Kesselring in a very comradely fashion in London and Venedig. In his booklet on the "Kesselring Case" he criticized the British court in the following words:

"All right-thinking men in England and Germany should form their own opinion of the court, which one could characterize as probably the worst informed which ever convened on His Majesty's order."

The field marshall, who became active as a writer, lived another eight years in Bad Wiessee. He died on July 16, 1960 of heart failure. Thousands accompanied him on his final journey. *General* Kammhuber, Inspector General of the new Luftwaffe delivered the eulogy for this extraordinary soldier at the open grave: "In earlier times I often had occasion to work with the deceased. I gained a picture of his training, which went far beyond the military, as well as of the outstanding clarity and logic of his thinking. He exercised the functions of his position with tireless effort, energy and confidence, and took to heart the principle of the general staff: work hard – don't stand out too much, be more than you seem!"

As the title of his book declared, Albert Kesselring remained a soldier to the final day.

CHAPTER XV

OBERSTLEUTNANT HELMUT LENT

The summer night was clear and bright. The commander of *Nachtjagdgeschwader 3*, *Oberstleutnant* Helmut Lent, looked at the clock. "The tommies must come soon," he said to his adjutant.

Then the telephone rang, long and loud. The adjutant picked up the receiver. "What's that . . .? Toward Stuttgart . . .? 600 aircraft! That can't be. Why am I just learning of this now?" There was silence on the other end of the line. There was some brief whispering, then a voice said, "*Herr Oberleutnant*, we've just received this report, couldn't believe it and asked for confirmation. I don't know why it wasn't reported earlier."

Lent quickly grasped what had happened. He didn't wait for the adjutant to fill in the details. The *Oberstleutnant* quickly left the command post, sounded the alarm and gave orders for the 1st *Gruppe* to make for Stuttgart. Then he took off and set course for Stuttgart, far ahead of the rest of the *Gruppe*.

The *Kommodore* knew how weak the night defenses were in the southern part of Germany. Formerly the British had flown their attacks from bases in England. Now that they and the Americans had occupied half of Italy, it was no longer difficult for them to send their bomber fleets across the Alps to Germany. The units stationed in Italy were responsible for attacking cities in southern Germany, while those based in England struck targets in northern Germany and Berlin. This division of the target area spared the enemy bombers long flights from the north and the associated heavy losses.

Even in summer the British flew across the Alps every night. Far ahead of his 1st *Gruppe*, Lent raced toward the threatened city. How far were the British from Stuttgart? The *Kommodore* demanded the utmost of his aircraft; he had to arrive over the city before the enemy. He recalled the telephone conversation his adjutant had had. Why were they informed so late of the enemy penetration? Why? Why? He would have to be very lucky if he was to pull it off.

Stuttgart! The crew saw clearly the bombers' objective, already illuminated by parachute flares. The pilots of the pathfinder machines had already done their work. The main force would arrive at any time. And that meant: attack! The weak night fighter units wouldn't be able to prevent it. 600 machines were approaching the city. Six-hundred! As well fighter control reported that fifty British long-range night fighters were accompanying the bomber stream and had already shot down several German night fighters.

Lent and his crew stared into the night. Where was the bomber stream? By his own calculation it must be in the same quadrant. Then, ahead, a ghostly shadow. And another, and then another. It was the tip of the bomber armada.

"I'm attacking!" called Lent. In an instant he was clinging to the tail of a Halifax. He pressed the firing buttons and seconds later the four-engined machine plunged into the depths. The spectacle was repeated three more times: bombers exploded in mid-air, glowing fragments of aircraft fell to earth. When the *Kommodore* landed back at base he was able to report his 96th to 100th night victories. A few days later, on July 31, 1944, Helmut Lent, the Luftwaffe's premiere and highest-scoring night fighter pilot, was awarded the Diamonds.

Helmut Lent was the son of a minister from the Warthebruch area. He was born on June 13, 1918 in Neumark, attended secondary school, and in 1937, after graduation, joined the Luftwaffe as an active officer. Lent was an enthusiastic glider pilot, and he quickly mastered the faster powered aircraft. Shortly before the Polish Campaign he became a *Leutnant* and was assigned to a *Zerstörer*, or heavy fighter, *Geschwader*. He flew day fighter missions at the outset of the campaign and shot down his first enemy aircraft on September 2. Lent attracted the interest of his superiors in the air war against England by shooting down three enemy aircraft in December.

Lent was convinced that he couldn't exploit his flying talents to the full as a *Zerstörer* pilot. His request for a transfer to single-engined fighters was not accepted. This young daredevil, who by now had eight kills, wanted to stay on the good side of his commanding officer. Good pilots were being sought for the newly-formed night fighter *Geschwader*, pilots who not only were masters of their aircraft, but who would dare to tackle the enemy "heavies" as well. Helmut Lent volunteered, and this time his *Geschwaderkommodore* was forced to let him go.

Lent shot down two four-engined bombers on his very first night fighter sortie, in May 1944. "A deuce," he said after landing. This was the beginning of an unbroken series of successes. Victory followed victory. The British sent their bombers to destroy supply dumps in Norway; they were intercepted by German night fighters. In a series of bitter fights, in which the British suffered heavy losses, Lent distinguished himself by shooting down thirteen enemy aircraft, the most of any German night fighter pilot. On August 30, 1941, after his twentieth kill, he was awarded the Knight's Cross. On June 6, 1942 he received the Oak Leaves, at which time his total stood at 36.

Lent became familiar to the British listening service. In those years his growing victory total made him a feared enemy of the bomber fleets. The British operational staffs counted on Lent, who they knew would always accept combat, no matter what the odds. Lent and his night fighters spread fear and terror among the British bomber crews. For his part the German ace admired the courage of the British who, although they flew in heavily-armed bombers, faced two enemies: flak and night fighters.

On August 3, 1943, Helmut Lent, by now a *Major* and considered *the* night fighter authority, was awarded the Swords. Far to the forefront of all night fighter pilots, he shot down one enemy aircraft after another. Fearless missions against superior numbers were his trademark.

During an air battle over the Zuider Zee Lent shot down three Halifax bombers. Then he scanned the sky for further enemy aircraft but found none. Suddenly a swift shadow whooshed past him. He was about to set out in pursuit when there was a crash and his aircraft was filled with the smell of burnt rubber.

"We've been hit!" cried his crew. They prepared to bail out. Lent felt a heavy blow against his shoulder. For a few seconds he lost consciousness and control of the aircraft. But then he came to and managed to regain control and return the Bf 110 to base. What had happened? A British long-range night fighter had crept up on Lent's machine unnoticed, then flown past to attract his attention. A second British machine had moved into position behind Lent and tried to shoot down the German aircraft. But the plan failed. The slightly-wounded Lent was able to land the damaged fighter safely.

It was unavoidable that the highest levels of command watched Lent closely. His outstanding technical knowledge and tactical ability caused people to sit up and take notice. It was no secret among Hitler's entourage that Helmut Lent would be the coming Inspector of Night Fighters. Following a conversation with the modest young officer which lasted several hours, Hitler came away impressed by Lent's ability. In one of his memos Hitler referred to Lent as the possible head of the night fighter arm; he planned to entrust him with the reorganization of the night fighter units.

This was not Lent's only discussion. He turned energetically to his immediate superiors. He needed more aircraft, better radar equipment and pilots who were dedicated to night fighting. Lent described the night fighters as the "troop of the upright", which took on an overpowering enemy, apparently without hope, but which nevertheless was successful. Were there in fact tactical recipes for success against the bomber strategy of the Allies? Were there enough German night fighters to enable them to achieve a success against the thousands and thousands of heavy bombers and their escorts which might bring about a turn in the bomber war? Helmut Lent asked himself these questions, and they were put to him. He knew that technical and tactical means were limited. Successfully engaging the enemy was for the most part a personal matter.

As to the question of how he envisioned defeating the large enemy formations, he replied: "Through personal courage! If we have a phalanx of night fighters and harass every enemy attack without pause, if we stay on the enemy continuously, we will make him so uncertain that he will either attack only by day or not at all. However, in order to carry out this mammoth operation our existing tactics will have to be changed."

There it was, simple and unembellished. Helmut Lent wanted to give the enemy no rest and attack him without pause. But that meant still more *Geschwader*, more outstanding pilots. Heavy losses had to be expected. But what was that against the unspeakable sacrifices of the civilian population, which faced the bombing attacks almost naked? The attacks on cities, in which women and children were burned alive, enraged him. To his comrades he said, "I find the war dreadful. But if it must be, then it should be conducted with fairness. Attacks on women and children, aerial mines and phosphorous on the peaceful populations of our cities and towns – all that is atrocious."

Helmut Lent died in tragic fashion. On October 5, 1944 he took off to visit his old friend, Oak Leaves wearer Jabs, who was based near Paderborn. The flight was uneventful until, just before landing, an engine failed. The aircraft lost height, stalled and dropped like a stone. It fell 50 meters and crashed to the ground. Lent's crew were killed instantly. He survived and was taken to hospital where he fought for his life for four days. Then he died, the participant in hundreds of air battles and victor in 102 combats.

CHAPTER XVI

GENERALOBERST DER WAFFEN-SS SEPP DIETRICH

O n April 24, 1966 heavy rain clouds hung over Ludwigsburg. The city, situated in the area surrounding Baden-Württemberg's capital, Stuttgart, was gripped by an unusual nervousness which few had ever experienced. Never before had the people seen so many police on foot and in cars. Bus after bus rolled through the city. In them sat mostly men. When the passengers got out near the new cemetery they effortlessly formed into groups. Many hobbled on crutches, others who could not see were guided by comrades.

Above the open grave sat a coffin, covered in flowers. It was surrounded by several thousand men. Silently they stared at the casket in which lay the body of their former commanding officer. His name was Sepp Dietrich, a man they had honored like a father and one who had cared for them as a father.

More than 5,000 had arrived from all over Germany as well as many who lived abroad. They came to say farewell to the man who had been for them a shining example of courage, bravery and comradeship during the battles of the last war.

Speeches were made by friends and former superiors. Then, as the casket was lowered into the grave, and without having been ordered to do so, they broke into song: *"Ich hat einen Kameraden"* followed by Germany's national anthem. It was a moving experience. As they sang pictures of the inferno of battle passed before them, as well as the faces of comrades who had been killed, gone missing or been taken prisoner. Then they saw a man standing before them who had demanded everything of each of them: Sepp Dietrich.

The police, who had tried to infiltrate the crowd of mourners unnoticed, gave up. They had been placed on alert and had been reinforced by police units from all over Germany. Some feared that something like an "SS revolt" was about to take place.

The young officers were surprised by the discipline of the former Waffen-SS soldiers. Their curiosity piqued, they listened reflectively to the words spoken at the grave by the men who had served and fought under the deceased. They saw the amputees, confined to their wheelchairs, and the many others who had come, men who had done their duty as soldiers, no more or no less. And many of them asked themselves who this man could have been that these men were taking their leave of him out of respect, twenty-one years after the war, following the degradation and defamation they had been forced to endure as former members of the Waffen-SS.

Sepp Dietrich was a born soldier. He possessed a natural talent for soldiering, which was unselfishly attested to by senior army commanders during the Second World War. In 1911 he joined the 4th Field Artillery Regiment 1 as a nineteen-year-old volunteer. In 1915 he served with the 6th Reserve Field Artillery Regiment and the 7th Field Artillery Regiment. When the German Army received its first tanks he volunteered for this modern service. In 1917/1918 he participated in attacks against the British and French with the Bavarian 13th Tank Battalion. Afterward, until 1919, he belonged to the 7th Field Artillery Regiment 1. Josef Dietrich, born on May 28, 1892 in Hawangen, Bavaria, had already distinguished himself through outstanding bravery. He earned both Iron Crosses, the Tank Assault Badge, the Bavarian Service Cross and the Austrian Medal for Bravery.

After the end of the war he joined the 1st Defense Regiment, a volunteer unit in Munich, as a technical sergeant. His unit played a substantial role in the defeat of the revolution and the removal of the communist government.

The same year he joined the *Freikorps* and the Bund "Oberland". In May 1921 he fought against the Polish insur-

Safe and sound. Walter Nowotny back from a combat mission with minor wounds and a riddled machine.

Helmut Lent (left) and another officer on the canopy of a Ju 52.

At the time of his death on October 5, 1944, Helmut Lent was 26 years old and an Oberstleutnant. At that time he led the list of German night fighter pilots with 102 kills.

SS-Oberstgruppenführer and Generaloberst der Waffen-SS Sepp Dietrich decorates members of the SS-Leibstandarte Adolf Hitler.

Sepp Dietrich, commander of the Leibstandarte Adolf Hitler, during surrender negotiations with Greek officers in May 1941.

Sepp Dietrich during a situation briefing with the Ia of a panzer division during the Battle of Normandy.

At the scissors during the Orel battle, July 1943.

Army Group North, January 1944 (left SS-Hauptsturmführer Macker).
▼

In conversation with grenadiers at the front, autumn 1944.

Field Marshall Walter Model, Commander-in-Chief of Army Group B, in conversation with soldiers in the winter of 1944/45.

October 9, 1944. FM Model inspects the forward command post of the 246th Volksgrenadier Division near Aachen.

GenFM Walter Model in early summer 1944 as Commander-in-Chief of Army Group North Ukraine.

Commander-in-Chief of Army Group B, FM Model, briefs the newly-appointed Commander-in-Chief West, FM Kesselring, in March 1945.

Reichsmarschall Göring and General der Jagdflieger Adolf Galland visit Gruppenkommandeur Erich Hartmann (summer 1944).

Ground personnel greet Erich Hartmann with flowers following his 301st victory on August 25, 1944.

On August 25, 1944 Oblt Erich Hartmann received the Oak Leaves with Swords and Diamonds after his 301st victory.

GFM von Rundstedt at the headquarters of General Balck.

Generaloberst Guderian listens to a description of the situation in the headquarters of Army Group Balck outside Budapest in early 1945.

During the campaign in France in 1940 some of Oberstleutnant Balck's soldiers captured a French flag. Here Balck presents the flag to General der Panzertruppen Heinz Guderian.

General Ramcke distinguished himself as a paratrooper in Crete and in Africa.

In Africa Ramcke and his troops traversed 50 kilometers of enemy-held territory, successfully adapting to life in the desert.

General Ramcke on his way into captivity after the surrender of the fortress of Brest. Ramcke was awarded the Swords and the Diamonds on the same day.

Schnaufer exchanges experiences with members of a neighboring night fighter unit.

Wolfgang Schnaufer was 22 years old when he became a Major. The English called him the "night ghost." He was the most successful night fighter pilot in the world.

Every bar represented a bomber. Major Wolfgang Schnaufer was able to paint 126 such bars on the tail surfaces of his aircraft.

After a successful sortie – the beaming captain and his crew.

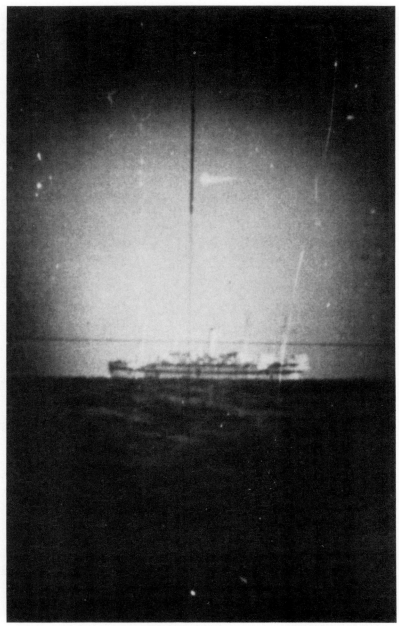

An enemy ship in the cross-hairs of a submarine's periscope. At the last second Brandi recognized this large vessel as a hospital ship.

„Albert Bergmann"

*Brandi travelled from internment in Spain to France and Germany under the name
Albert Bergmann.*

When the popular GenOb Dietl (right) was killed in an airplane crash, General Schörner assumed command of the troops on the polar sea front. Both men were members of the mountain infantry.

On February 28, 1945 the Soviet 3rd Guards Army captured the Silesian city of Lauban. On March 5 it was liberated by German troops. Third Reich propaganda trumpeted this as the longed-for turning of the tide. Reich Defense Commissar Goebbels congratulates the Commander-in-Chief of the successful army group, GenOb Schörner, in the city's marketplace.

Always in the front line: General von Manteuffel during the defensive battle at the Seret River in Rumania.

Von Manteuffel as guest of President Eisenhower, his former opponent in the war.

Situation briefing among officers of the Grossdeutschland Panzer-Grenadier Division. GenLt von Manteuffel (center) with regimental commanders Oberst Niemack (wearer of the Swords, left) and Oberst Langkeit (Oak Leaves, right).

After the war von Manteuffel was a deputy in the German Bundestag. Here he is congratulated by Bundeskanzler Adenauer in 1956.

Generalmajor Theodor Tolsdorff receives the Diamonds on March 18, 1945.

Tolsdorff observes an enemy attack from the roof of a house on the Jülich-Aachen road, just outside Jülich.

Theodor Tolsdorff lived as a pensioner at his home in Wuppertal with his wife Lore.

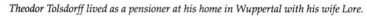

General Mauss distributes front packages to troops fighting on the Elbing (February 1945).

The last commander of the 7th Panzer Division, Dr. Karl Mauss was a dentist. At the end of 1944 his panzers covered the retreat of German soldiers and civilians north of Menzig (Menschikat).

In the front lines – General Mauss with an "Ofenrohr" anti-tank weapon and its users north of Könitz in February 1945.

After the war Dr. Mauss again opened a dentistry practice.

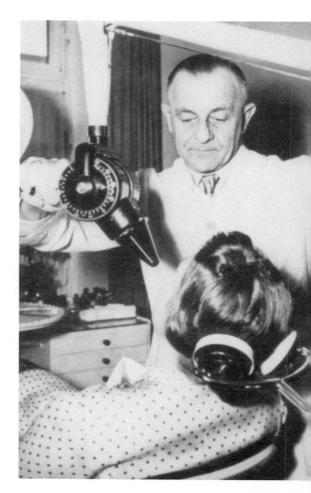

Situation briefing. Von Saucken (right) reports to the Commander-in-Chief of the army group, GenOb Reinhard (center), at the command post of GenLt Betzel (4th Panzer Division).

With Oberst von der Damerau near Teploye.

Final instructions before the attack. Von Saucken was one of those armor commanders who always accompanied an attack.

Von Saucken and the crew of his command vehicle.

gents in Upper Silesia and there received the Order of the Silesian Eagle, First and Second Class. As a member of one of the storm battalions formed by "*Oberland*", he participated in the putsch led by Adolf Hitler and *General* Ludendorff in Munich on November 9, 1923.

After leaving the Munich State Police, Dietrich accepted a position as a bonded warehouseman in a tobacco factory. Afterward he worked for two years as a forwarding clerk in the Nazi-owned Franz-Eher Publishing Company in Munich.

In May 1928 he joined the NSDAP and was accepted into the *Schutzstaffel* (SS), a defensive force which was just being formed, with the membership number 1177. Hitler recognized the soldierly qualities in Sepp Dietrich and on June 1 promoted him to *Sturmführer*. A *Sturmbannführer* by August 1, he was given the job of forming the 1st *SS-Standarte* in Munich and was promoted to *Standartenführer*. Dietrich's star was ascending rapidly. In 1930 Sepp Dietrich entered the Reichstag as a deputy of the National-Socialist German Workers Party (NSDAP). The same year he became an *SS-Oberführer*. On December 18, 1931 *Gruppenführer* Sepp Dietrich prevented blood from being spilled in the Stennes putsch through his calm behavior. From October 1933 to 1934 he commanded the *SS-Oberabschnitt Nord* of the *Allgemeine SS*. In the same year he became a member of the Prussian Privy Council, a city councillor of the Reich Capital Berlin and honorary judge on the Supreme Honor and Disciplinary Court of the German Labor Front. On July 1, 1934 Dietrich was promoted to *SS-Obergruppenführer*.

As early as the spring of 1933 Hitler and the former Minister of Defense von Blomberg had instructed him to form a guard unit for the Reich Chancellery made up of carefully selected men. From this guard unit later arose the *SS-Leibstandarte Adolf Hitler*, a reinforced infantry regiment. The *Leibstandarte* was under Hitler's direct command and was an elite formation. Its commander was *SS-Obergruppenführer* Sepp Dietrich. His task was to create a special sort of modern unit. With the help of his officers and NCOs Dietrich molded these men on the parade ground and in the field. He was the first to dive from the ten-meter tower and was also the best shot. He provided his men with an example of true soldierly behavior and good comradeship. He used the familiar "du" form of address with everyone, dropping the customary formalities. He was a father to his "tall fellows" and won their trust in a way few unit leaders have ever done.

On March 1, 1935, during the reincorporation of the Saar Region into the Reich, the *Leibstandarte* moved into Saarbrücken, and during the march into Austria on March 11, 1938 they were met with undisguised enthusiasm from the population during the drive from Linz to Vienna. On October 3, 1938 the SS unit marched through Eger and Karlsbad into the Sudetenland as part of *Generaloberst* Guderian's armored unit. On March 15, 1939, during the German occupation of Bohemia and Moravia, the unit marched into Mährisch-Ostrau.

In the Polish Campaign of 1939 the *Leibstandarte* was employed as a motorized infantry regiment. The average ages of the soldiers and NCOs were nineteen and twenty-five, respectively. This elite unit broke through the central Polish defensive position near Pabianiece and distinguished itself in the closing of the Kutno pocket.

Operating within the 4th Panzer Division, it prevented the desperate Polish attempt to break out of Warsaw and blocked the Fortress of Modlin on the south bank of the Vistula. For these actions Sepp Dietrich received the bar to both Iron Crosses.

At the beginning of the 1940 campaign the *Leibstandarte* fought in Holland, north of Rotterdam. Its armored units drove to the Aa Canal and established a bridgehead there. This was followed by the breakthrough to Dunkirk, where the British were surrounded. In the course of the fighting in this theater the unit took part in the pursuit of the enemy across the Marne. It then broke through the French lines and took Clermont-Ferrand and St. Etienne. Always at its head was the commanding officer, who received the Knight's Cross on July 4, 1940.

It was in France where the unit, which was marked by unequalled aggressiveness and recklessness, made a name for itself. Advancing irresistibly, scarcely noticing its own losses, driven only by the idea of being the first to strike the enemy, the *Leibstandarte* represented a completely new kind of German soldier. The sociologist Werner Picht characterized them not as a new form of fighting man, rather as a close-knit team, ready for any task their leader set for them. Heinz Höhne wrote in his outstanding work *Der Orden unter dem Totenkopf*: "The army officers were shocked that the commanders of the Waffen-SS had apparently never learned to employ the men entrusted to them with circumspection. Many, but by no means all, SS leaders practiced in the field what had been impressed upon them in the Junkerschulen: to give death and to accept death, accept it as the highest order of the unit. The SS units therefore sustained losses which were unknown in the army. Even during the fighting in the West the officer ranks of the SS divisions were so decimated that the units had to draw their new officers straight from the classrooms of the Junkerschulen."

"The SS units as the military elite of the nation? Hitler wanted it so. But even had this not been the case the *Leibstandarte* at least would have become it."

Heinz Höhne was not the only one to make a striking comparison when he said that they could be compared to the leathernecks of the US Army or the French paras. "They were all enshrouded by a myth of toughness and courage, they were all electrified by the consciousness of being members of an aristocratic minority, a special collective with its own laws and its own loyalties."

Almost a year later the *SS-Leibstandarte* smashed through British, Yugoslavian and Greek troops in daring attacks after they were called upon to help Germany's hard-pressed ally Italy in Greece. They stormed the Klidi Pass, considered impregnable, against hard-fighting Australian and New Zealand troops and stormed up to the Katava Pass, where the Greek Northern Army surrendered under pressure of the *Leibstandarte*'s rapid advance. The Gulf of Patras was crossed in fishing boats, Patras was seized and the Peleponnes occupied.

SS-Obergruppenführer Sepp Dietrich expressed to the Patriarch of Janina his admiration for the conduct of the Greek troops. A furious Dietrich rejected a request from the Italian High Command for him to "loan" them 50,000 Greek soldiers. "If you need 50,000 prisoners, why didn't you take them during the fighting?" This answer resulted in an energetic protest to Hitler against Dietrich. But the commander stuck to his decision and convinced those in headquarters. The Greeks weren't held as prisoners, instead were immediately released with their officers.

Following the Balkan Campaign began the great conflict with the Soviet Union. The soldiers of the *Leibstandarte* fought bravely wherever they were committed. The initial assault was a race against time. The Uman Pocket was closed, Novo-Danzig was reached, the city of Kherson was taken and the Dniepr crossed near Berislav. The next objective was Perekop.

Advancing far ahead of the main force the *Leibstandarte* drove into the enemy. The industrial city of Mariupol with the huge Azov steel works and shipyards fell undamaged into German hands. Taganrog was captured and Rostov occupied. During the battle on the Sea of Azov 100,000 prisoners were taken and 212 tanks and 672 guns captured. The Commander-in-Chief of the Soviet 18th Army was killed in the fighting. On December 31, 1941 Sepp Dietrich was awarded the Oak Leaves for the outstanding achievements of the unit and for personal bravery.

In June 1942 the remnants of the battered *Standarte* were pulled out of the front and transferred to France for rest and reorganization. The unit was to become a panzer-grenadier division. With 20,000 men – all volunteers – it fought between the Don and Donets with the same bravado as the soldiers of 1941-42 and took the city of Kharkov together with the *Das Reich* Division.

The officers made all the preparations for the attack in a small command post. By about two o'clock in the morning they were through. The preparations were carried out so quietly that the enemy took no notice. The *SS-Obergruppenführer* stepped out into the open. "Go," he said to his driver. "To the front."

A half-hour later the tanks of the *Leibstandarte* overran the Soviet positions, but soon were in danger of being cut off and encircled. However the commanding officer was up front with his men; he did not yield. There was no going back. Kharkov had to be taken! Skirting the city to the north, the Leibstandarte drove into the enemy, who defended grimly. The Soviet defenders were well aware of the value of this industrial city in the Donets region. The attack came to a halt for a moment, when enemy tanks emerged from the grey morning mist on the *Leibstandarte*'s left flank and launched a heavy attack. When the commanding officer received news of this he closed his eyes tight and thought. The flank was open. But must he not accept this risk if he was to break through? The Soviets had discovered the weak spot immediately. They tried to stop the attack, hoping at least to drive a wedge between the spearhead and the main body.

"Wait, I'm coming with you," said Dietrich to a dispatch rider. He jumped down from his command car, climbed into the motorcycle's side-car and sped off into the grey morning.

At the endangered point the grenadiers grappled with the Soviet forces which attacked relentlessly. The enemy had achieved a minor penetration which threatened the entire attack. The commanding officer grasped the situation immediately. He scraped together a panzer battalion and a battalion of grenadiers and attacked the Soviets, who had pulled back, in the flank.

When it became morning Dietrich was again at the head of his division and drove with it to the Red Square in the center of the city, meeting no serious opposition. The breakthrough surprised the Soviet command, which realized too late that this attack had sealed the fate of Kharkov. They threw all available forces into the attack area but the *Leibstandarte* held on, took the rail station and waited until the following army units entered the city. It was subsequently deployed to the north to take part in the capture of Belgorod. For this act of personal bravery, on March 16, 1943 Sepp Dietrich received the Oak Leaves with Swords.

The 1st SS-Panzer Division *Leibstandarte Adolf Hitler* was badly battered once more in the heavy fighting west of Belgorod ("Operation Citadel"). On July 12, 1943, after a massive artillery bombardment, 150 Soviet T 34s of General Rotmistrov's 5th Guards Tank Army overran a 500-meter-wide section of the division's front. The Soviets drove one kilometer into the German positions. But there they were engaged by the panzers of the SS. Ninety Soviet tanks were destroyed in a bitterly-fought engagement. A further 30 T 34s were destroyed by grenadiers from close range. Following these battles the division was pulled out of the front and transferred to northern Italy.

By this time the SS units, and not only the *Leibstandarte* Division, had become the core of the German Eastern Front. The American historian Stein credited them with having prevented another Stalingrad. "Wherever the SS units were deployed, they attacked. Sometimes they fought with great success, sometimes with limited or no success. But no matter how each individual action ended, the final result was the same: the enemy advance was stopped."

The losses of the Waffen-SS and the *Leibstandarte* were high. Nevertheless these units possessed an unbreakable offensive spirit and an unwavering ability to hold on in defense, which they did not lose until the day of Germany's surrender.

Sepp Dietrich, legendary figure and symbol of all the soldierly virtues of the Waffen-SS, was the outstanding personality of this "order." Alongside *SS-Oberstgruppenführer* Hausser and *SS-Obergruppenführer* Bittrich, Steiner and Gille, he was one of the very few who refused to allow themselves to be pressed in the ideological straightjacket of *Reichsführer-SS* Heinrich Himmler. Although one of the "old fighters" of the Nazi movement and a true paladin of Hitler, he had no time for the clique of Himmler, Kaltenbrunner and Heydrich. When he learned of the death of Heydrich, chief of the security service, he said, "Finally the swine is dead." Brutality was distasteful to him. When he heard of excesses against civilians or prisoners of war in his area of command he stepped in hard. His motto was: "We are soldiers and not marauders, we are German men and must conduct ourselves in a civilized manner wherever we are ordered."

His loyalty to the officers of the army brought him the nearly unlimited sympathy of the generals. In many cases where the party or security service threatened the life of another, officer comrades turned to Sepp Dietrich. He had no qualms about seeking out Hitler personally to "clear up the case." He forbade the operations of the "snooping agencies", referred to

Himmler quite openly as the *Reichsheini* and the "biggest zero to wear a uniform", and ignored his orders and decrees. Dietrich purposely kept his distance from the SS zealots, whom he considered soulless robots, war profiteers or "brutal swine", who had nothing at all to do with the soldierly Waffen-SS.

Twice Dietrich protested to Hitler against the shooting of Jews, of which he had heard on the Eastern Front. "You worry about your unit and keep out of it," answered his Commander-in-Chief. But Dietrich stood his ground. "You're making a great mistake, *mein Führer*," he answered. "Apart from the fact that shooting innocent people is a rotten thing to do and impossible to reconcile with the German soldier's concept of honor, these excesses damage the image of yourself and the Reich leadership. The German soldier and especially the soldiers of the Waffen-SS will have to pay bitterly for this some day."

Stunned, Hitler stared at him. "Have you become a defeatist?" he asked softly. "As I said, you concern yourself with your affairs and don't worry about the future." But Sepp Dietrich did worry. He made no secret of his opinion in conversations with generals and army commanders-in-chief. Dietrich could surely get away with more than any mortal. Such was his standing that no one would have dared lay a hand on him.

Generals and historians have tried to test, evaluate and analyze Sepp Dietrich's military ability. Their views differ. While one wouldn't have entrusted him with a regiment, others conceded a division, even a corps. *SS-Obergruppenführer* Bittrich, wearer of the Oak Leaves with Swords, declared that Dietrich had never been at all capable of following his situation briefings. In anecdotes Dietrich was compared to General Blücher, a soldier of old who supposedly couldn't read. ("We'll take the place I have my finger on.") In any case it is clear that Dietrich had outstanding and extremely capable general staff officers, who took care of the "tactical business" for him. One of these was the twenty-eight-year-old *Obersturmbannführer* Rudolf Lehmann, Ia of the *Leibstandarte*, later *Standartenführer* and finally division commander of the 2nd SS-Panzer Division *Das Reich*. Sepp Dietrich owed the greatest part of his success as a commander to this highly-qualified officer.

Sepp Dietrich led in the grand style, on a long leash so to speak. He lived with his soldiers – up front where the fighting was and where the situation was most serious. Possessing extraordinary personal bravery, he pulled engagements and battles out of the fire, an outstanding complement to his tactical staff officer Rudolf Lehmann.

Sepp Dietrich's reputation in the Waffen-SS can only be compared to the popularity of Field Marshall Rommel. Hitler knew how to best exploit the aura of the old fighter and ordered him to form the 1st SS-Panzer Corps. Dietrich was simultaneously promoted to the ranks of *Oberstgruppenführer* and *Generaloberst der Waffen-SS*. He was assigned General Staff *Oberst* Fritz Krämer to assist him.

Under the command of the 1st SS-Panzer Corps were the SS-Panzer Divisions *Leibstandarte* and *Hitlerjugend*. During the Allied invasion in 1944 the corps frustrated enemy attacks in the area north of Caen for two months, its troops countering the tremendous enemy assault through their self-sacrificial efforts. The corps held its positions in spite of furious fire from the Allied fleet and heavy bombing.

During the fighting on June 10, 1944 the headquarters of *Panzergruppe West*, under *General* Geyr von Schweppenburg, were destroyed. Two days later Sepp Dietrich assumed command of *Panzergruppe West*, which had been renamed the Fifth Panzer Army.

Sepp Dietrich proved himself once again in the battles in France. He repeatedly turned up where the fighting was heaviest, speaking to wounded, issuing orders and assembling reserves, which he committed at decisive points to prevent enemy breakthroughs. For these personal efforts and in recognition of the heroic efforts of his forces, on August 6, 1944 Dietrich was awarded the Diamonds.

During the bitterly-fought battles on the invasion front Dietrich recognized the senselessness of the fight against the western allies. The enemy's tremendous superiority on land, water and in the air paralyzed all movement. The heavy losses suffered by the German troops shocked the *Oberstgruppenführer*. At the outset of the invasion Dietrich spoke with *Feldmarschall* Rommel, Commander-in-Chief of the Atlantic Wall and an army group. The two had known each other for years and were on friendly terms. Rommel, who like Dietrich had viewed Hitler as the saviour of the nation, expressed doubts about the way the war was being conducted from Führer Headquarters. Dietrich revealed that he felt the same doubts. The two officers agreed that something had to be done to prevent Germany's soldiers from bleeding to death on the Western Front while the Soviets marched toward the German frontier.

In a subsequent conversation – the Allies had long since overrun the German positions – Dietrich and Rommel decided to compose a memorandum calling upon Hitler to conclude a cease-fire with the Americans and British. Once this had been done all German forces would be sent east. Sepp Dietrich declared himself ready to present the document to Hitler personally. Rommel wanted to accompany him to lend more weight to the entire affair. However the plan was overtaken by events and the two men did not see each other again until a few days before Rommel's accident. The field marshall visited Dietrich in his command post. He had news, he said, which made it appear inadvisable to go to Hitler with the memo: the latter would refuse to see them as he had decided to fight against the Anglo-Americans to the last man.

The field marshall remained silent when Dietrich asked him who had provided this information. Then, to Dietrich's surprise, he said: "Sepp Dietrich, we must act! We're both popular, we must make it clear to the Führer that he should end the war . . ." Dietrich nodded and asked Rommel what he understood "act" to mean. The field marshall: "If the Führer will not end it – and I can no longer take responsibility for allowing thousands of young men to bleed to death – then we must force him to step down." Dietrich stared at his opposite number. "And if the Führer has us shot . . .?" Rommel shook his head. "He wouldn't dare. That would unleash a mutiny."

Seconds later Sepp Dietrich had decided to go to Hitler with Rommel and confront him with the facts that the war in the west was lost and that he must request a cease-fire from General Eisenhower immediately. On July 16 Rommel called Dietrich once again. "Is it still on?" he asked. And Sepp Dietrich answered, "Yes, it's the best solution."

Rommel asked back what they should do if Hitler rejected their proposal. Then, before Dietrich could answer, he said, "Then we will just have to take over." Dietrich's reaction: "I'll only go along with it if no force is used." Rommel: "I agree. House arrest is sufficient . . ."

These were the last words exchanged by the two soldiers. A day later Rommel was injured when his car crashed after being attacked by fighter-bombers. Three days later Count Stauffenberg's bomb exploded in Hitler's *Wolfsschanze* headquarters in East Prussia. Much later Himmler branded the field marshall as a fellow-conspirator and imprisoned his Chief-of-Staff Speidel. Sepp Dietrich had him released immediately. And how did Sepp Dietrich behave in the time that followed? Was there not the possibility that his conspiracy with Rommel might be discovered if the field marshall unsuspectingly spoke of it from his sickbed?

"I wouldn't have changed my opinion one iota," Dietrich said later. "I had absolutely no idea what Rommel's condition was and what they planned to do with him. After I heard of the coercion with which Rommel was driven to commit suicide, I saw Hitler in a different light. This was no longer the man for whom I had once fought. That I held out and stayed was something I did only because of my soldiers. To undertake something against Hitler without Rommel would have been suicide. It wouldn't have benefited anyone."

Sepp Dietrich saw no other way out but to carry on. Everything he did, he believed he had to do in service to his fatherland. But the days when he would have allowed himself to be torn to pieces for his leader were over. The four war years were more than an interval to him. "I no longer saw any sense in the battle against the Allies and tried to obtain another command. Only the battle against the bolsheviks justified the continuation of the war to me," he said to the author. But he had to wait several more months.

On November 4 Sepp Dietrich handed the Fifth Panzer Army over to *General* von Manteuffel in order to assume command of the newly-formed Sixth SS-Panzer Army. On November 10 he and his new command were placed under the command of the Commander-in-Chief West. When the Ardennes offensive was ordered Dietrich spoke out against it and was supported by *Generalfeldmarschall* Model, Commander-in-Chief of Army Group B. But Dietrich's reservations were cast aside and the attack, code-named "Operation Watch on the Rhine", was ordered to go ahead.

The West-European volunteers serving with the Waffen-SS were immediately transferred, as they were obligated to participate only in the struggle against the Soviet Union and bolshevism.

The attacking spearheads of Dietrich's units drove ahead to north of la Roche and overran the US 1st Army. 20,000 prisoners were taken, 379 tanks destroyed and 124 enemy aircraft shot down. But supply difficulties, a turn in the weather and strong enemy attacks from the flank brought the advance to a standstill. An orderly retreat was made to the Westwall.

Then, finally, the OKW called Sepp Dietrich to the Eastern Front. The Soviets had launched a major offensive in Hungary. Dietrich was to transfer his Sixth SS-Panzer Army to this theater.

The Soviets achieved deep penetrations when several units of the Hungarian Fifth Army, which was on the left wing, went over to the enemy. The Soviets pushed into the resulting empty space and tried to encircle the SS army.

Dietrich was ordered to stand fast and allow himself to be encircled. His SS troops faced the threat of destruction. But the army's Commander-in-Chief was unwilling to carry out the order. He occupied a new position. In Führer Headquarters his independence was the subject of much adverse comment. Hitler ordered that the SS divisions should take off their cuff bands. Dietrich was taken by surprise by the order, which he received by radio at two in the morning on March 10. He called on his commanders and informed them of Hitler's order. Then he dispatched an SS officer to Führer Headquarters with a situation map and a hand-written note. Speaking on behalf of Dietrich the courier said:

"The soldiers of the Sixth SS-Panzer Army have fought bravely from the first day of the war, often to the end of their physical strength. They never deserved such an insult. *Oberstgruppenführer* Dietrich therefore requests that you rescind the order."

Hitler reluctantly withdrew his decree.

A new attack was ordered against the advancing Soviet tank armies, to be made toward the narrows of Lake Balaton. However on March 18 the Soviets broke through in the Vertes Mountains, raising the specter of a new Stalingrad. As a result the German attack had to be cancelled and a withdrawal begun to the edge of the Alps, in the Vienna area. The surrender, which followed on May 8, in the St. Pölten-Krems area, was taken by US General Patton. Sepp Dietrich and his soldiers became prisoners of war.

It casts a characteristic light on the soldier Dietrich that he was never required to sign a single death sentence in any of his commands. The following incident illustrates his understanding in dealing with problems and internal conflicts: an eighteen-year-old volunteer, from a well-to-do family and educated by a private tutor, was assigned to a tank crew, who had little regard for the young man and made his life miserable. The youth was unable to deal with the stress or the bullying and went home to his mother. On the way he was caught and brought before a military court. The sentence was death by firing squad.

Oberstgruppenführer Dietrich was supposed to confirm the death sentence with his signature. He read the document, saw the date of birth of the condemned man and summoned the youth, who described the case and his inner turmoil. Afterward Dietrich stood up, boxed the condemned man's ears and dressed him down: "So, that's enough! Now go, go where you want – to your mother. Stay there a week and come back and become a proper soldier!"

The young man went on leave, came back and in fact became an outstanding soldier. No one said anything more about the sentence, which Sepp Dietrich had lifted with a boxing of the young man's ears.

On July 16, 1946, Sepp Dietrich was sentenced to life imprisonment by an American court, the General Military Court, in the so-called Malmedy Trial. The sentence was reduced to

25 years on August 10, 1951. Finally, on October 22, 1955, Dietrich was released from Landsberg as part of the parole process. There was no justification of the verdict, only the supposition that he had broken the rules of war.

Barely two years later Sepp Dietrich was brought to trial once more. This time it was the German justice system which put him on the defendant's bench. On May 14, 1957, in the so-called Röhm Trial, he was sentenced by the 1st Munich Jury Court to eighteen months in prison for having participated in the murder.

What had happened? On June 30, 1934 a firing squad commanded by Sepp Dietrich had been ordered to execute six senior leaders of the SA on Hitler's order. The SA leaders had been accused of high and state treason by Hitler and were in Munich-Stadelheim prison.

Dietrich served part of his sentence in Landsberg prison, until he was released on February 2, 1959.

Although it was not easy, Sepp Dietrich mastered civilian life. At first he was active in the lumber trade, then he earned his living as an industrial mediator. His comrades had not forgotten him and often showered him with gifts. Until the day of his death, April 21, 1966, he remained the father of his "tall fellows."

CHAPTER XVII

GENERALFELDMARSCHALL WALTER MODEL

On April 21, 1945 a pistol shot ended the life of one of the best and most controversial soldiers of the German Wehrmacht. *Generalfeldmarschall* Walter Model shot himself in a clearing near Duisburg because he did not wish to see the end of his army group and because he believed in the maxim: "A field marshall is never taken prisoner."

Walter Model, one of the best-known field marshalls of World War II, remained true to himself to the final hour of his life. The pistol shot that ended his life was the marshall's response to a defeat for which he was not to blame, but whose consequences made it seem that life was not worth living.

As a young *Hauptmann* in the Grand General Staff in World War One, Model attracted the attention of *Generalfeldmarschall* von Hindenburg. After the war he remained in the 100,000-man army and in 1926, after holding several posts with the general staff, he took command of a rifle company in the 8th Infantry Regiment in Görlitz. In 1928 he transferred to the Ministry of Defense, where he was active in the training department as a lecturer on military history and later as a member of the "Reich Board of Trustees for Youth Fitness."

However Model's heart belonged with the field units. He took command of the 2nd Infantry Regiment's II Battalion in Allenstein and then the regiment itself, and later, as a *Generalmajor*, became head of 8 (Technical) Department in the Army General Staff. Model participated in the war against

Poland as Chief-of-Staff of IV Army Corps Dresden. During the French Campaign he was Chief-of-Staff of the Sixteenth Army.

During the German advance into Russia Model became known for his dynamic leadership in the most difficult situations. On July 9, 1941 he received the Knight's Cross while commanding the 3rd Panzer Division.

Fearless in his military decisions, Model was also forthright with his superiors. He was in no way a man who followed orders without question, contradicting them when he was convinced that his superiors had wrongly assessed the situation.

On February 20, 1942 there was a serious disagreement between Hitler and Model at Führer Headquarters over the question of adding a panzer corps to the defensive forces fighting at Rzhev. Both men expressed their views spiritedly. Model saw the situation from the perspective of a front-line officer, while Hitler viewed it from the map table perspective. The officers present couldn't believe what they were hearing when Model suddenly interrupted his presentation, turned to Hitler and said, "*Mein Führer*, are you commanding the Ninth Army or I?"

Hitler was surprised by Model's self-assurance. "You are to move the panzer corps into Gzhask! I can assess the situation better than you!" he answered.

Model stepped back from the map and moved close to Hitler. "I must refuse," he said gruffly. "You sit here far from the shooting. But I know what's going on up front!"

Hitler stopped short for a moment, then looked at Model and nodded. "Very well, Model. Do as you wish. But you'll owe me your head if things go wrong!"

Things did not go wrong. Model's assessment of the situation was proved correct. The Soviets attempted to break through where he had predicted. Now he had a reserve corps on hand and with it was able to head off the enemy thrust.

Immediately following this battle Model was wounded when his Fieseler *Storch* was shot down by partisans. It was the fifth time he had been wounded and the injuries were life-threatening.

The awarding of the Oak Leaves on February 13, 1942 and the Swords on April 3, 1943 were well-deserved rewards for a brave officer and outstanding leader.

Model was promoted to *Generalfeldmarschall* on March 31, 1944. While commanding Army Group North and then Army Group North Ukraine, he repeatedly frustrated the intentions of the Soviets.

Then, in June 1944, Army Group Center collapsed under hammer blows delivered by Soviet artillery, close-support aircraft, tanks and motorized infantry divisions. Totally unexpectedly and quite inexplicably, the pillars of the carefully-assembled defensive position crumbled. Even though the date of the attack was known and the Soviets stuck to their schedule, and aerial reconnaissance had revealed tremendous masses of tanks and infantry, the army group command failed to react. On the contrary: *Generalfeldmarschall* Busch ignored the reports and acted unconcerned. When informed forcefully of the danger facing him, he informed Führer Headquarters. Hitler thought it was a Soviet deception and Busch adopted this view.

For their part the Soviets did in fact carry out a deception on a grand scale. Although they could not totally conceal their buildup, they did succeed in shifting strong artillery forces by night, positioning them in very well camouflaged positions in the selected points of main effort. They also moved forces freed up from the Caucasus Front into the attack area, unbeknownst to the Germans. Some of these troops wore khaki-colored uniforms, while prisoners stated that their base was in the Caucasus and that they were members of a camel-equipped unit. These rested, well-trained and very well-equipped soldiers – a total of 146 rifle divisions and 43 tank units took part – subsequently overran the German positions on June 22, 1944.

The question as to why the German command resigned itself to the attack and waited, instead of abandoning the forward trenches and positions and evacuating men and materiel, allowing the enemy to drive into open space and then destroying him with well-prepared counterattacks, was never answered. Army Group Center was almost totally destroyed as a result, 25 divisions were lost. Afterward Hitler sacked

Generalfeldmarschall Busch – small consolation for such catastrophic losses. The way to East Prussia was open to the Red
Army.

It was at this time that *Oberst* Graf Stauffenberg's bomb
exploded beneath Hitler's map table in Führer Headquarters.
In the situation that followed, Field Marshall Model was tasked
with leading the shattered Army Group Center as well as Army
Group North Ukraine.

It was no simple matter for the field marshall to halt the
retreat of the harried and pursued troops. Unfavorable conditions and the enemy's materiel superiority created desperate
situations. Sealing off the Soviet breakthrough was a tough
assignment, and establishing a barrier and halting the superior enemy with a wiped-out army group seemed impossible
even to the greatest optimist. But Model did it. With no reserves to speak of he halted the Soviet steamroller before East
Prussia's borders. He organized and committed battle groups,
inspired his officers and men and always seemed to turn up
wherever the situation was most dangerous. For these acts
Walter Model was awarded the Diamonds on August 17, 1944.

This small, almost delicate man with a full head of black
hair and large, lively eyes, which viewed things skeptical and
appraising manner, was like a steel spring: always tense and
full of energy, sharp-witted, gifted with outstanding intelligence and an unsurpassed steadfastness.

Born in 1891 in Genthin in the Mark Brandenburg, Model
was a perfect example of the Prussian concept of a soldier. He
was a man who stood by his word, who scrutinized orders
and opinions ruthlessly, but who was equally ruthless toward
himself. This officer's rapid rise drew attention. Many of his
comrades envied his climb, others accused him – not until after the war of course – of a certain servility to Hitler.

The notion that Model saw in Hitler the supreme commander and accepted him as such cannot be ruled out. He made
no secret of his enthusiasm for the building up of the armed
forces and for Hitler's elimination of the unemployment problem. And in war he obeyed, was true to his oath to the flag, for
he didn't want to and in any case couldn't have done anything

else. However, all of this prevented him from speaking his mind openly to Hitler.

He reacted with outrage to the attempt on Hitler's life on July 20, 1944. "The forces fight, bleed and do the seemingly impossible, while in the rear an officer attacks his supreme commander with a bomb. That has never happened before in German history."

In January 1944 Model created something of a sensation, which went down as a novelty in the history of the German officer corps. Model wanted to "procure" a personal adjutant. He asked *General* Schmundt, Chief of the Army Personnel Office to make available a young officer from the officer reserve. Schmundt refused. Commanders of army groups were not entitled to "personal" staff.

Furious, while at Führer Headquarters Model told Himmler and *SS-Gruppenführer* Fegelein, Hitler's Waffen-SS liaison officer and later his brother-in-law, of the affair. "Then take one of my men," said Himmler.

Model accepted the offer. *Hauptsturmführer* Rudolf Maeker, a former tournament rider, became Model's personal adjutant.

The atmosphere in the German command structure was increasingly poisoned by Hitler's laudatory addresses to the Waffen-SS and his statements to the effect that these were the only soldiers he could depend on, as well as by his now barely suppressed mistrust of the army general staff, indeed of all the army's generals. The attempt on his life on July 20 and the fact that it had been planned and carried out by army officers, as well as the results of the initial investigation and subsequent inquiry, must have had a crushing effect on Hitler. Now he mistrusted almost every army general and felt lied to and double-crossed.

However one might assess Model's loyalty toward his Commander-in-Chief, it is clear that his accomplishments as an officer and army commander are undisputed and were acknowledged even by the enemy.

Generalfeldmarschall von Manstein, who knew Model well, wrote in his book *Verlorene Siege*: "Model's outstanding quality was an extraordinary energy, which did not dispense with ruthlessness. With it he combined great aplomb and precision in expressing his opinion. Temperamentally he was an optimist, who refused to acknowledge difficulties. He expressed his views openly, even to Hitler. In any case Model was a brave soldier who acted without regard to his own person and who demanded the same of his subordinates, often in brusque fashion. He was always to be found at the critical points of the front under his command."

Wherever Model was, the front held. And because the field marshall elevated perseverance and holding out to a maxim, he had to achieve success. A man who dealt with himself so energetically and unsparingly had to win the hearts of his soldiers and convince them that they were capable of doing more.

Never had he made it easy on himself. It's true that Model lived his life alone and that no one in his personal circle succeeded in getting close to him. It's also true that he surrounded himself with an armor of reserve, not because he wished it so, but because he knew no other way. It was part of his personality and belonged to his character that he tried to fight his way through everything alone. Before his soldiers, before his conscience and before God he wished to alone bear the responsibility for his actions and his conduct.

The field marshall with the nonchalant-ironical tone, who terrified staff officers and tore through the rear echelons like a whirlwind, was a father to his soldiers, who idolized him. He was happiest when he was among them. Those who had the opportunity to observe him and see how he treated and spoke of the men entrusted to him, were suddenly capable of seeing sympathy and emotion in the icy and seemingly unapproachable Model. His men became extremely attached to him.

Hitler once tried warily to speak to Model about the morale and apparent decrease in fighting ability of the troops. Model snapped his head around and said sharply, "You are mistaken, *mein Führer*! Whoever told you such rubbish doesn't know what it means to be on intimate terms with death for four years. By the way I would be happy to have you come and see for yourself sometime."

Hitler immediately changed his tone. "I don't wish to make any judgements as to their value, but I don't think that the German soldier is as good as that of 1941."

Model looked at Hitler with surprise. "The German soldier of 1941 is dead. Yes he is dead, fallen somewhere in Russia. But the soldiers we have now are not one bit worse. It's just that they are facing an enemy who is on the advance."

When a staff officer endorsed Hitler's views, Model lost all patience. "What do you know of filth, mud, icy cold and barrage fire? And tanks, tanks! You have absolutely no right to criticize my soldiers. I forbid you to do that! Only one who has fought and suffered with those brave men can talk about the soldiers. But not a man like you, who can sleep every night in a soft bed!" Then he turned to Hitler. "I would like to ask you emphatically, *mein Führer*, to see to it that neither the honor nor the bravery of the soldiers is questioned. Men who are ready to die for the Fatherland also have the right to be protected against stupid twaddle and vile gossip!"

The rear echelon called the field marshall *"Terrorflieger."* For Model enjoyed taking to the air in his Fieseler *Storch* and dropping in unexpectedly on rear area services. He combed headquarters for shirkers and excess personnel, sending any he found to the front where they were forced to endure the dangers and deprivations of the desperate struggle. He looked after foodstuffs and munitions and kept an especially sharp eye on the officers. Woe to any of them he found occupying a "cushy job."

Model built a lovely, large rest home for his army, where the exhausted soldiers could go to rest and regain their strength.

It was June 1943, before the Kursk offensive. Model informed the then Army Chief-of-Staff, *Generaloberst* Zeitzler, that he was refusing to carry out an attack which had been ordered, because he could not accept responsibility for conducting warfare with "a few boys." Afterward the head of the OKW referred to Hitler's express order to carry out the offensive. "I have no intention of doing it! Tell the Führer that. I know better than to carry out offensives which are senseless from the outset and which only cost valuable human lives," he observed. In fact the offensive was postponed until Model was sent sufficient reserves.

Soon afterward, when the attack bogged down, *Generaloberst* Jodl called and demanded that he attack again immediately on Hitler's order. Incensed, Model shouted into the telephone: "You can tell your Führer that Model will not carry out such an order!"

Later he said exactly the same thing in the presence of *General der Panzertruppe* Hasso von Manteuffel, when both were invited to speak in the Reich Chancellery.

Sometimes the flood of orders from Führer Headquarters was unending. Contradictory opinions, colorless information and fearful evasiveness during the answering of questions which were connected with the withdrawal of the front, led the *Generalfeldmarschall* to send Hitler a memorandum and several energetic protests. The memos passed through *Generaloberst* Jodl's hands, who immediately phoned Model to ask if he was serious about bringing Hitler's attention to mistakes in such blunt language. He dared not present the documents to Hitler. Model thought for a moment and said, "Tell the Führer that I'll come."

There was a mood of alarm in Führer Headquarters during Model's visit. He straightforwardly told Hitler and his advisors everything he had put in writing. Undeterred by the presence of the supreme commander, he pointed out Hitler's errors and in conclusion said, "How can you demand of the exhausted men at the front that they allow themselves to be smashed by the masses of materiel of the Americans and Russians, when you, *mein Führer*, refuse to understand that my orders and operations serve only the well-being of these troops and the general situation?"

Impressed by the field marshall's words, Hitler gave him sweeping authority to act as he saw fit. He valued Model's straightforwardness and respect for the truth. Because of Model's success and personal courage he was allowed to speak bluntly to Hitler and withdraw the front. To Hitler Model was "the saviour of the Eastern Front."

When Model received the Diamonds on August 17, 1944, Hitler said to him, "Without you, your heroic actions and the skillful leadership of your brave soldiers, the Soviets would be in East Prussia today and even standing at the gates of Berlin. The German people have you to thank."

The same day Model was ordered to the Western Front to take over the army group formerly commanded by *Generalfeldmarschall* Günter von Kluge, who had taken his own life with poison.

Model was never happy with the command of Army Group B, for he was an eastern specialist. Nevertheless he did his best. In Belgium, in Holland (Arnheim), in Germany (Aachen) and in the Ardennes offensive he called upon all his skill, but achieved only partial success.

Generalfeldmarschall von Manstein wrote: "Model failed to succeed in plucking the laurels of victory as the leader of a daring operation. More and more he became the man whom Hitler used to restore the situation in a front which was threatened or shaken and in these situations he did an extraordinary job." Model was the great "defensive lion" on all fronts.

In the Ruhr pocket, with the *Generalfeldmarschall* and his army group surrounded and facing a hopeless situation, Model lost hope for the first time. He saw that the end was near and ordered all the units under his command to issue release papers to their soldiers in order to prevent them from being taken prisoner.

Just as he had made his decisions on all fronts alone, he now remained alone as he watched the end approach. There was nowhere left to go. For Model, therefore, there was only one option: he must die on the battlefield.

He calmly wrote a last letter to his wife and children. Then he informed his closest associates that he had decided to seek death. Model appeared wherever there was fighting, but death refused to take him.

His opponent on this front was the American General Matthew Ridgeway. This commander of the 17th Airborne Corps was later to play a role in postwar West Germany and Europe. Ridgeway dispatched Captain Brandstetter, a member of his staff, as an emissary to Model in hope of convincing him to surrender. Model refused. A little later Ridgeway again sent Brandstetter to Model, this time with a personal letter. He asked Model to see that the German defeat was total and that there was nothing dishonorable in surrender in a situation such as existed then. As well there was the matter of saving the lives of German and American soldiers and preventing further destruction of towns and villages. But Model once again refused. He did not know the word surrender. His oath to the flag was the supreme law. His soldiers were to go home and not into POW camps.

It was the night of April 17/18. With Model were the IIa, *Oberst* Pilling, the Ic, General Staff *Oberstleutnant* Michael, and the Id, General Staff *Major* Behr. They drove in an armored car. Near Ratingen they broke through the steadily advancing columns of the Americans and disappeared into a wood which seemed untouched by the pitilessness of the war.

On April 20, 1945, Hitler's 56th birthday, Model had the radio set switched on. Reich Minister Goebbels was speaking. As the Soviet artillery pounded the capital, Goebbels criticized the Ruhr Army, accusing it of cowardice. Model shook his head. Bitterly, he said, "I could never have believed that I would be so disappointed, for I served only Germany." Then he stood up, determined to end his life there and then.

Once again the officers tried to talk the field marshall into another course of action. But Model remained determined. He refused when the others suggested they break through the enemy lines to central Germany.

The next day he went into the wood with *Oberst* Pilling. Model selected his burial site; it was beneath a group of mighty oaks. Then the field marshall drew his pistol and shot himself. *Oberst* Pilling and *Oberstleutnant* Michael buried him there. Among his personal possessions they found a card with the first line of a poem:

"I will come as victor, or not at all . . ."

In 1955 Model was reinterred in Vossenack.

CHAPTER XVIII

MAJOR ERICH HARTMANN

They called him *"Bubi."* He was young, twenty-two years old, slim, with a fresh face beneath light blonde hair, an *Oberleutnant* when he received the Knight's Cross with Oak Leaves, Swords and Diamonds. He was the most successful fighter pilot in the world. Experts called him a phenomenon and he went into military history as such. The Soviets had placed a bounty of 10,000 Rubles on the head of this "boy." The reason: within 30 months Erich Hartmann shot down 352 aircraft! Flying with *Jagdgeschwader* 52 – the most successful fighter unit of the war with nearly 11,000 aerial victories – he completed 1,428 combat missions and participated in more than 800 aerial combats.

Following the German surrender on May 8, 1945, the Americans handed the entire *Geschwader* over to the Soviets. They were astonished when they saw the "Black Devil", as they called Hartmann (his aircraft had a black nose), alive before them. This youngster was supposed to have shot 352 "red falcons" out of the sky? At first they didn't want to believe it. They thought it impossible that this young officer with the child's face had destroyed the equivalent of five Soviet wings. Then, when they were convinced that they had the right one, they put him on trial and on December 27, 1949 sentenced him to twenty-five years forced labor. Several months later followed a second conviction: ". . . is sentenced to a further twenty-five years forced labor."

October 1955

The bells rang in the Friedland reception camp located at the border between the occupation zones. Trains were arriving with prisoners of war from the Soviet Union. People cried, celebrated and hugged one another, choked with emotion at the joy of being reunited with a son, a husband or a father.

Things were more businesslike in the administration buildings. Registration cards sat in piles. Numbers were called out, money issued, food and cigarettes distributed. Somewhere else suits were tried on and then names were called out. Once again the former soldiers formed up into ranks.

"Your name?"

"Hartmann . . . Erich Hartmann."

The old woman, a brooch with the red-cross pinned to her collar, looked up from the registration form for a moment. Her dark eyes looked into a face wrinkled and furrowed by ten years of captivity and confinement.

"Hartmann?" she asked.

The young returnee from Russia in the tattered flying jacket nodded. "Erich Hartmann, Major, retired . . ." He smiled and added casually: "That was then . . . what's past is past."

"I . . . I . . . that is my son, always spoke of a flying officer named Hartmann. One with many victories."

She stroked the paper softly. "It just occurred to me as I read your name."

The returnee looked at the old woman with interest. "I was a flying officer," he said after a brief pause.

The woman raised her head. She sized up the young man with the serious face and the pale eyes.

"So, you were a pilot? Perhaps you're the Hartmann of whom my son always spoke? He wanted to be able to fly like you."

"Well, perhaps we'll be able to fly again – I mean perhaps I can speak with your son some day, we can talk."

He didn't see how the woman pressed her lips together, and then how, as if a thought had just come to her, a smile flitted across her lips. "My . . . boy was killed . . . just before the end of the war."

The returnee drew on his cigarette. What could he say to her? The woman felt his embarrassment, sensed what he was thinking. She didn't want to keep the young man any longer.

"But I'm happy that I had the chance to talk with you. If only my boy could have experienced that," she said. "He told us that you were the most successful flier of all. You were a fighter pilot, were you not? So was my boy."

The returnee nodded. Suddenly the woman asked: "You were highly decorated? I remember . . ."

She looked at the place where once the Knight's Cross with the Oak Leaves, Swords and Diamonds had hung.

"Yes, I guess you could say so," he said.

As returnee Erich Hartmann left she called after him: "Good luck and all the best for the future."

A single man shot 352 enemy aircraft out of the sky. One man! And this in an incredibly short space of time. Erich Hartmann took little more than two years to do it. His career as a fighter pilot began just as the end at Stalingrad was announced. The Soviet pilots had closed the gap as far as flying ability was concerned and now took to the air in machines which were almost the equal of those flown by the Luftwaffe. The days when the "Ratas" fell from the sky were gone. For the German units were weaker, losses climbed and the vast front consumed men and materiel.

Erich Hartmann preferred combat at an altitude of 8,000 meters. It was there that he felt most comfortable. There were fighter pilots who did not fly above 3,000 meters. Others were outstanding pilots, but less successful in combat. They lacked the nerve to press the triggers at the right moment.

Hartmann was no aerobatic flier, nor a technical expert like Mölders, Gollob or Galland. In 1943, when Hartmann opened his score, one couldn't do either exclusively. Time was of the essence and the watchword was: destroy the enemy!

352 times Erich Hartmann returned to base victorious. 352 times a blazing torch lit up the Russian sky. 352 times an enemy fell before his guns.

Hartmann's victims included 261 fighters and 91 twin-engined bombers. Almost every type in the Soviet inventory was included in his victory list: the dangerous Il-2 "Stormavik" close-support aircraft, the MiG-1, the U-2, the I-16 "Rata", the Airacobra, the Boston (lend-lease from the USA), the LaGG-3 and 5, the Yak-7, the Pe-2.

Those in the *Geschwader* knew that Hartmann had had difficulties with the Bf 109 at the beginning of his career. But that didn't last long. Born in Weissach, Württemberg on April 19, 1922, Erich Hartmann was an outstanding glider pilot. The doctor's son was "tainted with an inherited disease" where flying was concerned. For his mother was an outstanding aviatrix, who had earned her pilot's license and flew a Klemm 27. Every Sunday one could see the pretty young woman at Böblingen airfield – the family had since moved to Weil in Schönbuch – flying with her two sons. It's no wonder then that Hartmann, who became well-acquainted with aircraft as a child, later slipped easily into the seat of a fighter aircraft?

When, in 1940, Hartmann entered the Luftwaffe as an officer candidate after leaving school, he had no way of knowing that he would one day exceed the victory total of the beloved Mölders. Not even in his wildest dreams did he have such thoughts. On October 8, 1942, at the age of twenty, Hartmann, who had become a *Leutnant* on March 31, was transferred to Jagdgeschwader 52, commanded by *Major* Hrabak, which was operating in the Caucasus. Two days later he was sent to *Major* von Bonin's III Gruppe and from there to 7 *Staffel* in Soldatska, which was led by the later *Oberleutnant* Krupinski.

Hartmann had bad luck right at the outset: he crash-landed on his very first combat sortie on October 14. He realized he was being pursued and thought that his hour had come – then he put his aircraft down in a forced landing. On his return to the *Gruppe* he was balled out by *Major* von Bonin. In the heat of battle he had taken his own element leader Rossmann for a "red falcon."

Hartmann never forgot this false start. Nothing like it ever happened to him again. He wanted to learn, learn, learn, and he had plenty of opportunity to do that.

Hartmann's unit included a number of well-known aces. There was *Oberleutnant* Krupinski with 70 kills (eventual total 197), Knight's Cross wearers *Feldwebel* "Paule" Rossmann and

Feldwebel Dammers, *Major* von Bonin, *Leutnant* Grislawski and *Oberleutnant* Rall (total of 275 kills). All were thoroughly experienced fighter pilots, outstanding fliers, daring men with iron nerves. Hartmann wanted to and was able to learn from them. It was *Leutnant* Grislawski who taught him how to successfully engage the heavily-armored Il-2, which seemed almost impossible to shoot down. Grislawski was something of an Il-2 specialist. "You must hit the oil cooler," he said. "And you can only do that when you fly under the Il-2."

On November 5, 1942 there was a scramble. Eighteen Il-2s were attacking the advancing German infantry without pause. Ten LaGGs provided fighter cover. The Soviets were numerically superior, as always, but the men of JG 52 attacked.

That afternoon Hartmann was flying with *Oberleutnant* Trepte, the *Gruppenkommandeur*'s adjutant. They intercepted the enemy over Digora. Hartmann selected an Il-2 and attacked, but his bullets bounced off the aircraft's armor. Then he remembered Grislawski's instructions. He dropped beneath the Russian machine, and when he was sixty meters away opened fire. Hit! A black cloud of smoke exploded from the Il-2 which immediately turned and headed east. Hartmann followed and fired again. The Il-2 exploded. It was his first confirmed kill.

It was a long time before Hartmann was able to score victory number two. On February 27, 1943 he shot down a MiG-1 over Armavir. Small, blinking stars appeared from out of the sun. They dove at increasing speed toward the German aircraft, which were searching the sky for the enemy.

"*Achtung*, Indians from out of the sun!" Hartmann flew on calmly. He wanted to wait until the Soviets flew in front of him. Then he spotted a lone enemy aircraft. The Messerschmitt accelerated. Hartmann heard in his headset: "Watch out, that's dangerous." But Hartmann saw only the lone enemy aircraft, which by now had spotted him as well. Hartmann positioned himself behind the MiG. But the Soviet pilot was an old fox who could fly; he wasn't about to be fooled so easily. Hartmann climbed higher and higher. The needle on the altimeter showed 6,500 meters. The two aircraft twisted and turned, painting wild condensation trail patterns against the sky.

The altimeter showed 8,000 meters. Hartmann had to stay alert if this wasn't to be his last mission, for the enemy knew something about flying.

Then he saw the enemy aircraft above him again. Why didn't he fire? When he instinctively jerked his head around he saw the MiG coming toward him in a dive. He must be crazy, thought Hartmann. He saw the enemy aircraft grow larger as it raced toward him. He had at most three seconds before . . .

Hartmann was so fascinated by the enemy's maneuvers that he stared at the MiG as if paralyzed. Suddenly there was a crackling in his headset. The sudden noise woke him from his nearly fatal dream.

Now he did something the enemy hadn't counted on. He pulled up and raced toward the enemy. The two aircraft nearly brushed wings as Hartmann zoomed over the MiG. Hartmann made a wide turn, got on the MiG's tail and opened fire as soon as the enemy aircraft was in his sight.

The shock of such coolness, the astonishment at such calm and cheek on the part of his opponent, must have shaken the Russian pilot. He had no more time for defense, for his aircraft was now hurtling toward the earth in flames.

After this duel at 8,000 meters the young *Leutnant* knew what he had to do to be successful. Hartmann accumulated victories like pearls on a string. Four or five kills in one day in the course of five missions was not unusual. In a single week he shot down 17, in the month of August 45. On August 20 Hartmann was looking for his 89th and 90th kills.

Scramble! Forty Il-2s were circling over the front lines, making life hell for the infantry. The fighters were supposed to clear the air.

It was about six o'clock in the morning when the *Staffel* of Bf 109s sighted the enemy. Hartmann positioned himself behind an Il-2, shot it down, and attacked a second. The Il-2 burst into flames – his 90th kill. But suddenly his motor quit. Smoke filled the cockpit. Hartmann hadn't felt his aircraft being hit. There was only one hope of escaping – he had to make a forced landing.

The Messerschmitt touched down in a field of sunflowers and slid to a halt. Hartmann thought he was safe. A truck of German make approached the aircraft. Two men jumped down and came toward him. Russians!

His first thought was: captivity. Hartmann placed everything on one card. He feigned being wounded. The Soviets carefully lifted him from the Messerschmitt and laid him on the bed of the truck. Then something happened that might have come from a Karl May novel. Hartmann struck one of the Soviet soldiers, jumped from the truck and ran into the field of sunflowers. Flabbergasted, the Soviets chased him, shooting and yelling. But for Hartmann it was a matter of life or death.

The artillery fire was Hartmann's compass. He slipped through the Soviet lines. Thirty-six hours after his forced landing, long after the missing-in-action report had been filed, he reported to his commanding officer: "*Leutnant* Hartmann reporting back from combat mission."

In September Hartmann assumed command of a *Staffel*. On October 29, 1943, after shooting down a LaGG-7 and an Airacobra over Kirovograd for his 147th and 148th victories, he was awarded the Knight's Cross. By March 2, 1944 he had shot down 202 Soviet aircraft, for which he received the Oak Leaves, along with *Oberleutnant* Krupinski. Promotion to *Oberleutnant* followed on March 18, 1944. On July 1 he shot down his 250th enemy aircraft. Hartmann was awarded the Oak Leaves with Swords.

On August 25 his comrades painted the number 300 in icing on a huge butter-cream cake. That afternoon Hartmann had waggled his wings five times as he flew over the airfield. The command post, which monitored the fighters' radio transmissions, had heard that *Oberleutnant* Hartmann had shot down his 300th enemy aircraft. Hartmann was awarded the Diamonds the same day. He was the most successful fighter pilot in the world!

Hartmann flew to *Wolfsschanze* Führer Headquarters, where the attempt on Hitler's life had taken place on July 20. Hartmann had seen Hitler soon after the assassination attempt on August 3, when he received the Swords. Only three weeks later, on August 26, he was back to receive the Diamonds.

As was the rule after the assassination attempt, no officer was permitted to wear his pistol in Hitler's presence. Pistols were surrendered and each visitor had to undergo a body search. Hartmann had no intention of participating in this unworthy spectacle. Just as *Oberst* Rudel had done, he forbade the search and said to *Oberst* von Below, Hitler's Luftwaffe adjutant, "Please tell the Führer that I don't want the Diamonds if he has no faith in his front-line officers."

The *Oberst* spoke with the security officer and Hartmann was allowed to enter Hitler's office wearing his pistol. There he removed his pistol belt, hung it on the coat rack and went in to see Hitler. Later, in the dining room, Hitler declared to the astonished *Oberleutnant* that the war was lost militarily, but that there was hope of splitting the Americans and Russians, which might enable Germany to conclude a fair cessation of hostilities. "We can't allow ourselves to be overrun by the bolshevik hordes," said Hitler. "That would be the end of Europe."

On September 1, 1944 Hartmann was promoted to *Hauptmann* and on November 1 he assumed command of I *Gruppe* of JG 52. On March 1, 1945 he was detached from his unit and taught to fly the legendary Me 262 jet fighter. He did not stay away long, for his commanding officer, Diamonds wearer *Oberst* Hermann Graf, soon recalled him. Hartmann shot down 52 more enemy aircraft by May 8, the day of Germany's surrender. The last came on May 8. It was a Yak-11, whose pilot, in view of Germany's imminent surrender, was performing loops to celebrate the Red Army's victory. As he said later, Hartmann suddenly felt hatred rise in him. He had heard of the atrocities of the Soviets, and he saw red. Later, after taking time to reflect, he said, "I have one victory too many."

Oberst Graf intended that the unit should surrender to the Americans. There was unrest in Deutsch-Brod where the unit was based and where many relatives, women and children were staying. On May 8 *Kommodore* Graf received a radioed order which was to decisively affect the fates of the two men. "Graf and Hartmann are to fly to Dortmund immediately and surrender to the British forces there. Remaining JG 52 personnel will surrender to Soviet forces in Deutsch-Brod. Seidemann, Commanding General of the Flying Corps."

Oberst Graf held the piece of paper in his hand as he informed Hartmann of the order he had just received. "The general doesn't want us, as wearers of the Diamonds, to be taken prisoner by the Russians. They'd make short work of us and put us up against the wall straight away. Together we two have shot down 550 Soviet machines, think of that."

Hartmann asked whether they should obey the order. Graf shook his head, went to the door of the tent and opened it a crack. "Out there are more than 2,000 relatives of our men, old people, women, children, refugees. They depend on us, trust us. These people are completely defenseless. Do you really think I could climb into an Bf 109, leave them here and fly to Dortmund?" Hartmann understood. "That would be a betrayal," he answered. Graf sighed with relief. "I'm glad that you're of the same opinion as I. Actually I hadn't expected anything else. We'll forget the order, say nothing to the people and try to surrender to the Americans."

Then the *Kommodore* gave the order to set fire to the unit's aircraft. He assembled a convoy and led it to Pisek, about 100 kilometers away, where there were troops of the American 90th Infantry Division.

Eight days later the Americans handed JG 52, with the women and children, over to the Soviets. The martyrdom began, first for the women and children, who were separated from their husbands and fathers. The Soviet soldiers looked on them as personal booty. The German soldiers were forced to watch how the *soldateska* raped and murdered their wives and daughters.

This first stop of a ten-and-a-half-year passion stamped itself upon Hartmann's memory forever. Whatever was to come, no matter how personally hard and difficult, was nothing compared to the horror of what he had seen and experienced there.

Erich Hartmann's odyssey through the prisoner-of-war camps would fill the pages of a book. In those years he passed through all the highs and lows a man is capable of experiencing: the general who had become a toady of the NKVD and the Antifa, and the unknown Feldwebel who became an example through his great humanity. Hartmann learned for the first time who was really "true", and what sorts of personalities had previously been concealed behind decorations, medals and ranks.

It didn't take the Soviets long to recognize the "market value" of prisoner Erich Hartmann. First they tried flattery, praising him as the most successful fighter pilot in the world. When Hartmann failed to fall for this ploy, and instead kept his distance, they plucked other strings.

The officers camp at Gryasovets was run by NKVD Captain Uvarov and his comrade Klingbeil, a German communist emigre. One day Klingbeil had Hartmann brought to see him. After offering him a seat and a cigarette, he said, smiling cordially, "Do you know, my dear fellow, that we've wanted to send you home for a long time?" He waited for Hartmann's reaction. "Yes, we wanted to . . . even though we're sure that you would immediately take up with the west, am I right?"

Hartmann shook his head. "No, I'm fed up with it all. Anyway they have other people at the top. I'm a pilot, but no tactical leader."

"To be sure they have others in the West. Men who have led larger formations. But you, Hartmann, you know the Soviet Air Force better than almost anyone. You would be a threat to us if we let you go." He smiled and poured himself a glass of vodka. "But we're nevertheless giving you a chance to be released . . . a great chance."

"And what is that, may I ask?"

"Quite simple my dear fellow. You would agree to remain in East Germany. You would take over a command in the air force there. You could even choose your own post. Say yes and in the next few days we'll drive you to Moscow and introduce you to personalities of the DDR. Then you'll be informed of your duties – and you can go to Germany."

Hartmann wanted to gain time. If he was in East Germany he would soon have the opportunity to flee to the west. There was no question. Then he said, "I'll have to think about it . . . your proposal I mean."

"But my dear fellow, there's nothing to think about. You can be happy that you've been given this chance. The price to be paid is not very high at this moment." Hartmann looked up in surprise. "What kind of price? And how high is it, may I ask?"

Klingbeil leaned over the table slightly and looked into Hartmann's face. Slowly, emphasizing each word, he said, "You will provide us with proof that you're trustworthy, understood? We couldn't simply let you walk. We want to see if you are worthy of our trust."

Then the NKVD Captain took a list from his briefcase and read out ten names. They were all officers in the camp with Hartmann whom he knew well. "You'll give us a character sketch, Hartmann, understand?"

Then he asked the prisoner if he knew that these officers had contact with military posts in West Germany.

"I don't understand, *Herr Hauptmann*," said Hartmann. "You're asking me to be a low-down stool-pigeon. But I won't pay this price!"

Klingbeil tried to smooth things over; he pleaded, scolded, threatened. And then he said calmly, "Come Hartmann, sign this letter. That's all you have to do. Then you're a free man."

Hartmann stared at the piece of paper. If he signed it he would be released from the uncertainty of prison life. Just a signature! But he also knew that although he would probably safeguard his own life by signing, he would at the same time endanger the lives of ten of his fellow prisoners. "No, *Herr Hauptmann*, I won't take part in your rotten plan!"

Furious, Klingbeil jumped to his feet. "Go to the devil, you nazi swine!" he roared.

Only a few days later NKVD Captain Uvarov ordered Hartmann to him. He began the same game as Klingbeil. But this time Hartmann was asked to sign a paper written in the Russian language. "I won't do it if it's not translated," he answered. Uvarov became furious. "I am a Soviet officer and you must believe me," he shouted. But Hartmann refused to allow himself to be convinced. "Translate it first," he demanded. Furious, Uvarov pounded on the table with his fists. "You damned fascist swine, you'll pay for this. We can do anything we want with you, you filthy swine, anything. No one will ever learn what has happened to you. Russia is very large . . ."

Hartmann stuck to his guns. "No, I will not sign," he said, looking into the red face of the NKVD officer. That was too much for Uvarov. "You will work until your bones break . . . ," he raged.

Later, Hartmann was amazed that he was able to calmly ask, "Is that all?" He hadn't counted on Uvarov's reaction. The Russian stared at him and replied coldly, "No, you have insulted a Soviet officer. For that you get ten days in the bunker."

When the guard took Hartmann away he had no idea what lay in store for him in the bunker. He spent ten days in a stinking, filthy, stone dungeon, three meters long and one wide, with only a small tin for a toilet. He was forced to sleep on the floor and suffered terribly from the cold. Each day he was given two liters of water and 600 grams of bread.

On December 27, 1949 he and other German prisoners were put on trial. A "war court" convened, and the prosecutor read out the "sins register." It accused Hartmann of the destruction of 352 Soviet aircraft, the shooting of 780 Russian civilians and the sabotaging of the Russian economy. By shooting up a flour mill and a bakery Hartmann was supposed to have reduced daily production from 16 tonnes to 1 tonne.

Hartmann, who smiled as the charges were read, could prove that he had never been in the area where he had supposedly committed his "war crimes." He was a soldier, and had never fired on civilians. But the judge said, "That doesn't matter, you engaged in aerial combat and on occasion missed your target. These bullets then fell to earth and killed people, understand?"

When Hartmann shook his head the man, who wore the uniform of a captain, observed, "That doesn't matter either. Twenty-five years forced labor . . . understand now?"

Hartmann was not one of those who gave up or resigned himself to his fate. He tried to fight the system through his behavior. He went on a hunger strike because conditions in the camp were more than degrading. Speaking for his fellow prisoners, he never once submitted to the brute force of the NKVD. It was the same in the camp at Shakty, to which he was sent after his sentencing. Conditions there were so catastrophic that he organized a rebellion, something unique in the annals of German POWs in Russia. After asking the camp commandant in vain to address some of their grievances, Hartmann and a number of fellow prisoners occupied the administration building and disarmed the guards. He then phoned the commandant's superior, a general in Rostov, from his office, described the situation and asked him to send a commission to guarantee humane conditions in the camp.

The commission came, but Hartmann and the other ringleaders of the uprising were sent to Ivanovo prison and subsequently, with their hands bound like criminals, to Novocherkassk. Hartmann spent nine months there, five in solitary confinement. Then a kangaroo court was assembled. It accused him of "inciting a rebellion of the civilian population of Shakty against the Soviet government." The Soviets: "Furthermore we have proof that you support the efforts of the international bourgeoisie and maintain contacts with the counter-revolutionary Bandera bands."

Hartmann argued the charges. He didn't even know a man called Bandera. He was unaware that this Ukrainian had carried on a war of liberation for his people from the Soviet Union long after the war was over.

The court decided: "A further twenty-five years forced labor for this member of the international bourgeoisie!"

Hartmann listened calmly as the sentence was read. He knew that the Soviets would show no pity, unless of course he agreed to their proposal that he become an informer. But as he had told Captain Klingbeil, he had no intention of turning against his own people.

In 1953 Hartmann was moved to the camp at Diatevka. He stayed there for a year, but then they shipped him back to Novocherkassk prison again. Then, one day, something that all the prisoners had hoped for, but scarcely dared dream of, happened. The effects of the visit to Moscow by German Chancellor Dr. Konrad Adenauer were felt even in the camps. The verbal and physical abuse of the prisoners stopped, and they no longer had to stand facing the wall when a guard passed by. Now they were prisoners of war again.

The news of freedom almost took their breath away. Hartmann was given back his flight jacket and then he travelled to Germany. He was home after ten and a half years. The comrades he was supposed to denounce had gone home long ago. Several of his former fellow prisoners visited him a few days after his return. Most of them were soldiers again and wore a uniform. "Come join the Luftwaffe. You can fly again," they said. But Hartmann was uncertain. He first wanted to recover from the ordeal of captivity. Later he asked himself the question on which his future would depend: what will you do? He knew nothing else but flying. Learn another profession now? No, based on experience that was unlikely.

Naturally he was excited about flying again. It had been ten and a half years since he had sat at the controls of an aircraft. He also knew that the new Bundeswehr was flying jets. But he should soon be able to master them, after all he had flown the Me 262 in 1945. In 1956 he made his decision – and joined the Bundeswehr. He was accepted as a major. Not until four years later, on December 12, 1960, was he promoted to *Oberstleutnant*. This was undoubtedly due to the fact that Hartmann was not a comfortable subordinate. He called things by their proper names. He had always behaved that way, especially while a prisoner. Erich Hartmann backed down before no one.

Hartmann soon discovered that the Bundeswehr was administered rather than led. The level of training was inadequate, and measured against that of the Soviet soldier even catastrophic. This business was not to his taste. It bothered him that those with connections were favored over the capable. Mess mannerisms counted for more than soldierly behavior.

The bureaucrats in the Bundeswehr plotted against him, his superiors branded him "troublesome." But those in NATO held a different opinion: "Hartmann is a first-class flier and an outstanding air combat tactician as well!"

Hartmann trained *Jagdgeschwader 71 Richthofen*, which he took command of in the summer of 1959, to NATO standards within a year. The unit achieved excellent gunnery results, winning the admiration and praise of the allies. Only in the Bundeswehr was no notice taken.

Hartmann had to wait seven years before being promoted to *Oberst* in mid-1968. He carried on for another three years, until finally his enemies saw their chance. Hartmann was brought up on charges over the trifling matter of having moved his pilot's certificate and then being unable to find it when it was due for renewal. Grounds: expiration. An investigation was begun and there were three hearings, all of which Hartmann won hands down. His enemies wanted to "shoot him down" from their desks. However the plotters and enviers in the Bundeswehr were not about to succeed where the Soviets had failed.

It was embarrassing. Senior officers of the US Air Force shook their heads at the treatment being meted out to the most successful fighter pilot in the world. Luftwaffe Inspector General Panitzki was queried about this in Washington. His deprecating answer was: "Hartmann is a good fighter pilot, but not a good officer." To be sure Hartmann's casual and self-certain behavior didn't please every superior. No, Hartmann was young, temperamental and had an irrepressible drive for freedom. His difficulty in accepting the role of a subordinate was certainly a shortcoming where discipline was concerned, but in action he proved himself to be disciplined and an exemplary *Kommodore*.

On September 30, 1970 "Bubi" Hartmann left the Bundeswehr. Embittered? Certainly not – but disappointed. "If the Bundeswehr were properly led, if performance and effectiveness were placed above thoughts of career, then I would have stayed – at any price."

Hartmann went on, as always. From 1971 to 1974 he was active as chief flying instructor at Hangelar near Bonn. He remained an enthusiastic pilot and was happiest when with fellow members of the Herrenberg Flying Club in Swabia. There, working without pay, he taught enthusiasts to fly. Each day Erich Hartmann could be found at Poltringen airfield among his fellow pilots.

Erich Hartmann died on September 19, 1993.

The Blonde Knight of Germany was the name of a book about Erich Hartmann written by American authors Toliver and Constable. In the German version the title is "Bring Down

Hartmann", an order which the Soviet Air Force command had given its "red falcons" during the war. They did not bring "Bubi" down.

CHAPTER XIX

GENERAL DER PANZERTRUPPEN HERMANN BALCK

T
he slim, seemingly delicate, eighty-three-year-old gentleman in the dark blue blazer and light grey pants leafed through the diaries. He had kept them religiously during the First and Second World Wars; today they were historical sources for a book which retired *General* Hermann Balck had written but not yet published.

Balck said himself that his greatest accomplishment came at the end of the war. It was then, in May 1945, that he prevented the entire Sixth Army, 300,000 soldiers, from falling into Soviet hands and subsequently led it to surrender to the Americans.

At the beginning of 1945 Army Group Balck withdrew toward the Reich border, where there was a prepared position. Heavy fighting lay behind the soldiers. The enemy had been shaken off. On the right there was contact with the Second Panzer Army; on the left the Sixth SS Panzer Army had been unable to establish contact, but had informed the general of this. Balck himself gave the order, supported by his Chief-of-Staff *General* Gaedtke: the Reich frontier was to be held until the cease-fire, so that Steiermark would most likely fall into the hands of the western allies. Further: contact was to be maintained on the right, in order to keep open a path back to Germany for Army Group Southeast (E), parts of which were still deep in the Balkans (Sarajevo), and in the final stage ensure and carry out the withdrawal of the Sixth Army behind the old border of the Reich. More than 200,000 refugees were in the area held by the army group, believing themselves safe from the advancing Soviets in the valleys of Steiermark. With them were also the newly-formed 1st and 3rd Hungarian Armies, which were also under Balck's command.

After IV SS Panzer Corps had abandoned its positions without considering the consequences, an empty strip was created into which a Soviet tank corps immediately drove and headed toward Graz.

In this situation Balck received news that the Hungarian *St. Laszlo* Division, which had previously fought bravely, had gone over to the enemy and was now fighting against the German forces. Balck had no opportunity to confirm the accuracy of the report and issued an order of the day instructing his forces to disarm all Hungarian troops within the area of the Sixth Army.

What had happened? It was a fact that the Hungarian division, which was commanded by a brave officer, Major General Zoltan-vitez-Szügyi, to whom *General* Balck had presented the Knight's Cross on February 25, had moved to the right without informing the German army headquarters. The *St. Laszlo* Division thus moved out of the field of view of the army Commander-in-Chief. He had to believe what had been reported to him: like so many other Hungarian units, the division had gone over to the Soviets. Balck drew his conclusions from this assumption and ordered the immediate disarming of all Hungarian troops still present.

What *General* Balck did not know, and only learned thirty years after the war, was that the *St. Laszlo* Division had not deserted, rather it fought on against the Soviets until midnight of May 9, 1945. Not until May 10 did General Szügyi surrender to the British.

A gap had formed on the left wing of the Sixth SS Panzer Army. Into this gap, between Pinkafeld and the Semmering, moved five Soviet divisions, which headed for Graz. The front staggered. The danger of being cut off from the old Reich grew from hour to hour. *General* Balck decided to attack. He knew that in such situations only offensive action could be used. Defense meant his own destruction. Balck hurriedly scraped together his attack force: the outstanding 1st Panzer Division and a rocket brigade without launchers, as well as an officer with five tanks, the 117th Light Infantry Division and the 1st Alpine Division.

The commander of the Salzburg Military District, *General* Ringel, had established a defensive position at the Semmering. In *Oberst* Raithel, commander of the Dachstein Mountain Artillery School, he had an outstanding assistant.

When it was reported to Balck that the Soviet armored spearheads were not far away, he ordered *Oberstleutnant* Wolff, a tank officer on his staff, to load three men armed with Panzerfaust anti-tank weapons into a Kübelwagen and drive toward the Russians. Balck knew that extraordinary situations called for extraordinary measures.

Just ahead of the enemy armored spearhead Wolff and his men discovered a German hospital and a replacement unit (the 19th Driver Replacement Battalion from Graz). He armed everyone who could walk and took up the unequal battle against the Soviet tanks. In a few minutes the handful of German soldiers destroyed six tanks. The Soviets broke off the attack and withdrew. *General* Balck sent several units to reinforce the defenders and together they held the position.

Balck's forces attacked on April 16, 1945. South of the Semmering they encircled the five advancing Soviet divisions and destroyed them. The operation ended on April 27. Army and Waffen-SS troops, as well as the Volkssturm, had shown outstanding fighting spirit. When a village near Vorau was liberated from the Soviets, the local minister came up to the men of the Volkssturm and greeted them: "Comrades, I am cured!" Eight days of occupation by the Red Army had robbed the old man of all his illusions.

In the days that followed, Balck made preparations for a withdrawal to the Reich border, where he expected to surrender to the Americans. The Soviets withdrew forces for the battle for Vienna. The order Balck received from army group read: "Hold. With the West against the East." Balck considered such wishful thinking utopian and ignored the order.

General Balck and *Feldmarschall* Kesselring met in Judenburg during the night of May 6/7. The field marshall knew that the war was coming to an end but gave no clear orders. As well he did not defend his stand fast order. Quite certainly he didn't believe in it himself.

Balck's Chief-of-Staff, *General* Gaedtke, was sent by the army group to the American headquarters. But the American general refused to negotiate, instead he demanded a visit by the army group's Commander-in-Chief and its immediate, unconditional surrender.

On May 7 *General* Balck learned from his Ic, General Staff *Major* von Czernicki, who had intercepted a radio message, that an agreement had been reached between the Americans and Soviets, according to which all German forces which had fought against the Americans would be handed over to them, while all of those which had fought the Soviets would be delivered to the Red Army. The implementation date was May 8, 1945.

Balck immediately sent his forces toward the Americans. The weapons were left where they were. Only the rearguard, consisting of tanks, anti-tank guns and machine-guns, remained fully armed. Bridges were supposed to be destroyed only on orders from the army command. They remained intact. The Russians did not pursue because they failed to notice the German withdrawal. All the efforts to be taken prisoner by the Americans almost came to nothing at the Enns River. An American lieutenant stopped the march group and sent the units back into the Enns Valley, where they were to be handed over to the Russians.

General Balck learned of this and telephoned his opposite number, American General and division commander McBride. Balck briefly described the situation and asked for an immediate private meeting. Balck's surprise was great when he was greeted in Kirchdorf, where the American headquarters was located, with full military honors. The guard presented arms and Balck reviewed the American troops. McBride, at first rather reserved, offered his hand to his opponent: "General, I understand that you wish to surrender to us. Every American should be happy if as few German soldiers as possible surrender to the Soviets," he said.

The American was no less astonished when Balck answered in fluent English. Then the two generals retired to speak privately. Soon afterward Balck issued the necessary orders and instructions for the surrender to the American forces. 300,000 German soldiers were grateful to their commander-in-chief.

Hermann Balck came from an old military family. He was born in Danzig-Langfuhr on December 7, 1893. After graduating at the top of his class he joined the 10th Light Infantry Battalion in Goslar. The young officer was wounded seven times during the First World War. He wore the Wound Badge in Gold, received the Iron Cross, First and Second Class for exceptional bravery, and became one of the first officers to receive the Bavarian Service Order in October 1914. As well he received the Austrian Military Service Order, Third Class, the Knight's Cross with Swords to the House Order of Hohenzollern and was recommended for the Pour le Mérite in October 1918. His father, *Generalleutnant* Balck, received the Pour le Mérite from the Kaiser's hand for personal bravery and outstanding command of his troops.

After the war Hermann Balck and his company joined the *Grenzschutz Ost*. He fought as a company commander in the Hannover Volunteer Light Infantry Battalion in Posen province. In 1920 he was taken into the 100,000-man army, the first of all the *Leutnants* and *Oberleutnants* of X and VIII Army Corps. His unit distinguished itself several times during the fighting in Posen. Appointments and promotions followed. In 1935, as a *Major*, he became commander of the 1st Bicycle Battalion in Tilsit. Later he was assigned to the Army High Command and became officer in charge of cavalry and part of the motorized forces.

In the war against France in 1940 Balck caught the attention of his superiors through his personal bravery and outstanding command of his troops. Leading the 1st Rifle Regiment, he broke through the enemy lines near Sedan and stormed on to Dunkirk. In recognition of this daring attack Balck was awarded the Knight's Cross on June 3, 1940 and was mentioned by name in the Wehrmacht communique. At the Aisne he and his 1st Rifle Regiment broke through, rolled up the enemy positions in the Vosges and seized Belfort Fortress. For these feats his name was entered in the German Army's Book of Honor.

In the campaign against Yugoslavia and Greece in 1941 Balck, now commanding the 3rd Panzer Regiment, broke through the Metaxas Line, advanced up the Tempe Valley to central Greece and pushed into Salonika and Athens. The British news service reported: "The 3rd Panzer Regiment was able to cross terrain which we had considered absolutely tank-proof. We therefore dispensed with an anti-tank defense." Balck was awarded the Bulgarian Order of Valor 3rd Class with Swords.

On July 7, 1941 Balck was attached to the OKH with the special mission of clearing up the army's motor vehicle situation. He was given special full authority to overcome the confused situation. Hermann Balck was one of the Wehrmacht's outstanding commanders of armored forces. On November 1, 1941 he became "General of Fast Troops" in the OKH. *Generaloberst* Guderian said, "You couldn't find a better man."

On May 12, 1942 Balck took command of the famous 11th Panzer Division, with which he achieved great success. 91 enemy tanks were destroyed in one day in the defensive battle in the Sukhinichi bend. This figure was never equalled during the entire war! The "Eleventh" was present at the Chin, east of Smolensk and near Voronezh.

On July 4 seventeen T 34s drove into the 11th Panzer Division's flank and suddenly appeared before the division command post. The tanks shot up the wooden houses from a range of 800 meters. Confusion reigned among the staff officers and rear area personnel.

Only one man kept his head and summoned panzers by radio: the division commander, *Generalmajor* Hermann Balck. The history of the 15th Panzer Regiment, which belonged to the 11th Panzer Division, states: "He stood on the roof of his command bus, in a rather unusual display but nevertheless in commanding style, and called to the commanders of the tanks which had just arrived: 'Now see to it that you do something!' They did what could be done and banished the specter of the Russian tanks. *Major* von Burstin, commander of III Battalion, was killed during the brief but sharp tank battle, which *General* Balck directed from the roof of his bus. All seventeen T 34s were destroyed."

Moved into the Stalingrad area on December 17, the 11th Panzer Division drew praise for its outstanding bravery and its commander was mentioned in the Wehrmacht communique. Balck was awarded the Oak Leaves on December 22, 1942. On March 4, 1943 he received the Swords for the destruction of Army Group Popov, a force ten times stronger than his own.

In 1943 the Allies landed near Salerno, Italy and established a bridgehead. Balck received orders to take command of XIV Panzer Corps and destroy the Americans. The operations he began seemed to be leading to success. Then the general crashed in his Fieseler *Storch*. In spite of serious injuries he initially retained command of his corps, but was soon forced to relinquish command for health reasons. Consequently his attack plans could not be carried out.

March 13 to November 13, 1943 saw Balck in the officer reserve of the OKH. On November 1, 1943 he was named commanding general of XXXXVIII Panzer Corps. His Chief-of-Staff was the then *Oberst* von Mellenthin, who later became a close friend. The panzer corps played a major role in the offensive and defensive battles in the areas of Kiev, Zhitomir and Berdichev. Near Brusilov his troops destroyed the 60th Soviet Army and a further enemy army.

Balck and his corps fought near Shepetovka, Yampol and Luck, and took part in the heavy fighting near Ternopol, Kovel and Brody. On August 5, 1944 he became Commander-in-Chief of the Fourth Panzer Army, which distinguished itself in the battles near Baranov. When the Soviets broke through into southern Poland, Balck immediately counterattacked, stopped the enemy, and then drove him back to his starting position. On August 31, 1944 he was awarded the Diamonds and his name was again mentioned in the Wehrmacht communique.

In western Europe the Allied forces were advancing irresistibly. Driving into the retreating German forces, they neared the borders of the Reich. Army Group G was formed to halt this advance and was placed under the command of *General* Balck.

The renewed allied offensive began at dawn on a cold November day. Between Belfort and Luxembourg 700 American tanks ground their way across muddy fields. More than a million American and French troops advanced against a numerically inferior enemy. The German defenders numbered 700,000, with a mere 30 tanks.

Of Army Group G's battle in the west, English historian David Irving wrote in his book *Hitler and his Generals*: "His attack (Patton) began on November 8, but in pouring rain. In eight days he advanced only 25 kilometers through mud and minefields in the direction of the *Westwall*. Then *General* Balck's flexibly-conducted operations and the stubborn defense of Metz brought the attack to a halt." (Metz was under Balck's command.)

Thirty German tanks against 700 American! The American losses were tremendous – more than a third! One-third of their tanks had been destroyed. This outstanding defensive success was due to an inspiration on the part of *General* Balck. He knew that he couldn't count on the delivery of additional tanks, but he had as good as nothing with which to meet the enemy attack.

On the Eastern Front Balck had to deal with an enemy who was a master of improvisation. Many German unit leaders, Balck included, were surprised and began to learn. They employed the same means as the enemy and were successful.

It was at this time that Balck remembered something which had been part of a unit leader's daily bread in Russia – improvise! Why should he not try it on the Western Front? If the great American offensive was to be stopped in time – and there were signs that it was not far off – then Balck would have to resort to a trick. In a very brief time he came up with a plan to lay centrally-organized minefields. But to do this he needed men.

General Unruh (Heldenklau) and his aides scraped together regiments in the rear areas. The hospitals were combed and anyone could stand on two legs was "mobilized." Battalions formed from invalids were expected to halt a rampaging enemy equipped with the most modern weapons. *General* Balck was opposed to the idea. In his opinion it was irresponsible to send these men to the front. But as he needed troops in order to carry out his mine plan, he took command of the battalions unfit for duty at the front and renamed them "mine battalions." The soldiers were given a brief indoctrination on their future mission, which, by the way, they performed magnificently.

In order to halt Patton's tanks Balck's "mine specialists" rammed metal rods into the ground at the focal points of the US attack. The tanks' mine detectors at first identified them as mines. But soon the Americans were able to see through this obvious trick – and they were supposed to: for now they abandoned caution and drove into the real, well-concealed minefields, which lay behind the simulated ones. The surprise was perfect, the success assured. Patton's armored attack bogged down and collapsed under the fire of the German artillery and infantry.

Following this operation Balck was ordered back to the Eastern Front. In Hungary he commanded the German Sixth and the Hungarian First and Third Armies. Then came the heavy fighting for Budapest and the subsequent withdrawal movements, during which *General* Balck's forces successfully carried out the final German encirclement operation of the war east of Graz, in which several Soviet divisions were destroyed. This was followed by the surrender to American troops in Styria. *General* Balck considered the successful withdrawal of all German forces from Hungary and their surrender to the Americans as his greatest accomplishment.

Several years after Balck's release as a prisoner of war, the German police arrested the unsuspecting former general. He was brought to trial and charged with murder. What had happened?

When Hermann Balck commanded Army Group G on the Upper Rhine Front, the OKW gave him special powers to employ harsh measures in an emergency. Balck acted according to this special authority. From intercepted radio messages he had deduced that a major allied attack was imminent. Balck was convinced that only concentrated artillery fire could smash this attack. When the attack began he ordered the artillery to lay down fire on the enemy. Then a division commander reported to him that the artillery chief was lying drunk in his bunker. Balck dispatched an officer, who in fact found the *Oberstleutnant* completely drunk on a sofa. The officer reported that the latter was incapable of pulling himself together and had no idea where his batteries were located. The general knew that without artillery he had no chance of stopping the attack. He ordered the artillery officer shot. On the advice of the division commander, *General* von Knobelsdorf, he reviewed the facts of the case the following day. Nothing changed and the situation was confirmed. Afterward Balck repeated the order to execute the officer, which this time was carried out.

Balck became suspicious. Shortly before this incident a division commander had been exonerated in a similar situation. As it turned out the court had been filled with his relatives. This was not to be repeated. However under the pressure of events Balck was unable to convene a drumhead court martial, which, on the strength of the facts, would likewise have issued a death sentence.

Found guilty in the shooting of the artillery officer, Balck was sentenced by a Stuttgart court to three years in prison, of which he was made to serve only eighteen months. Balck knew the verdict three months earlier. It was established by the Americans, who likewise discharged the regular court and staffed it as required for this sentence. In no western army would he have been brought to trial.

The general's standing and the public popularity he enjoyed was underlined by the court's verdict in a de-nazification proceeding against him. Here are a few extracts:

> "He was a thoroughly irreproachable military personality, such as is highly respected and valued in every country which possesses effective armed forces. There is an abundance of sworn statements, which appear credible, which base his entire philosophy on a disciplined order and consciousness of duty . . . Even the current public prosecutor Kischke, who had the defendant as commanding officer, described him as the most loyal and proper officer he ever met, who was never regarded as a national-socialist . . . It would be improper to view an officer who made not the least concession to the reprehensible principles of national-socialism and who did not belong to the party as incriminated, simply because he was a good and brave general.

He has been formally examined by the court but not found to be incriminated: Central Denazification Tribunal North-Württemberg."

Balck never hesitated to act against members of the party, as in the winter of 1942/43, when he took action against the district propaganda head in Silesia. This resulted in a lengthy prison sentence and later assignment to a penal battalion.

Following his release Hermann Balck began work as a warehouse worker, but soon he obtained a position in the field service of a Swabian firm. Later he became independent as an economic and business consultant, established contacts for business transactions and was active primarily abroad.

But his true love remained South Africa – black and white. His longtime Chief-of-Staff *General* von Mellenthin, who had family in South Africa, had formed an airline together with South African pilots which operated between Luxembourg and Johannesburg. Hermann Balck represented the airline in Europe. Since getting to know South Africa he busied himself with the cultural history and economy of that part of the world. Five times he made lengthy trips across Africa south of the Zambezi. At the age of seventy he and his wife crossed the Kalahari Desert in a Volkswagen. Balck continued his studies and gave talks on South Africa in West Germany. He travelled often to the United States, where he was in demand as a guest speaker in politically-influential clubs. As proof of his outstanding condition he swam the Wisconsin River at the age of eighty.

A widower, Balck lived alone, pursuing historic studies and living on his lovely property in Asperg near Ludwigsburg. This was his favorite place, which he had built up over a period of sixteen years. *General* Hermann Balck died on November 29, 1982 at the age of 89.

CHAPTER XX

GENERAL HERMANN GERHARD RAMCKE

Bonn, June 26, 1951. Federal Chancellor Dr. Konrad Adenauer receives former *General der Fallschirmjäger* Hermann Bernhard Balck, who has just been released from a French prison, in Schaumburg Palace. This meeting between the chancellor of the federal republic and a former general of the German Wehrmacht was more than just a conciliatory gesture to the general, who had been imprisoned in France for six years.

The parachute general's daring flight from the *"Liberté Provisoire"* was intended to draw attention to the fate of German prisoners of war still imprisoned by the French. The reaction in the German press showed that Ramcke had succeeded in rousing the public with his sensational escape. Afterward the number of voices calling for the release of the German prisoners grew, especially in France. No longer was the spirit of revenge to prevail, finally it was to be replaced by reason and humanity.

Nevertheless the general returned to France after his flight. They had promised to finally open his trial. For six years the French had sought evidence against Ramcke, the defender of the French port city of Brest. Material had been assembled during the last months of his captivity, but Ramcke's French defender had refuted it and picked it apart.

The chancellor of the federal republic bore this in mind when he spoke with Ramcke about the fate of the German prisoners of war. Dr. Adenauer also knew of the impeccable testimonials which their former American enemies had provided for the paratroopers and the general, their brave and fair opponent at Brest.

The Ramckes are an old farming family which settled in Pinneberg at the beginning of the fifteenth century. But Bernhard Ramcke, born in Schleswig-Friedrichsberg on January 24, 1889, had no wish to become a farmer. He rebelled. Ramcke's love belonged neither to school nor to agriculture. The sea called to him. When Bernhard was in the second grade his teacher asked him what career he wanted to choose. Self-consciously the young boy, who could not have known the different military ranks, answered, "Admiral or general."

Ramcke must have thought of that day when, years later, he stood before the mustering commission in Friedrichsort, near Kiel. The officers smiled at the slender youth who, in answer to doubts about his constitution, answered self-confidently, "I can do it. Just let me go to sea." And he did do it.

The young Ramcke sailed around the world on the frigate SMS *Stosch* and was drilled hard. The young seaman then sailed the seas on the *Prinz Albert* and the *Blücher* before the outbreak of the First World War. Ramcke saw action against the British and French in Flanders as a member of the marine division. In 1916 acting officer Ramcke received the Iron Cross, First Class and the Prussian Military Service Cross in Gold. Bravery in the face of the enemy resulted in a promotion to *Leutnant*. Later, during the fighting in the Baltic states, he became an *Oberleutnant*. Ramcke served in the 100,000-man army as a *Hauptmann*, in the Wehrmacht as a *Major* and finally, as an *Oberstleutnant*, as commander of the Pomeranian troop training grounds at Gross-Born.

Germany's newest branch of the armed forces, the parachute troops, became famous through its daring and successful actions in the Western Campaign. This was the service which suited the daredevil Ramcke. Although he was already fifty-one years old and an *Oberst*, he volunteered and was immediately accepted by *General* Student, founder of the German paratroop force.

The young paratroop force faced its most severe trial by fire in 1941 during the invasion of the Mediterranean island of

Crete. Preparations for the capture of the British base lasted three weeks. The action was actually not part of the Balkan Campaign. It was an independent operation, in that control of the eastern Mediterranean was at stake, the gain or loss of decisive positions in the battle for the Suez Canal.

The attack from the air by paratroops and mountain infantry, which was carried out under the direction of the Luftwaffe High Command, began on May 20. Severe tactical difficulties had to be overcome and the troops suffered considerable losses.

It will be left to historians to assess whether this military operation was justified or not. The fact is that the German parachute troops never recovered from the losses they suffered during the bitter fighting in Crete. To rebuild the striking power and restore the full operational readiness of such a force after the difficult and heavy losses in Crete would have required years of basic training.

At the time of the Crete landings *Oberst* Ramcke was commander of the parachute replacement troops. He and a battle group of 500 men jumped near Malemes to relieve the hard-fighting men of the corps, who were locked in battle with the British. Ramcke succeeded in establishing contact with the other battle groups. Together with mountain infantry which had been flown in, the parachute troops rolled up the enemy in their positions and overcame the defenders.

In recognition of his personal efforts Ramcke was promoted to *Generalmajor* and on August 21, 1941 was decorated with the Knight's Cross. Subsequently, while spending time with the Royal Italian Armed Forces, Ramcke received orders to take a parachute brigade to North Africa to support the forces of *Generalfeldmarschall* Rommel. *General* Student protested this use of his troops as infantry in the desert, but the order stood. Arguments that the parachute troops were too valuable a force to be used on anything but specialized operations were to no avail.

Rommel wore a look of concern when he greeted the parachute general in the Libyan desert. "You know your mission and the situation, Ramcke. Come with your men as soon as possible so that I can finally take some of the pressure off my troops. By the way, have a good look around. This theater is quite unlike any other." Ramcke and his brigade went into position on Ruweisat Ridge near Deir el Schein and at the Qattara Depression in the southern sector of the German El Alamein front.

On October 23, 1942 General Montgomery and his 8th Army went on the offensive. At about 22.00 hours more than 1,000 guns opened the battle. 1,114 British tanks rolled against 230 German panzers. The massed employment of heavy weapons smashed the defensive front set up by Rommel.

The bravery of the German troops of *Panzerarmee Afrika* could not halt the assault by the British and their allies –Australians, Poles, South Africans, Indians and New Zealanders. Montgomery's tanks broke through in the northern sector of the front. Ramcke and his men were in the southern sector, 130 km from the sole coastal road, and without motor transport. That meant a march of 130 kilometers through the desert if they wished to avoid being cut off and captured. On foot!

Ramcke and his parachute troops withdrew cautiously. Soon exhausted by the sun and sand, the paratroops dug new positions, fought off British tanks and armored cars, marched, dug, marched. There was no time to rest. The enemy was behind and in front of them. The troops of *Panzerarmee Afrika* and the Italian 20th Corps were already in retreat to the Fuka Position, and soon afterward were on their way into Cyrenaica. There were only two possibilities for the paratroops: establish contact with the retreating panzer army or be taken prisoner.

Three British scout cars circled the exhausted paratroops at a distance. They were able to observe every movement. But they did not attack or call in stronger forces. Perhaps they believed that these German troops, cut off from the main body of the retreating army, would surrender and allow themselves to be taken prisoner.

The British did not know Ramcke and his paratroops. One night a column of trucks halted only a few hundred meters away from the paratroops. German? No, they were British. A second column drove up beside the first: British tanks! The time had come. Either die in the desert, be taken prisoner, or perhaps win. Silently the paratroopers formed into squads of three or four. Their orders: creep up to the British vehicles,

quietly overcome their crews, climb in and head west. There
was no be no shooting. Everyone was wide awake. Forgotten
were thirst, hunger and all the hardships, gone was their exhaustion. Pistols drawn, they crept toward the British who,
tired and suspecting nothing, dozed in the desert night. Not a
shot was fired. The British crews were overwhelmed. Motors
sprang to life. Seconds later the paratroops disappeared into
the night in their newly-acquired vehicles.

Some time later the first shot was fired. Bewildered, the
British tank crews, who were in the second column, climbed
into their vehicles. What was going on? Who had fired? Where
was the firing coming from? Why were the trucks driving
away? The tankers must have thought that their truck crews
were running to save themselves from Germans who had appeared from somewhere in the east. Confused, they gave the
fleeing trucks covering fire. They had no way of knowing that
Ramcke's men were in the British vehicles. The general called
a halt in a depression and assembled his men. The paratroops
went through the trucks and discovered that they contained
everything they needed: water, good food and fuel.

Early the next morning British fighter aircraft appeared.
They headed toward the column. Would the Spitfires destroy
all hope of salvation? But Ramcke's men knew what to do.
They waved up at the fighters. The pilots saw British vehicles
with British markings, so they waved back.

The adventurous drive through the desert continued at a
high tempo, always in pursuit of the withdrawing German and
Italian forces. Another column appeared. British! Unsuspecting, they drove toward Ramcke's vehicles. The paratroops
jumped out and took them prisoner. There was one more surprise: the trucks were carrying German and Italian POWs. They
couldn't believe their eyes when they saw the German soldiers.
Ramcke said, "The Germans and the Italians get in, the British
get out." The English soldiers were given water – more important than food in the desert – and left behind. The paratroops
continued their westward journey with the liberated Germans
and Italians.

Finally, after five days march behind the British offensive
front, they reached their objective. Ramcke and his courageous

men caught up with Field Marshall Rommel on the coastal road. Rommel had thought them lost. 2,000 paratroops rejoined Rommel's army and fought on. This great act of valor on the part of the paratroops was acknowledged on November 15, 1942 by the awarding of the Oak Leaves to *General* Ramcke.

Following the withdrawal of the Ramcke Parachute Brigade from Africa, it was reformed in the Auray area in France. Relations with the population were especially good. One day Ramcke had the mayor of the town draw up a list of fathers of large families still held as POWs by the Germans. He was given a list of eight names, which he passed on to the Chief-of-Staff of the Wehrmacht General Office with a request for their release.

Soon afterward Ramcke's paratroops were deployed to the southern sector of the Eastern Front. There was heavy fighting, resulting in heavy losses which necessitated a transfer to the Wahn training grounds. There the brigade was reformed.

On June 6, 1944 began the allied invasion on the Channel Coast. Ramcke was now commanding the 2nd Parachute Division. The new unit had not completed training when the order arrived: transfer to western Brittany; prevent the enemy from capturing the city and port of Brest. On the way to the front Ramcke visited Auray, where he received a warm welcome from the population. Eight men were especially grateful to him – they were former POWs whose release he had negotiated.

Meanwhile the Allies had broken through the German Atlantic Front near Avranches. All units in the Brest area were ordered into the fortress. Ramcke and the widely-separated elements of his division were still on the heights of Mont d'Areé. American units were also advancing on Brest and they occupied Guipavas airport. The danger existed that the paratroops might be cut off from Brest. On August 8, 1944 American emissaries called upon the commander of the fortress of Brest, *Oberst* von der Mosel, to surrender. Mosel refused. Ramcke's division moved into the approaches to Brest, where the paratroops occupied new positions. On orders from above Ramcke assumed command of the fortress of Brest; *Oberst* von der Mosel became his Chief-of-Staff. Inside the fortress, in addition to the 2nd Parachute Division, were the 243rd Infantry Division and troops of the naval commander. 35,000 Germans defended the French fortress of Brest against an American armored division, several artillery brigades and an armada of bombers and fighter-bombers. But Ramcke and his men carried out their orders to tie down massive enemy forces.

About one-half the population of Brest was still present, the rest having left the city. In view of the imminent battle for the fortress Ramcke wanted to evacuate the remaining 40,000 inhabitants as well. He opened negotiations with General Middleton, commander of the American 8th Army Corps, for a cease-fire. The Americans agreed. In four consecutive days the inhabitants of Brest were driven out of the city to safety in German vehicles.

As it soon turned out, not all the civilians had been taken out of the city. 5,000 to 7,000 Frenchmen indicated that they did not wish to leave their property – but many of them were members of the *Résistance*, General de Gaulle's resistance movement. They stayed in the fortress to take up the battle against the paratroops in darkness. The carried out acts of sabotage and ambushed German troops. *General* Ramcke hoped to negotiate another evacuation schedule with the Americans. Mayor Eusen went to American headquarters. But this time General Middleton refused.

Heavy fighting began, losses were heavy on both sides. The garrison of the fortress held on even though their position was hopeless. They knew that they were tying up allied forces which could not now move east, but they also knew that they could not hold out indefinitely and would have to surrender sooner or later.

Even with the strong forces at his disposal, General Middleton was unable to take the fortress. He received reinforcements: an infantry division and combat engineer and mortar battalions. The Americans attacked repeatedly beneath the hail of shells from their artillery. The few minor penetrations they achieved were soon eliminated by the defenders. Ramcke held on.

One day an American medical column took the wrong turn and ended up in the German lines. *General* Ramcke did not take the Americans prisoner, instead he sent the bewildered boys from Texas back to General Middleton, who thanked Ramcke by radio for this friendly gesture.

The battle went on. The defenders of Brest held the fortress against an overwhelming superiority, against waves of bombing attacks, against partisans, against the artillery – all the while conscious that they were cut off from other German forces. On September 13, 1944 General Middleton sent three officers as emissaries with a letter for *General* Ramcke:

> "To: Generalleutnant Ramcke, Commanding General of the German forces in Brest.
> From: Commanding General of the American forces before Brest.
>
> As always in war, the military situation reaches a point at which a commander can no longer justify further loss of blood and the sacrifice of his men.
> We have discussed the situation of the German garrison of Brest with some of your officers and men captured by us. All are convinced that the military situation is hopeless and that nothing can be achieved by prolonging the battle. We are therefore of the opinion that the garrison of Brest has no justifiable grounds for holding out any longer.
> Your soldiers have fought well. About 10,000 men are now prisoners of war. You know your own losses. Furthermore you have lost much vital war materiel and your forces are surrounded in a small, confined area. You have thus fully and totally fulfilled your duty to the Fatherland.
> In view of the preceding I ask you, as one career soldier to another, to cease this unequal battle. We hope that you, as a senior and responsible officer who has served honorably and done his duty, will give this proposal your favorable consideration.
>
> signed Troy H. Middleton"

Ramcke's answer to this letter was to the point:

"To the Commanding General of the 8th American Army Corps, General Troy H. Middleton.

General:
I reject your proposal.

signed Ramcke"

The fortress commander still believed that each day he held out brought relief to the homeland and gave the German command the opportunity to build a new front. He thus intended to hold as long as possible. But Ramcke had no way of knowing that Germany's fate in France had long been sealed and that his men were being sacrificed to no purpose because the holding of Brest had lost any strategic value.

The Americans now pounded every sector of the German fortress front. Attack after attack struck the defenders. Hard, costly close-quarters fighting broke out. The enemy pressed ever closer to the city. Finally the American artillery began using phosphorous rounds in an attempt to smoke the Germans out of the burning city. There was now no longer any possibility of holding off further penetrations by the enemy.

Ramcke heard by radio, his last link to home and the German command, of his promotion to commanding general and the awarding of the Knight's Cross with Oak Leaves and Swords. A day later, on September 21, 1944, it was reported to him by radio that he had been awarded the Diamonds. But by then the fortress of Brest had been forced to surrender.

General Ramcke and General Middleton faced each other in the headquarters of the American commander. The American asked what he could do for Ramcke. The German answered, "See to it that my men are treated well as prisoners."

Speaking to his men for the final time, Ramcke thanked them for their loyalty and their courageous actions. When he bade them farewell a thousand German soldiers shouted, "Father Ramcke, father Ramcke!" The general, who truly was a father to his soldiers, now began his journey into captivity, which initially ended in Camp Clinton in the state of Missouri.

Ramcke read in an American newspaper that Senators Price

and Eastland were critical of the notorious "Morgenthau Plan." The two men called for a proper and reasonable policy toward Germany. Ramcke then wrote a letter to the two senators – it was just before Christmas 1945 – and described the situation in the camp. But who was to smuggle the letter out? Finally Ramcke himself took on this difficult job of letter carrier. With the help of two confederates Ramcke slipped through the wire. He then hitched a ride into the nearby city of Jackson, but was unable to obtain stamps at the local post office as it had closed for the day. Ramcke pretended that he was hard of hearing and suffered from a speech impediment. Some kindly people directed him to a drugstore which was open on Friday and he was able to obtain the necessary stamps. Ramcke returned to the camp the same way, unnoticed and just in time for evening roll call. He now decided on escape. The general planned his breakout carefully. He hoped to reach South America. Meanwhile the camp commander learned who had written to the two senators. Ramcke was moved to another camp. A period of wandering now began which saw him go from America to England, from there to Munsterlager in Germany and finally to France. Handcuffed, Ramcke was turned over to the French authorities as "the murderer of Brest."

In six years as a prisoner of war Ramcke was forced to endure humiliation and degradation, before finally, after his escape and voluntary return, he was placed on trial. The court sentenced the general, who was the father of seven children, to five years in prison. However the French justice authorities set Ramcke free, as the years he had spent as a captive were deducted from his sentence.

Following his release Ramcke was active as a leading employee in an industrial concern and wrote several books on his experiences during the war. He died on July 5, 1968 in Kappeln, Schleswig.

CHAPTER XXI

MAJOR HEINZ
WOLFGANG SCHNAUFER

July 13, 1950. The Mercedes convertible glided over the shining asphalt of the wide road leading from Biarritz to Bordeaux. The dark-haired, slender man with the serious, but still youthful face glanced at the speedometer. 80 kilometers per hour.

Suddenly a truck emerged at considerable speed from a side road, whose entrance was hidden by a forest cafe. Ignoring the right of way, it tried to cross the road. There was the sound of squealing brakes as the driver of the car tried to avoid the truck, followed by the dull thump of the impact. The convertible flipped over. At the same instant the truck's cargo of heavy oxygen tanks, which had been improperly loaded, rolled onto the road and into the ditch, in which the unconscious driver of the Mercedes lay.

The fire department arrived, as well as an ambulance. Some time later the duty doctor at the clinic began looking for the German's identity papers. All he knew was that the injured man's car was of German origin. He found the papers, which identified the man as Heinz-Wolfgang Schnaufer, born on February 16, 1922, place of residence Calw in Württemberg, Germany. Two days later, on July 15, 1950, the young man died. It was another forty-eight hours before his mother was informed of the death of her son.

In the small Black Forest city of Calw, news of the fatal accident involving the local hero spread like wildfire. Rumors began to circulate.

The famous night-fighter pilot had been murdered!

Belated revenge by the French resistance!

Lured into a trap!

These rumors were nourished when the French Sûreté sealed the dead man's coffin and released it to his family only after lengthy negotiations. But a subsequent medical inquest proved that the suspicions were unfounded. Furthermore, reconstruction of the accident turned up no clues which might suggest a plot or an assassination.

The population of the small city of Calw escorted the young man to his final resting place. To further honor his memory the main street of a new residential district was named after him.

February 16, 1945. It was the birthday of the *Kommodore*, *Major* Wolfgang Schnaufer. The night fighter crews waited for mission orders. The weather was bad, too bad – nevertheless they were ready to take off. "Congratulations on your twenty-third," called the men. Someone fiddled with the radio set and found a hit song, dance music.

"Where did you find that?" asked Schnaufer. "The other side. Calais armed forces transmitter." Then the music stopped and a voice came on the air.

"Hello comrades of the 4th Night Fighter Wing in Gütersloh. We admire your daring actions, but why do you go on risking your necks? Your commander is the best and most successful night fighter pilot in the world. Heinz Wolfgang Schnaufer! *Herr Major*, we beg to offer you congratulations today on your twenty-third birthday."

There was a brief pause.

The men of the night fighter *Geschwader* looked at each other in amazement. How did the English know . . .?

"You know, *Herr Major*," the voice continued, "That our bomber crews have given you the honorary title of 'night ghost.' We endeavor to be fair. We respect the enemy. And because we know that your actions are also fair we respect you. On this your birthday the BBC dance orchestra will play for you the hit song "The night ghost, the night ghost, he haunts our castle."

The night fighter crews were beside themselves. They shot down British heavy bombers almost every night, and yet here they were being congratulated by them!

Schnaufer had expected this honor least of all. It was a great distinction for the enemy to acknowledge his achievements, hold him in high esteem and speak of him with great respect. Behind the name "night ghost" there lay a high degree of respect, admiration and also a little fear of the German night fighter ace. The air force was less sentimental, simply admitting that he was the outstanding night fighter pilot of the German Luftwaffe.

Each attack carried out by the young *Kommodore* unfolded with clockwork precision. While a *Gruppenkommandeur* his unit was able to rack up the considerable total of 700 kills. It is not surprising, therefore, that the British sent swarms of Mosquito long-range night fighters especially to combat Schnaufer and his *Gruppe*, and later his *Geschwader*. Before each of their bombing attacks over the Reich they dispatched a number of aircraft whose sole purpose was to prevent these successful night fighters from taking off. Incendiary and high-explosive bombs were dropped on airfields thought to be used by Schnaufer. Success eluded them, however, for 126 heavy bombers, the majority of them four-engined Lancaster and Boeing heavy bombers, fell to the guns of the German hero of the night sky.

The weather service reported dense fog. Enemy bombers were approaching over the North Sea. Schnaufer gave his crews the order to take off. The night fighters quickly climbed through the layer of fog and found themselves beneath a clear, starry sky.

Suddenly a dark shadow appeared before him. An enemy aircraft! Schnaufer positioned himself behind the intruder and identified it as a Lancaster. The bomber was flying alone, far ahead of the main formation. As a so-called "pathfinder," it was this aircraft's job to locate and mark the selected target using parachute flares and "Christmas trees." As a rule the commander of the bomber force flew in this aircraft.

Shooting down such a "master of ceremonies" was equivalent to a battle won. For on failing to find an illuminated target area the following bombers released their bombs haphazardly, often before they reached the actual release area. Schnaufer was well aware of the possibilities. But he also knew how dangerous it was to engage in battle with the heavily-armed enemy machine. Most of those manning the rear turrets were officer cadets, young men who readily accepted any one-on-one confrontation and who were extraordinarily brave.

Schnaufer had no time to lose. The farther from the target he stopped the enemy bomber, the greater the likelihood of forcing the main formation to drop its bombs over forests or fields. He slowly approached the tail of the Lancaster. 200 meters, 100 meters. The tail gunner hadn't spotted him yet. 50 meters.

Now – Schnaufer fired his cannon. The shells struck the fuselage of the enemy machine. His second burst hit a fuel tank. Seconds later the black giant exploded. Burning pieces of the aircraft fell past the Bf 110 like gold and silver rain. The burning bomber's ammunition and illumination flares exploded, transforming the wreckage into a glowing fireball falling toward the earth.

Seconds later another four-engined bomber appeared. Schnaufer turned toward the Lancaster and dove beneath it. As he did so he fired a burst into its fuselage. The English tail gunner spotted the Bf 110 at the same instant. Although his own aircraft was now ablaze, he opened fire with his four machine-guns, scoring hits on Schnaufer's aircraft. The gunner continued firing as the blazing Lancaster plunged earthward.

The main force must come any time now! Schnaufer turned toward the northwest to meet the British bombers. In the darkness he saw a fast-moving four-engined aircraft in front of him. He moved into position beneath the bomber, matching its course, and opened fire, setting the rear fuselage on fire. But the aircraft flew on. He was now close behind the bomber. Just then the machine blew apart. The force of the shock wave was so great and the heat from the exploding bombload so great, that Schnaufer feared that the Bf 110's fuel tanks might catch fire.

For a fraction of a second Schnaufer lost control of his machine, which fell away into a steep dive, but after several difficult maneuvers he was able to recover. "We're going home," he announced over the intercom. But flight engineer Wilhelm Gänsler had sighted another Lancaster.

Although exhausted from the three previous attacks, Schnaufer crept up on the new enemy. Perhaps he was a little more nervous than usual, for he shot past the target on his first approach. The bomber's tail gunner sprayed bullets in the direction of the night fighter. The heavy bomber tried to take evasive action by climbing and diving, but Schnaufer was not to be shaken off. From thirty meters he opened fire on the British bomber and set its fuel tanks on fire.

The ground was still covered with fog when the crew landed after forty minutes in the air. Four victories in less than an hour! Worn out and exhausted, the men threw themselves down on their cots. But barely an hour later the alarm bells once again sounded in the hall: "The Tommies are coming again!"

There are some men who, although well-educated, knowledgeable and intelligent, remain dependent on others. Often they are completely helpless even in simple situations. Heinz-Wolfgang Schnaufer was the opposite type, combining keen intelligence with a pronounced sense of the practical. He was quick to comprehend, evaluating new findings and experiences with astonishing accuracy and care to the advantage of those around him, and did not shy away from unfamiliar tasks.

At the age of fourteen he expressed a desire to become an officer. He saw this career not as being cared for by the state, but as a calling. Schoolmates maintained that mentally he was three to five years ahead of friends of the same age. He graduated with honors in November 1939 at the age of seventeen.

After being accepted as an officer candidate, Schnaufer had the opportunity to fly almost every type of German aircraft during flight training. Not only did he receive first-class instruction in piloting a fighter, but was schooled in dive-bombing and instrument flying for single- and twin-engined fighters, solo and formation. Night fighter school stressed night instrument flying as well as night interception tactics. On April 1, 1941 Schnaufer was made a *Leutnant* and assigned to a front-line unit. He was just twenty years old when he was awarded the Iron Cross, Second Class for his first victory near Grenz-Donau on June 2, 1942 and the Iron Cross, First Class for his sixth. At that time he had no idea that he would accumulate another 120 victories. The German Cross in Gold was awarded to *Oberleutnant* Schnaufer in 1943 after fifteen victories. The Knight's Cross followed on January 15, 1944, when he shot down his 40th and 41st victims.

It was then that Schnaufer began his great run of success. He shot down four heavy bombers in each of five consecutive nights. On May 1, 1944 he was promoted to *Hauptmann*. The Oak Leaves were awarded on June 27, 1944, after his 80th victory, and the Swords a little later, on July 30. On October 8 he reported his "one-hundredth" and was decorated with the Diamonds.

In a single night, within the space of fourteen minutes, he shot down five four-engined bombers over Aachen! The incoming British and Americans who witnessed the slaughter of the RAF crews reported to their bases in England: "That could only have been Schnaufer!"

Captured British officers who had flown missions to Germany and fought against Schnaufer the German expressed astonishment. How was it possible that this one man and his crew stuck to the enemy night after night, and often more than once in a night, tireless and undaunted.

The English knew how difficult it was to attack a four-engined heavy bomber, because the radar and navigational aids carried by the German fighters had not been sufficiently developed. The success achieved by those fighters must be rated even higher when one considers that they flew by night in all types of weather, and in spite of unfavorable conditions accepted battle with the well-armed and protected heavy bombers of the RAF.

"British formations, suspected target Stuttgart!" There was no holding Schnaufer back when this information was received by night fighter headquarters in St. Trond in Holland. He had to try and intercept and break up the bomber stream. But the British were already deep inside Reich territory.

Schnaufer demanded everything the Bf 110 could give. Meanwhile his radio operator, *Oberleutnant* Fritz Rumpelhard, who like Schnaufer's gunner, *Oberfeldwebel* Wilhelm Gänsler, had been awarded the Knight's Cross, tried to locate the bomber stream using the new search equipment. Finally, a few kilometers from Stuttgart, the first aircraft appeared on the radar screen. Schnaufer attacked from behind and set the enemy aircraft on fire on his first pass. But he wanted to catch up with the front of the stream and shoot down the "master of ceremonies," in order to keep the main force from reaching Stuttgart. The *Hauptmann* managed to fly beneath the bomber stream unnoticed. Then –still beyond the city – a Lancaster left the huge stream of bombers and flew toward the target.

The radar operator tracked the enemy aircraft precisely in his radar set. But the crew of the bomber appeared to have spotted the German night fighter as well. The bomber evaded wildly, diving, rolling and climbing in its efforts to shake off the Messerschmitt. But it was all in vain; Schnaufer stayed with the Lancaster.

The radio operator calmly called out the distance to the target: "600 meters . . . 400 meters . . . 200 meters. Now 80 meters."

Then a brilliant flash lit the night sky. It couldn't have been caused by tracing ammunition; it was much brighter, more like an exploding fuel tank. The harsh, stabbing light blinded the crew. What had happened?

At the last moment, just before Schnaufer opened fire, the British bomber had released a flash bomb, which was intended to blind the pursuing night fighter and deflect it from its target.

At the same instant there was a crash in the cockpit.

The tail gunner fired on the now-visible Bf 110. His first burst smashed the fighter's radio and radar equipment. Schnaufer instinctively let the aircraft fall, and dove away into the clear sky beneath the Lancaster.

Where had the "master of ceremonies" gone? He had to get him, dared not lose sight of him, otherwise Stuttgart would be bombed. It was high time. Schnaufer searched the dark background. He held his course, guessing that the British would do the same. Seconds later his aircraft was bounced about as it flew through the slipstream of another machine. Then a dark

shadow appeared in front of him: it was the "master of ceremonies."

"I'm attacking!" Schnaufer called to his two companions.
He dropped slightly below the Lancaster, which flew on calmly.
Schnaufer climbed the Bf 110 slowly until the huge belly of the
bomber was right above him.

The British gunner opened fire as Schnaufer began his attack. Tracing ammunition pierced the darkness. The bullets
only just missed the target. Schnaufer saw the bright flashes
from the bomber's guns. He flew into the enemy fire. It was as
if he had no nerves at all. The English gunner must have received a frightful shock, for he had surely never witnessed such
cold-bloodedness before.

Then Schnaufer pressed the firing buttons for his cannon.
A single burst was enough to cause the Lancaster to blow up.
The bomber's deadly load, consisting of flash, illumination and
incendiary bombs, "Christmas Trees" and illumination flares,
were blown into the air, falling to earth like fireworks. Incendiaries struck the engine of the German fighter.

"We've lost an engine – it's on fire!" called Schnaufer, simultaneously switching off the ignition. They flew on with
one engine. As he maneuvered the crippled aircraft out of the
following bomber stream, another Lancaster appeared in his
field of fire, illuminated by the exploding incendiaries and
"Christmas Trees." But Schnaufer dared not approach the
heavily-armed enemy aircraft with his battered machine.

"A little faster and I'll shoot him down," urged gunner
Gänsler. The *Hauptmann* pushed the throttle forward. Faster,
Wilhelm had said. Good, he would fly faster. Then Wilhelm
Gänsler's machine-gun opened up. Continuous fire. A few
seconds later they heard an explosion. The bomber blew apart.
Meanwhile the bomber stream had reached the spot over which
hung the parachute flares, which were used to mark the bomb-
release point. The pilots of the 400 to 500 bombers no longer
had a "master of ceremonies," but they saw the "Christmas
Trees" and several burning aircraft falling to earth. Their leader
was gone – and so they dropped their bombs, not on Stuttgart,
but in the forests between Renningen, Malmsheim and
Münklingen. Schnaufer breathed a sigh of relief. The long flight

and the difficulties had been worth it. The major attack on the city had been deflected, the British bombers turned for home. Now they would be intercepted by other night fighters.

Schnaufer landed his damaged machine at Echterdingen airfield near Stuttgart. He intended to fly back to base the next day following repairs. But first, in the late evening hours, he called his mother in Calw.

"Schnaufer here."

"Schnaufer here too," said Heinz-Wolfgang.

"Son, where are you calling from?"

"I'm in Echterdingen. I was over you . . ."

"Aren't you still in St. Trond?"

"I flew right across Germany when I heard that a bomber force was going to attack Stuttgart. But I spoiled it for them . . ."

"Are you coming by?"

"Unfortunately no. My machine's just being overhauled, and I'll be flying back in a few hours. I landed on one engine."

Schnaufer's mother didn't try to change her son's mind, she knew it was pointless.

On an ice-cold February night in 1945, *Geschwaderkommodore* Schnaufer, by now promoted to *Hauptmann*, achieved his crowning success. The war was lost. The Soviets were marching on Silesia, Brandenburg and Berlin. The Reich capital lay under a rain of bombs night after night, day after day.

Schnaufer's *Geschwader* was based in Gütersloh when he received news of the approach of strong Anglo-American formations. Course: Berlin. The German fighters took off, even though they knew that their firepower was inadequate against the overpowering enemy. But they were eager to try and tear apart the mighty bomber stream, deflect it from the Reich capital. They could do no more. Naturally they would shoot down as many enemy machines as possible.

The leading aircraft of the bomber stream were nearing the outer fringes of Berlin when Schnaufer's *Geschwader* reached it.

"Attack! Just attack!" he ordered. He himself immediately dived on a four-engined Boeing. It exploded in mid-air before the enemy tail gunner could fire a single burst.

Below the city was ablaze. It had been heavily bombed the previous afternoon. Feeling the tremendous heat from the fires, the crews of the night fighters could only what tragedies might be being played out in the cellars and ruins of Berlin. Schnaufer flew until his ammunition was gone. But by then he had shot down a further six four-engined bombers. His *Geschwader* had succeeded in splitting up the huge formation, sparing Berlin from a concentrated attack. The bombs fell haphazardly in the forests, lakes and fields around Berlin. Only a few bombers succeeded in reaching the city core.

One of Schnaufer's tactics was to approach an enemy bomber from below, climb like an arrow and fire into its fuel tanks. This was made all the more difficult by the fact that the defensive gun positions of the four-engined bombers were so arranged that night fighters attacking from below could be engaged as well. Schnaufer came up with an idea which allowed him to dispense with this attack from a steep climb: mounting additional cannon in such a way that they fired vertically above. The barrels of four 20-millimeter cannon projected upwards from the canopy of the aircraft. No longer did he need to attack the enemy from in front or behind. Now he flew beneath the enemy and pressed the triggers when he had the bomber above him in his gunsight.

In March 1945, on orders from above, he evaluated the Do 335 for use in the night-fighting role. His last combat mission took place on April 9, 1945. He took off from Fassberg at 22.00 and landed 79 minutes later, at 23.19. In vain he pursued the Lancasters, which were guarded by a strong fighter escort. On April 19 Schnaufer flew cover over the base at Eggeberg while part of the *Geschwader* flew to Fassberg. This was also his last flight.

Germany's most successful night fighter pilot ended his career as a flight officer with a total of 2,300 flights and 1,133 flying hours.

Nachtjagdgeschwader 4 and its commander *Major* Schnaufer surrendered to the British. Finally they had the "night ghost," the legendary night fighter pilot who had become the terror of their bomber pilots. He became something of a prodigy. Interrogation followed interrogation. Allied flying officers came to have a look at Schnaufer. So it had been this young, good-looking man who shot down the 126 bombers!

During the war British propaganda had spread the story that Schnaufer was given with drugs (Laktal-B) before takeoff. For normally no man could withstand this nervous strain. The English considered it abnormal that a single man could shoot down four or six bombers in a single night. Something wasn't right. While a prisoner Schnaufer was asked which drugs he was injected with. When the interrogating officer was told that he had taken no stimulants he didn't want to believe it. Schnaufer was released in November 1945 following a bout of diphtheria.

But the British hadn't forgotten the "night ghost." And he was to experience an honor of a special sort. The Royal Air Force put Schnaufer's aircraft, on which was painted a tally of the bombers he had shot down, on display in Hyde Park, the most visited spot in London, inside a roped-off square. A placard was placed above the Bf 110: "This Bf 110 was flown by the world's most successful night fighter pilot, 23-year-old Major Heinz-Wolfgang Schnaufer."

British communists tried to destroy the aircraft. When they failed in this they placed a poster near the aircraft in an attempt to detract from the reputation of the German pilot. But the police intervened and the poster disappeared. Hundreds of thousands made the pilgrimage to Hyde Park to gaze in wonder at the Bf 110 and the 126 victory markings painted on it. They could scarcely conceive of how one man could shoot down 126 heavy bombers. A single man and his crew. One of the aircraft's tail fins, the one wearing the 126 victory markings, is today a prized exhibit in the Imperial War Museum in London.

Following his release Schnaufer and a number of his former *Geschwader* comrades established a transport operation in northern Germany, which they soon gave up. The first thing he did was contact his family, after which he began establishing outlets for the family's distillery and winery. At that time it was considered risky to invest even in businesses which seemed to have a future, for Germany was one great pile of rubble.

But Schnaufer had only one goal: to build up his father's firm. He had thought about it even while still in captivity. One basic element of his plan was to take as many former members of his unit as possible to Calw with him to work in his father's business. Others came later when they were unable to return to their homes in East Germany. Within two years the small distillery in Calw had become a major operation, whose "*spiritus rector* was Heinz-Wolfgang Schnaufer.

Heinz-Wolfgang Schnaufer embodied all the virtues of a good soldier. For him the ideals of a soldier were reflected, not in blind obedience, but in setting an example as an individual in discipline and order, in the respect of the dignity of man and the law, in the love of fatherland and in one's own actions.

CHAPTER XXII

FREGGETENKAPITÄN ALBRECHT BRANDI

His men nicknamed him "Cherry Brandi," trusted his good eyes, and were infected with his radiant calmness. When the Commander of U-Boats ordered him to "harass convoys in the Mediterranean," it was as good as a death sentence. Brandi nevertheless scored a fabulous success: three cruisers, 12 destroyers and 21 merchant ships, totalling 118,000 tonnes, as well as two enemy aircraft shot down.

(Many years after the war doubts were expressed about the sinking of the warships. They were not mentioned in the loss lists of the Royal Navy and therefore could not have been sunk. So much for the statisticians. Available sources, and especially Brandi's personal documents, confirm the success, however.)

No other branch of the German Armed Forces suffered such high losses in the last war as the U-Boat arm. Of the 39,000 men who served aboard submarines only 6,000 survived. One of those who did survive was also one of its bravest. For only two *Kriegsmarine* officers wore the Diamonds: Wolfgang Lüth, who was killed in an accidental shooting, and Albrecht Brandi, the last commander of the submarine battle groups.

Brandi himself said, "The awarding of the Diamonds was more a symbolic act. To be sure we have given our best and have lived through some difficult hours. But I believe that they awarded me the Diamonds because I continued to enjoy success against the enemy at a time when, by and large, there were as good as no U-Boat successes to report any more."

The blonde Westphalian with the kind face and striking blue eyes was modest enough to acknowledge that the leaders in the race to achieve the highest total of sinkings were those captains who had been hunting convoys since the beginning of the war.

The total tonnages sunk racked up by U-Boat aces Kretschmer, Topp, Mohr, Endrass, Prien, Hardegen, Liebe, Lüth, Merten, Suhren, Scheppke, Schnee, Schultze and others were achieved in the Atlantic, off the American coast or in the seas around Great Britain. Brandi, however, served in the Mediterranean, where there was little "free hunting." The U-Boats operated alone, and their objective was to pick off vessels sailing in heavily-guarded convoys. In the Mediterranean the submarines had less freedom of movement than in the Atlantic. The dense net of enemy aerial reconnaissance made it nearly impossible for them to slip through unseen. It is therefore not surprising that Brandi's U-Boat often had to remain submerged for more than eighteen hours at a time. The enemy anti-submarine aircraft, which operated from nearby bases, were equipped with the latest detection equipment: airborne radar which could locate a surfaced submarine. This made Brandi's success even more impressive. He was a specialist in attacking warships. Destroyers were the hounds which chased the submarines, and there were few U-Boat captains who would select them as targets. One of them was Albrecht Brandi, who commanded three submarines in action before being based ashore as commander of the U-Boat battle groups.

He was no Günther Prien, no beaming hero whose name was on everyone's lips and whose picture was widely circulated by the press. Brandi's mission also did not include special operations, such as Prien's sortie into Scapa Flow. His mission was to harass convoy traffic in the Mediterranean, but he was no less bold than Prien.

Albrecht Brandi first went to sea in 1935. His first voyage abroad was on the *Emden*, and before the war he served with Captain Bartels on minesweeper M 1 as I WO. The M 1 saw action during the capture of the Westernplatte at the outset of the Polish Campaign and off Norway. Bartels received the

Knight's Cross and in June 1940 Brandi was given command of the M 1, which was active in the waters off Norway. This was followed in 1941 by his "confirmation cruise" aboard the submarine commanded by the well-known Erich Topp. Serving with Topp, Brandi learned everything a commander of a U-Boat must know and be able to do. Topp, an extremely bold captain, chased allied convoys in the Atlantic and enjoyed the reputation of having nerves like "steel cable."

When Brandi received his first U-Boat in autumn 1942 his mission was to keep his eyes open in the North Atlantic. The young captain knew that his main task on this cruise was to build trust between himself and his crew, bound together as they were for better or worse. A submarine crew without mutual trust could achieve nothing, and had no hope of surviving a depth charge attack or other critical life-and-death situation. Nowhere more than on a submarine did success depend on trust, which was something the captain had to earn from his men.

At seven o'clock in the morning on August 29, 1942, U-617 left Kiel on its first operational sortie. Two other boats sailed with it. Brandi knew that the other two were equipped with devices which could indicate when they had been picked up by the enemy radar. A third set had not been available. At first he was disappointed, but then said to himself: who knows, perhaps it's just as well. By keeping a sharp lookout day and night and trusting in his luck, Brandi hoped to be able to make good this shortcoming. The three submarines sailed together until the evening of August 31, when they departed at five hour intervals for the southern tip of Norway. Finally they had done it! Alone at last!

During the voyage Brandi repeatedly delved into the contents of the red folder: orders and experiences from the war so far. It was a lot, but he had to know it in his sleep. Heavy seas made the going difficult. The wave crests were blown horizontal by the strong winds. The horizon was visible at best after every third wave. Half of the porcelain dishes had already been tossed over the side in shards. Everything not tied down had to be held onto. Against such a sea the U-Boat made only 8-9 kilometers per hour.

On September 5 the weather was still bad. The island passage, the so-called "rose garden," made its presence felt through five crash-dives necessitated by the appearance of aircraft. These dropped sixty bombs and depth charges but all fell at a harmless distance. The motion of the sea had taken on such uncomfortable forms that the 1st watch Officer was nearly tossed overboard during a nighttime alert. He landed on the deck near the ship's gun.

The U-617 was supposed to engage enemy convoys far out in the Atlantic, and contact with the enemy was to be expected after five days. The crew was thus all the happier when, on the 7th, a lookout reported: weak smoke trail off the port bow. Brandi immediately called for increased speed and set off in the direction of the suspected ship. It turned out to be a lone, small freighter on course for Reykjavik. It was a fast ship, zigzagging energetically as it sailed toward its destination.

It took six long hours for U-617 to position itself in front of the freighter. "Torpedo weapons ready! Tubes 1 and 2." But then the target altered course and it was all for nought. Brandi submerged and set off on a reciprocal course. After surfacing all that was visible of the freighter was its masts, stack and bridge. Brandi had to steam for another nine hours at top speed before he could begin a second attack. The freighter again changed course, and once more Brandi saw all his hopes wrecked. But he was on the general course of the roughly 1,400-tonne "small" freighter. It came nearer. "Tubes 1 and 2 ready." – "Tube 1, fire! – Tube 2, fire!" There was a long wait, about fifty seconds. To the crew it seemed like an eternity. Then there were two huge explosions. Beneath the surface the crew showed its relief with a loud cheer.

For days Force 10 gales and sea states of 7 and 8 prevailed. The submarine travelled submerged, for on the surface revolutions for seven knots produced a speed of only one knot. Naturally there were limits on sailing underwater with the electric engines because of the resulting lack of oxygen. The bad weather continued. The men in the submarine were tossed about, scarcely able to sleep, let alone read. The captain was concerned about the high rate of fuel consumption with no corresponding progress or opportunities to sink enemy shipping.

Brandi was assigned a new position by the Commander of U-Boats: "Proceed to St. Georges Channel." Too bad about the fuel. Brandi hoped for greater success in the St. Georges Channel. The U-Boat was welcomed by a hurricane, the like of which Brandi had never seen. U-617 had to ride out the terrific storm. The devil really was loose. Only two men could man the bridge at a time, in fully sealed diving suits, safety lines attached and wearing lead boots. Flying spray made it almost impossible to see. Brandi ran submerged by night, the rolling continued until it had reached a depth of 70 meters. Then something happened which no one thought possible: a convoy appeared. With Force 9 and 10 gales and a Sea State of 8, Brandi launched a night surface attack and sank a 10,000-tonne tanker and a 5,500-tonne freighter. Soon afterward a straggler, unable to keep up in the rough seas, came into sight. It was hit amidships by Brandi's torpedo, began listing heavily and ten minutes later sank by the stern. Brandi's luck held: the 3,600-tonne *Ronmanie* appeared. It was carrying a cargo of food, autos and gasoline for England. A textbook attack followed: two torpedoes, two hits. The Commander-in-Chief of U-Boats congratulated U-617 on its success. Brandi was now assigned a fixed area of operations and had to wait, just wait.

Two days after the sinking of the *Ronmanie* the watch officer sighted mastheads in heavy seas and very strong winds. Brandi turned toward the sighting and spotted an entire convoy, consisting of 30 to 40 steamers and destroyers. Brandi sought out the fattest target and fired: nothing was heard. The next torpedo was fired at a 5,000-tonne freighter. After a long run it reached its target and the steamer went up in a huge column of spray. The third and last "eel" left the tube. Brandi heard the explosion but saw nothing. He surfaced in order to remain in contact with the convoy. The submarine came up like a rubber ball in a bathtub. But there, 300 to 500 meters away, sat a destroyer at full stop. Brandi abandoned the attempt to run on the surface and ordered a crash-dive. The distance was so small that the destroyer hadn't attained sufficient speed to release depth charges when it reached the spot where the submarine had submerged, and U-617 had time to go deep. Then the hunt began. 104 depth charges were dropped over a six-hour period, some in double salvoes, and well aimed to boot. Nevertheless the mood on board was excellent.

After six and a half hours it was dark; Brandi took a chance and ordered the boat to surface. The destroyer was still there, again at full stop. Its crew seemed to be asleep. U-617 turned and disappeared into the night. Fuel was running low, but fortunately the order was received to head home. The submarine reached the Bay of Biscay on October 3, and five days later the boat sailed into St. Nazaire. Result: 4 steamers totalling 20,122 tonnes sunk, 2 steamers totalling 8,000 tonnes torpedoed, one torpedoed with failure to detonate. The sinkings of the first six were as good as certain. That was 28,000 tonnes, which meant six pennants!

The great slaughter of the U-Boats began in the Atlantic. The majority of the German submarines were sunk in the Bay of Biscay, between Europe and Canada and off Gibraltar. Each sailing meant a "one-way ticket to heaven" and the likelihood of returning home dropped from day to day. In May 1943 alone, thirty-eight U-Boats failed to return to their home ports. The enemy had new radar. Against this sinister enemy the submarines were helpless. No longer were guns and torpedoes and daring enough to assure success. At this time Brandi received orders to slip through the Strait of Gibraltar into the Mediterranean and harass enemy operations there. In those days the Gibraltar narrows were impassable. Anti-submarine nets and destroyer patrols made passage impossible. Yet Brandi was supposed to slip through. The young captain had no choice but to trust in luck as he set sail on this seemingly impossible mission. In the Atlantic he came upon some fat targets, many unguarded. But Brandi was not allowed to attack. The torpedoes on board were meant for ships in the Mediterranean. Sailing off the coast of Africa he witnessed a spectacle such as had never been seen before. The Americans had landed near Oran. Offshore was a tremendous mass of vessels of every type and size, from small tugs to 20,000-tonne transports, from destroyers to heavy battleships, like the British *Rodney* and *Nelson*, and aircraft carriers. All spewed out men, vehicles, foodstuffs and munitions.

Brandi slipped innocuously past the dangerous enemy, for he was on another mission. What good would it have done if he had attacked one of the big ships? He surely wouldn't have got away alive. For the enemy would have immediately located Brandi's submarine with their modern radar and destroyed it with depth charges. No, there would really have been no purpose in playing hero given the certainty of his own destruction. He set course for Gibraltar and passed through the narrows without referring to the charts. In the Mediterranean he lay in wait to attack lone vessels and transports, ignoring ships which were well-defended. But the sea between Africa and Europe couldn't be compared to the Atlantic. One couldn't operate as freely there, for the sea contained many shoals. A submarine lying on the bottom was often visible to the naked eye.

Brandi received the Knight's Cross on January 21, 1943 and the Oak Leaves on April 11 the same year. The Commander of U-Boats, *Grossadmiral* Dönitz, thought highly of the quiet U-Boat captain. He had proved to be a skilled officer on operations, achieving success in spite of heavy enemy defenses.

Brandi sailed aboard U-617 from April 1942 to September 9, 1943. In that eighteen-month period captain and crew came to know each other well. There were almost no secrets among the men. Albrecht Brandi was the one constant factor. His excellent eyesight was well-known, but even more so were the patience and determination with which he pursued the enemy, the courage with which he lay in wait, and the coolness with which he sought out and employed the best firing position.

A depth-charge attack could not only shatter the nerves of the crew – in most cases the boat was damaged, forced to surface or torn apart by the shockwaves. In such dangerous situations Brandi sat among his men and played with a stick-puppet as if nothing in the world – or more accurately under the water – could bother him. The tiny figure flipped repeatedly over the small wooden stick. This time left, the next right. The men stared at their captain. Nothing could unnerve him.

Albrecht Brandi made the puppet dance as the depth charges
fell and the boat shook, the dull rumble of the explosions clearly
audible. After the attack was over he made a point of saying,
"Well, that's that," and then put the puppet away and discussed
further operations with his officers.

The game with the puppet mesmerized the men. It had a
stimulating effect on them, and the calm which Brandi radi-
ated was passed on to the crew. Scarcely anyone thought of
the end as the depth charges rumbled and roared, no one
cracked up or lost his nerve. Extreme discipline and calm
reigned on U-617. The men trusted their captain.

Only an officer such as this could be considered for the difficult tasks which had to be carried out. Certainly Brandi, who
was called "the old fox," "the great shark" and "the silent
stalker," was well-known in Dönitz's headquarters. There were
enough bold, brave officers who wouldn't have shied away
from picking tankers and transports out of Mediterranean convoys. But – and this was the question motivating the "Operations Director Mediterranean" – did they possess the unshakable calm to creep up to radar-equipped units, attack not a
minute too soon or too late and disappear at the right moment?
Of this they were not so sure.

Most of the famous captains, those who were still alive,
had gone on to command larger units and had left the hunting
of convoys to the "young." They had sunk many tonnes of
enemy shipping, danced among the mountainous waves for
months or glided through the deeps. Submarine duty was hard
on the nerves, for the enemy now possessed defensive weapons which gave the German submarines little chance of success. Furthermore the few boats had to be spread around the
huge theater of the world's oceans. So it wasn't surprising that
the Commander of Submarines ordered *Kapitänleutnant* Brandi
to take up position in the Mediterranean.

"Cherry Brandi" had an especially good eye for ships which
were important and significant to the course of military operations. It might be a steamer carrying munitions, foodstuffs
or troops. Brandi didn't fire at every ship – he selected his victims carefully. But he stood alone against the enemy. It wasn't
the warships that he feared, but the enemy's new detection

equipment which could locate a submarine on the sea bottom, even at night and in the thickest fog. How was he supposed to creep up on a convoy or lone destroyer? Yet he did it. Once he sent three escorted steamers to the bottom in the period of twilight between night and day. The next day he spotted three corvettes and two freighters. He crept up on the enemy, measured the range and fired his torpedoes. In a matter of seconds mountains of fire spewed from the stricken ships. Sixty seconds later a destroyer steamed past. Attacking such a fast, heavily-armed, depth-charge-equipped ship was very difficult. But Brandi was an expert in underwater attack. The destroyer failed to discover U-617. The British didn't credit any German boat with the cheek and daring required to operate in waters swarming with Allied ships. Besides, there were several corvettes in the area as well. Who was going to attack them? Slowly and with infinite care Brandi maneuvered the submarine into firing position. He observed the enemy ship through the periscope. The lookouts on the destroyer appeared to be asleep. There was no movement on deck. Did the British really feel so safe? Brandi knew they were wrong. When he had the enemy ship in his sights he ordered softly, as if he didn't wish to wake the crew of the enemy ship: "Torpedoes one and two –fire!" Swift as arrows the "eels" slid through the water. In the submarine the men waited for the explosion. Running time . . .? Stopwatch . . .? Any time now. Then the boom of two explosions struck the ship's side. The destroyer fell apart like a pencil snapped in two. In the course of this Mediterranean cruise Brandi sank another seven freighters and a tug.

On August 28, 1943, U-617 sailed from Toulon. Its mission: operate against heavy warships operating just off Gibraltar. It was to be the boat's last cruise and last action. Unfortunately the nest was empty. All that he found was a destroyer, whose detection equipment soon picked up the submarine. Brandi sank the enemy warship. It all happened so quickly that the operator probably had no time to pass a report of his findings; there was no pursuit. Apparently the enemy assumed that the destroyer had struck a mine. After a time the captain sank two further destroyers at the same spot, before withdrawing to the east to give the crew a rest.

During the night of September 11/12, 1943 an aircraft suddenly appeared over U-617. It had not switched on its search equipment, as this would have been noticed immediately aboard the submarine. Apparently it had spotted the surfaced submarine in the moonlight and dropped its bombs. The third struck the water a few meters from the hull, but due to the angle of impact and a delayed-action fuse, it detonated beneath the submarine, which was raised about a meter out of the water. The lookout on the upper deck had just been able to shout "air attack," and the captain was just about to go above, when the explosion of the bomb knocked out the electricity and with it the lights. Anything made of glass or porcelain, the armatures for example, was shattered; the floor plates (which enabled the crew to walk over the tubes) were somewhere, but not over the tubes, so that feet became wedged somewhere in the darkness. Everyone wanted to get topside of course, but this was impossible because a huge stream of water shot through the open hatch and the upper ladder – coming from above – and the lower were on opposite sides. Two men couldn't climb up at the same time as the conning tower was too narrow. It seemed that everyone below in the boat was going to drown.

Chlorine gas developed from the bursting of the batteries and the inflow of sea water – but then all of a sudden the inflow of water stopped. Voices could be heard, and when the captain arrived topside, having climbed up somehow, the men who were manning the anti-aircraft reported enthusiastically that they had shot down the attacking aircraft.

Nevertheless all was not well, for the ship was completely disabled. Amazingly, no one had been hurt. In spite of all the gear which had been knocked out, Brandi finally was able to steer the U-617 toward the African coast at minimum speed. He hoped to carry out further repairs in a protected location somewhere near the coast.

Suddenly, another aircraft appeared. The submarine's anti-aircraft guns barked as it approached and dropped its bombs. The last, a phosphorous bomb, scored a direct hit on the conning tower. The aircraft did not attack a second time, apparently content to shadow the submarine at a respectful distance. The U-boat then ran aground on a submerged rock only 200 meters from shore. All efforts to free it proved fruitless. The crew were sent ashore in rubber boats. The only personnel to stay on board, apart from Brandi, were the 1st Watch Officer and *Unteroffizier* Alfred Haremsa. Both were reluctant to leave U-617 and wished to stand by their captain. They knew that the boat had to be destroyed. The explosive charge on board was only sufficient to blow a hole in the hull, which would sink the ship but not totally destroy it.

The three men finally decided to detonate a torpedo in the stern of the ship. They decided that, since the fuse was only ten minutes "long," not enough time to reach shore, their chances of survival would be greater if they stayed aboard during the explosion. The 1st Watch Officer began counting, but soon gave up as there was no way of telling how many minutes had already passed. First the small explosive charges on the individual instruments went up. Huge jets of flame shot from the conning tower. Then the torpedo exploded, destroying the entire ship aft of the conning tower. The three men found themselves in the water and swam to shore.

At the moment the ship blew up the crew on the beach had little hope for the survival of those still on board. Pieces of the vessel were thrown the 200 meters to the shore. But Brandi and his two comrades had been improbably lucky, as they were shielded from the direct effects of the blast. Their luck continued to hold, in that the oil which flowed from the submarine failed to catch fire. The three were met by the men on shore, who had themselves just taken cover from flying pieces of wreckage. At first they thought they were seeing ghosts, until they realized to their joy that the three "demolition experts" were still alive.

The first order of business now was to burn the bag of secret material which had been brought ashore in the inflatable boat. A bedouin appeared and tried to stop the submariners. He was seized quickly. After everything had been burned he was released after agreeing to lead the Germans to the nearest government outpost.

The crew, which had just spent fourteen days in their submarine with no daylight, now began a long, difficult march under the hot sun. Some had no shoes or wore only rags wrapped around their feet as they walked through trackless terrain littered with sharp stones or over rocks. But fortunately for them they had been stranded in neutral territory, namely Spanish-Morocco. They were welcomed warmly by the Spanish unit stationed there and were interned in the closest large city, Mellila. Some time later they were taken to Xuan, dressed in civilian clothes, and from there were shipped from Centa to Cadiz on the European mainland. Not until they were on the pier in Spain did the captain separate himself from his men. The 1st Watch Officer, Georg Gantier, took over while the captain slipped away discretely and joined a group of men who had previously identified themselves. He drove with them to the German naval attache in Madrid. Brandi remained there as a guest for several days while they furnished him with a passport under the name Albert Bergmann, consulate employee. Albrecht Brandi, alias Albert Bergmann, was then taken to and across the Spanish-French border.

Brandi continued on to Toulon, from there to Paris and then to Germany. Dönitz showed his appreciation for the act of friendship which the Spanish government and Franco had shown him – it couldn't be made public as Spain was a neutral country and had violated its neutrality by freeing Brandi. He had a priceless set of Rosenthal china presented to Franco.

In January 1944 Brandi assumed command of U-380, which was destroyed by enemy aircraft in Toulon harbor on March 11, 1944. Subsequently he sailed aboard U-967, again into the Mediterranean, from April to July 1944. (Brandi received the Swords on May 13, 1944.) Then he became director of submarine operations in the Gulf of Finland. (On November 24, 1944 he received the Diamonds.) With sixteen submarines under his command, Brandi was to forestall Soviet naval operations in the gulf. Nothing came of it, however, as the Soviet ships remained in port.

Talk in Germany now turned increasingly to miracle weapons. Albrecht Brandi, scarcely occupied in the northern Baltic, seemed to the senior naval commanders to be the right man to command the newly-formed special attack units. Diamonds wearer Brandi, meanwhile promoted to *Korvetten-* and then

Fregattenkapitän, accepted the new position, fully aware of the great responsibility he was taking on.

It wasn't easy for him to make clear to his men that in every action the odds would be almost 100% against them, just as they had been when he blew up U-617 from under his feet. The men understood. They had come voluntarily, not in pursuit of adventure but to fight. Even the OKM was surprised that thousands volunteered for the special attack units. Thousands! They volunteered knowing that the war was already lost and that their chances of survival were slim.

In Führer Headquarters the news that 3,000 officers alone had volunteered gave new hope that the outcome of the war might yet be altered. The volunteers were ready to take on the Allied fleet and escorted convoys in one- and two-man boats called "Seals," and as armed divers. Additional targets were bridges and supply dumps, and as well they were ready to operate in the enemy's rear until killed or captured.

With 3,000 superbly fit and battle-tested men, Brandi practiced the "multiplication tables" of naval close combat. The success achieved in the first missions was amazing. His "Seals" sank 60,000 tonnes of shipping in the Thames Estuary in the first three days. But what was 60,000 tonnes to an enemy who had carried out the invasion of France with tonnages in the millions and whose industry was running in high gear? The *Fregattenkapitän* was filled with worry. For now his own losses climbed from day to day. The time for the employment of these daring, death-defying men had passed. They had nothing with which to oppose the technically-superior enemy apart from a tiny boat, two torpedoes, their courage and their lives. Furthermore, in addition to the enemy, they had to contend with the technical inadequacy of their own weapons. Torpedoes failed to strike the target or ran in circles, endangering the boats which had launched them.

The war was lost, Germany capitulated. Brandi and his unit surrendered to a Canadian unit in Holland. He demonstrated military order from the moment of the surrender. Wearing clean uniforms, with the highly-decorated in the front rank, the men marched through a cordon of Dutch civilians and Canadian soldiers, past the flags of the victors. Brandi and his men left behind an outstanding impression, and soon afterward the *Fregattenkapitän* was named camp commandant of Ymeuiden, where every night he had to feed and shelter 10,000 soldiers. A few weeks later he was transferred to the Emden Minesweeper Flotilla, where he was placed in charge of a 12,000-man internment camp. This lasted until September 1945. Then Albrecht Brandi was a free man. It was time to build a new life.

Brandi had always been interested in architecture. Perceptively he saw that shattered Germany needed engineers, architects and technicians. He learned bricklaying with a construction firm in the Sauerland in preparation for his future career as an architect. He hauled cement, stone and mortar. After his journeyman's examination he applied for enrollment to the technical high school in Aachen. But they wanted nothing to do with the former naval officer with the highest German decoration for bravery. Their answer was brief and final: rejected because you are a militarist! He received the same answer from the state school of architecture in Essen. Brandi refused to allow this to discourage him. He had a profession with which he could keep his head above water and worked part-time in the architectural office of his cousin, Professor Brandi of Göttingen. Then he came to know the British city commandant through Essen's city architect. The Englishman saw to it personally that Brandi was immediately accepted into the Essen State School of Architecture. Brandi went into business on his own in 1950. He dedicated himself to his new mission in life with great zeal. Germany was experiencing an economic upturn, and hard work and energy were demanded of everyone. Brandi pitched in with both hands. He became a sought-after and highly-esteemed architect. Brandi designed a number of well-known buildings in his home town of Dortmund. He made a name for himself far beyond the boundaries of the city by winning numerous contracts. His friends said that rarely had a man exuded so much sympathy, love of life and humor as Albrecht Brandi. Nothing meant more to him than community life. His family was everything to him, and he was happiest with his wife Eva and their six children.

Albrecht Brandi died on January 6, 1966 at the age of fifty-one. Once, a year before he died, he said to his friends, as if he had had a premonition of death: "Even though I am a young man, I am, as it were, comparable to a man who has lived almost all of his life and who must draw up a self-critical balance of all the things he has done right and wrong..." And in the same connection: "We are not linked together by a religion or even an ideology, not by common political or economic interests, rather we understand one another through the common ideals of service, humility, tolerance, understanding and responsibility in service to the whole. These virtues are valid everywhere, timeless and therefore necessary to us today. We live in an exciting time. The old western systems were simply too limited. The security which our fathers felt behind national boundaries can no longer satisfy us. The assurances which all common people are given by an awareness of standing and property are visibly diminished, indeed all the safeguards which part of the people build against other parts will, if they are to be considered valid today, have to be overhauled tomorrow. Perhaps it's good that way."

Once, when asked his position on decorations for bravery, he answered: "The measures and acts which are acknowledged through the awarding of a decoration are performed by a sworn soldier as a matter of course. He will always be proud and glad that he had and exploited the opportunity to achieve military success. Many equally brave soldiers never had such an opportunity and often played a role in the success of those who were publicly decorated. A submarine commander always received his decorations in the name of and for his crew. Consequently I do not believe in a special group of decorated soldiers within a military community. In this day of stereotyping I am in favor of the formation of an elite, but not in respect to past achievements, rather with a view toward a specific objective."

CHAPTER XXIII

GENRALFELDMARSCHALL FERDINAND SCHÖRNER

erdinand Schörner has been the subject of more untruthful, shady and controversial press than any other general of the German Wehrmacht. Many would have had him go into the history of the last war as a monster in uniform. Not all the legends and ghastly tales were invented by the rear-echelon services, which Schörner combed ruthlessly for shirkers and by whom he was therefore hated; some were the work of communist propaganda, which systematically defamed him after he turned down an offer to become Inspector General of the East German People's Army following his release from Soviet captivity in 1955. This personally very brave officer, who had been awarded the Pour le Mérite after the Twelfth Battle of the Isonzo in World War I, was unfairly humiliated in his old age.

His services on the Eastern Front are uncontested. Schörner led with a firm hand, driving his field forces to high levels of achievement, forces which feared but also respected him, because they knew that he was concerned for their welfare. "Schörner will do it," was the watchword when the situation looked hopeless. And he did it. It is attributable to his skill as a commander and his unyielding will to defend that it proved possible to evacuate 1.6 million refugees to safety from Silesia and the Sudetenland. This historical fact alone may well offset all the accusations against him, whether they are justified or not.

When the war was over the Soviets sentenced Schörner to 50 years forced labor; released in 1955, his wife and oldest son having died while he was a POW, there followed defamation and four and a half years in prison, of which he spent two years in Landsberg. Destitute – his soldiers sent him money and food – he survived the worst of times. He wanted to be left in peace and live only in the circle of his friends. Schörner died on July 2, 1973 in Munich.

At the end of January 1955 there was a sudden uproar in public opinion in the Federal Republic of Germany. The lead articles in the West German press outdid each other in their commentaries. Rumors circulated and there was a great deal of speculation. What had happened?

On January 28, 1955 an average-sized man came back from Soviet captivity. His eyes gazed wearily through the lenses of metal-framed glasses. He wore an old, threadbare winter coat, a woollen muffler and a black beret. He was an inconspicuous man, a man like thousands of others.

The man was Ferdinand Schörner, *Generalfeldmarschall* of the former German Wehrmacht. What caused the uproar in public opinion? What moved the bulk of West Germany's commentators to attack this man? Who was he?

Schörner was born in Munich on June 12, 1892. Actually he was supposed to become a teacher. He studied foreign languages in the Universities of Munich, Lausanne and Grenoble and prepared himself for his future career.

The outbreak of the First World War ended Schörner's studies. On August 1, 1918, he went to the front as a reserve officer candidate with the King's Own Infantry Regiment of Bavaria. Within three months he was promoted to *Leutnant*.

The young Schörner was an extremely brave soldier. During the Battle of Hermannstadt he and his 12th Company barred the retreat of elements of the Rumanian 1st Army by blocking the Red Tower Passes, preventing a withdrawal to Transylvania. A year later, during the Twelfth Battle of the Isonzo, he and his 12th Company broke through near Tolmein and captured the commanding Hill 1114. The high command had not reckoned on this success and instead had made preparations for a long, hard battle. Young *Leutnant* Schörner's battle-winning action was thus of even greater significance. For this feat of personal bravery and extraordinary daring, he was awarded the Pour le Mérite, becoming the only Bavarian infantry *Leutnant* to receive the decoration. The young officer, who was three times wounded seriously, once again drew attention to himself when, on April 12, 1918, he played a major role in the storming of the Kemmelberg in Flanders.

After the war Schörner fought as a member of the *Freikorps Epp* in the liberation of Munich from the communist government and in the Ruhr. Afterward he was taken in by the 19th Reichswehr Infantry Regiment. The multilingual young officer attended classes at the military college. From 1923 to 1926 he was active as a "Command Assistant" in the Munich Military District and in the *Reichswehrministerium*. On July 1, 1926 he was promoted to the rank of *Hauptmann*, simultaneously taking command of a company in Landshut an der Isar and soon afterward in the Allgäu region of Bavaria.

In 1931 Schörner became the first German officer to be detached to the Italian Army as an interpreter, before being called up as an instructor in tactics at the military college in Dresden. In 1934 he was promoted to *Major* and a year later was made a group leader in Department 3 of the Army General Staff (foreign armies). There Schörner gained an insight into the military apparatuses of other nations and learned to recognize the methods of the various foreign intelligence services. Schörner was no desk officer. His heart was with the field forces. His fondest wish was fulfilled when he was promoted to *Oberstleutnant* in 1937 and given command of the 98th Mountain Infantry Division.

In the war against Poland, Schörner, now an *Oberst*, and his mountain infantry distinguished themselves, especially in the encirclement and capture of Lvov (Lemberg) on September 12, 1939. This operation, which was dubbed the "storming of Lvov," was characteristic of Schörner. His order: "Off to Lemberg, at Reichsautobahn speed, while creating as much dust as possible!"

Four weeks after the start of the Western Campaign Schörner was given command of the recently-formed 6th Mountain Infantry Division. The unit stood ready to take part in Operation *Seelöwe*, the invasion of England. But things turned out differently.

Promoted to *Generalmajor* in August 1940, Ferdinand Schörner once again demonstrated his tactical skill in the campaign against Greece. His mountain infantry struck destructive blows against Greek, New Zealand, Australian and English forces. On April 20, 1941 Schörner was awarded the Knight's Cross. On April 27 his advance battalion raised the Reich war flag on the Acropolis.

Schörner's favored tactic was to move swiftly and take the enemy by surprise and above all spare the blood of his own forces. His number one rule was to achieve the greatest possible success with the minimum losses. This was evidence of his great sense of responsibility, which was balanced by his concern for the welfare of his soldiers.

In June 1941 war broke out with the Soviet Union. Schörner and his 6th Mountain Infantry Division were sent to the Murmansk Front in the autumn of 1941. Following the tragic accidental death of the legendary *General* Dietl, Schörner was promoted to *Generalleutnant* and made commanding general of XIX Army Corps. The corps' mission in this treeless, ice-cold steppe was to disrupt the enemy convoys which travelled over the north cape of the Fischer Peninsula to Murmansk, and guard the nickel mines near Kolosjoki, south of the Petsamo region. During Schörner's period of action in the north there was heavy fighting as Soviet attacks were repeatedly beaten off in an area which even the tough Finns were reluctant to try and hold. Even elite Soviet mountain units brought in from the Far East were unable to break through the front held by Schörner's troops.

Another characteristic of Schörner's was that he wasn't one to lead from the background. His command post was located in the midst of his troops, even in especially difficult situations. In this war, which was fought under completely abnormal conditions, the German mountain infantry, the coastal defenses and the Luftwaffe achieved a success unique in the annals of warfare. As Schörner was well aware that fighting morale and defensive strength depended on the discipline of his forces, he made light of the difficulties of the missions given him and his soldiers with a motto he invented and which later made the rounds as a familiar quotation: "The arctic is nothing!"

Even then his reputation as an extremely strict and tough unit commander preceded him. He became the terror of the rear-echelon services, carrying out checks and ordering staff officers to the front. He soon earned the nickname "wild Ferdinand," for the man with the ever-present sunglasses, the breeches and the crooked walking stick concerned himself with every detail. His motto was: everything for the front-line troops! The way he saw it, those who fought at the front and risked their lives had the right to be properly fed and equipped. This made the general popular with the fighting forces, but feared by the rear echelon.

When Ferdinand Schörner assumed command of Army Group Nikopol in the southern Ukraine in autumn 1943, he handed over his former command on the Murmansk Front without having allowed the enemy to capture a single meter of ground.

In October 1943, as Commander-in-Chief of the newly-formed *Armeeabteilung* Nikopol, Schörner repelled every Soviet attack. Then, in January 1944, the enemy broke into the positions of the neighboring XXX Army Corps. The danger of encirclement loomed. Schörner managed to hold onto a three-kilometer-wide corridor, through which he led his men out of danger. Afterward he was supposed to hold a bridgehead on the east side of the Dniepr. Schörner considered the order impossible to carry out. Other commanders felt the same way, but dared not revolt against an order from the Führer. Schörner took matters into his own hands, abandoned the bridgehead and saved his men.

On February 17, 1944 Schörner received the Knight's Cross with Oak Leaves, and on March 31 he became a *Generaloberst* and Commander-in-Chief of Army Group Ukraine. Here too his reputation, of wanting to stand everything which had previously worked on its head, preceded him. This may be exaggerated, but it is clear that Schörner, as related by English historian David Irving in his book *Hitler and His Generals*, used unconventional methods of command. According to Irving, he interlocked one Romanian division after another into the German front, mixing the German and Romanian units so irrevocably that Antonescu (marshall and head of state of Romania) couldn't have withdrawn them even if he'd wanted to. He ordered anyone who abandoned his position shot for cowardice in the face of the enemy; if Russian tanks overran one of the last positions they were to be knocked out in the rear while the gap in the front was sealed off as quickly as possible. Every soldier who destroyed an enemy tank with a bazooka or *Panzerfaust* was immediately given three weeks leave on the mainland.

On taking command of the newly-formed Sixth Army, he found it facing encirclement and destruction in the Odessa area. Schörner called Führer Headquarters and requested permission to abandon the city. But the request was refused out of consideration to Germany's Romanian ally. The political fallout from an evacuation of Odessa could have serious consequences, for Turkey would also disapprove of this decision, quite apart from the loss of the Crimea, which would be unavoidable with the abandonment of the city.

Schörner could not accept these arguments and flew to meet with *Generaloberst* Jodl at Führer Headquarters. The hopelessness of the situation and the threat that Odessa might be surrounded led Schörner to withdraw the Sixth Army beyond the Dniepr contrary to Hitler's orders. This move enabled the Germans to establish a new front along the south side of the river. Odessa was lost but the Sixth Army was saved. The new front held until August 20, 1944.

From Army Group South Schörner was sent north to take command of Army Group Courland. But he arrived too late and was unable to prevent the Soviets from breaking through. Schörner faced a decision: either fight to the last man or withdraw and build up a new front. He made his decision: the Sixteenth Army, which was in positions north of Riga-Dünaburg, and *Armeeabteilung* Narva were to be disengaged from the enemy as quickly as possible and, abandoning the northern Baltic provinces, moved south across the Riga narrows to Courland.

But there were difficulties with Führer Headquarters, which refused to agree to Schörner's proposals. Schörner stood his ground. He saw clearly the dangerous situation in which his forces found themselves. The Sixteenth and Eighteenth German Armies were opposed by twenty Soviet armies. He therefore gave orders for the withdrawal of the Sixteenth Army and *Armeeabteilung* Narva and regrouped his forces south of Riga. Schörner's actions saved every unit to the last man and all their materiel. On August 28, 1944 he was decorated with the Swords.

Equally dramatic was the action involving the island of Oesel. *Generaloberst* Schörner knew that the island could not be held; he was also aware of Hitler's orders concerning the island. Nevertheless he dared evacuate it, even though he informed none of his officers of the plan. One day in autumn 1944 he sailed to Oesel in a motor-torpedo boat with the "Admiral Baltic," *Vizeadmiral* Bernhardi, and visited the division headquarters there as well as various officers at the fighting front.

The regimental commander of the most forward infantry unit and his staff were housed in a huge shell crater. Schörner talked with the officers and men. Based on what he was shown on maps and sketches, but primarily on his own observations and impressions, he determined that Oesel could only be held for a few more days.

During the return trip Soviet fighters attacked the vessel as Schörner was discussing the situation with his aide, *Major* Schmidt. Schmidt was wounded and the boat set on fire. There was no choice but to transfer to another ship on the high sea. The maneuver succeeded in spite of continuous air attacks. German fighters were summoned by radio, but it was hours before Schörner and his party finally arrived in the port of Windau that evening. Immediately after going ashore the *Generalmajor* dictated a message to the wounded *Major* Schmidt addressed to Hitler. He informed him that he had ordered the evacuation of Oesel as the island could no longer be held. As a result of this action 30,000 German soldiers avoided capture by the Soviets.

All of Schörner's attempts to force a corridor through to East Prussia failed. His army group was again cut off and the 26 German divisions were forced to fight off a numerically far superior enemy in desperate fighting in the Courland. Hitler's express order, that the now encircled Army Group North was to maintain an all-round defense, was accepted by Schörner. He knew that in doing so more than 100 Soviet divisions were tied down in the north and kept away from the main front. As related by historian David Irving, the German soldiers fought with exemplary bravery to the bitter end, undefeated in six large-scale and bloody Courland battles, which ended in bitter defeats for Stalin.

For *Generaloberst* Ferdinand Schörner the fateful year of 1945 began with the awarding of the Diamonds on January 1, and after the Soviet offensive from the Baranov bridgehead on January 12 made unexpected progress, with the assumption of command of Army Group Center. At the beginning of the January offensive, true to the motto "Death to the German occupiers!," Marshall Zhukov issued the following order to his forces:

> "The great hour has struck! The time has come to deliver the final, decisive blow and fulfill the historic mission which was set by Comrade Stalin: to finish off the fascist animal in his own lair and raise the flag of victory over Berlin!"
>
> The time has come to settle accounts with the German-fascist brutes. Great and burning is our hate! We have not forgotten the pain and suffering which the Hitlerite cannibals inflicted on our people. We have not forgotten our burned-down cities and villages. We think of our brothers and sisters, our mothers and fathers, our wives and children, who were tortured to death by the Germans. We will revenge ourselves for those burned in the devil's ovens, for those who died in the gas chambers, for those shot and martyred. We will exact a terrible revenge for everything."
>
> We go to Germany, and behind us lies Stalingrad, the Ukraine and White Russia; we go through the ashes of our cities and villages, on the traces of blood of our Soviet

people, who were tortured to death and torn to pieces by the fascist animals."

"Woe the land of the murderers!"

"Nothing will stop us now!"

"We have promised our dead friends, our children, not to lay down our weapons until the evil-doers are finished. The fascist robbers shall pay many times over with their dirty, black blood for the deaths, for the blood of our Soviet people."

"The time has come, comrades, to free from German slavery millions of our Soviet people who were forcibly driven into forced labor by the fascist oppressors. Their lives are in danger. And the sooner we are in Germany, the more of them we will be able to save. At the same time we will help our brothers, the Poles, the Czechs and other oppressed peoples, to throw off the chains of German oppression. In destroying the fascist animals we are fulfilling to the end our role as an army of liberation."

"The war cannot be ended as long as Soviet people languish in German slavery, as long as the German robber nest is not completely smashed."

"Comrades!"

"There remains bitter enemy resistance to be overcome. Caught in the vice of two fronts, between us and our allies, the enemy will resist with the desperation of those condemned to death. But for us defeating the Germans is nothing new. The troops of our front have already beaten them at Stalingrad and Kursk, at the Dniepr and in White Russia, at the Vistula and at the Narev. We even defeated them when they were on the advance with their accomplices, the Hungarians and the Finns, the Romanians and the Bulgarians. Now, after having been taught a hard lesson by the Red Army, they have all turned their weapons on the Germans. The German is now alone, like a hunted animal. We defeated the Germans when we were still fighting alone, but the Americans and the English, the French and the Belgians, are now defeating them together with us."

"This time the German brood will be smashed for good."

"Glorious and daring fighters of our front!"

"In order to complete this task, each of us must be brave, daring, courageous, determined and heroic on the battlefield. We are bound to act as Comrade Stalin demands of us. To force open the enemy defense in its entire depth through a combination of fire and movement, to give the enemy no time to rest, to liquidate enemy attempts to halt our advance through counterattacks, to skillfully organize the pursuit of the enemy, to prevent him from taking with him his heavy weapons, to attack the enemy's flanks through daring maneuvers, to drive into his rear, surround, split up and destroy him."

"Dear Comrades, we have everything necessary to do this."

"We are stronger than the enemy. Our guns, aircraft and tanks are better than the Germans' and we have more of them than the enemy. This first-class equipment has been given to us by the people, who through their heroic performances have assured our victory."

"We are stronger than the enemy because we are fighting for a just cause, against slavery and oppression. We are educated, organized and encouraged to heroism by our Leninist-Stalinist party, the party of victory."

"We are stronger than the enemy through the wisdom of our Commander-in-Chief, Marshall of the Soviet Union, Comrade Stalin, who directs the struggle of our people and the Red Army. We know that Stalin is with us – victory is with us."

"Our objective is clear. The days of Hitlerite Germany are numbered. The keys to victory are in our hands."

"On to the final and decisive battle, glorious heroes!"

"Through heroic acts we will increase the glory of our fighting banner, the glory of our Red Army."

"For our Soviet fatherland, for our heroic people, for our beloved Stalin – forward, comrades in arms!"

"Death to the German conquerors!"

"Long live victory!"

Schörner was now seen as a saviour. He became a legendary figure. When Schörner arrived at his headquarters on January

18 and found Reich Ministers Speer (armaments) and Dorpmüller (transport) present, he knew what they were there for. They told him in plain words of the Führer's order that the industrial region of Upper Silesia had to be held, no matter what the cost. "If we lose Upper Silesia we can make an end of it. The steel production and coal deliveries from this region are all that's keeping our war machine running," said Speer. Schörner looked at the map and wasn't frightened. Another commander with weaker nerves would probably have resigned. But Schörner said to his Chief-of-Staff, *General* von Xylander, "It will be very difficult to do achieve anything here. But in any case we must hold until the people are evacuated from the combat zone."

The ratio of German to Soviet forces was 1:7 in tanks, 1:11 in infantry, in artillery 1:20 and in aircraft 1:40. Schörner was only able to parry the continuous enemy attacks by skillfully withdrawing and giving up the industrial region which Hitler had ordered held at all costs. This was the only way the Seventeenth Army could be saved from destruction and the Soviets prevented from breaking through into Moravia. The front which Schörner commanded extended from the area south of Brunn to Frankfurt on the Oder. After lengthy consideration he decided to give up the industrial region and withdraw the Seventeenth Army to the Oder between Ratibor and Cosel.

The *Generaloberst's* soldiers assisted in and guarded the evacuation of the women and children. The refugees moved in huge columns in temperatures of minus 20 degrees, flanked by Schörner's soldiers. All those seeking to escape the Soviets marched west along the highways and the field and forest roads of Silesia. At about two o'clock in the morning on January 23, the *Generaloberst* telephoned Hitler's headquarters. "*Mein Führer*, I have just ordered the evacuation of the Upper Silesian industrial region. My forces have fought bitterly there for days; they can do no more. If we do not evacuate we will lose an entire army, and the way to Moravia and Bohemia will be open for the Soviets. We are falling back to the Oder and will hold there."

The officers around the *Generaloberst* looked at each other with concern. *Generalleutnant* von Xylander was sure he would be relieved, possibly even court-martialled and shot. For a few seconds all they heard was a slight clicking in the receiver. Schörner waited for the answer. He had resigned himself to the fact that he would be disciplined. But from the other end of the line came the voice of a tired and obviously exhausted man. "Yes, very well Schörner, if you say so. You have acted correctly." The *Generaloberst* placed the receiver back on the cradle. He ran his hand over his combed-back hair and stared at the telephone in silence . . .

In order to now save the industrial region of Moravian-Ostrau, Schörner and his troops fought a twenty-day defensive battle, and once again inflicted a destructive defeat on the Soviets. On April 3, 1945 the Soviets called off their attack and regrouped. They had gained no ground whatsoever and their losses in tanks and troops had been terrific. On April 5 Hitler promoted *Generaloberst* Ferdinand Schörner to the rank of *Generalfeldmarschall*.

On April 25, south of berlin, Schörner's troops recaptured Bautzen and Weissenberg. The Soviets suffered heavy losses. In Führer Headquarters they again dreamed of a change in Germany's fortunes. But the end could not be halted. Just before committing suicide, and after throwing Himmler and Göring out of the party and appointing *Grossadmiral* Dönitz as his successor, Hitler named Schörner to the post of Commander-in-Chief of the Army. On April 28, 1945 Hitler said of the field marshall: "On the entire front only one man has shown himself to be a true general and that is Schörner. His services cannot be rated highly enough. If we had had more such officers . . ."

The evacuation of the women and children depended on holding every city, every village and every strip of land. Schörner was now less concerned with military success than with the necessity of employing his troops to save as many people as possible from the irresistibly advancing enemy. The writers of history will one day have to declare that it was on account of the resistance of these troops that 1.6 million people were evacuated to safety from Germany's eastern provinces, people who would otherwise have inevitably fallen into the hands of the Soviets or the rebelling Poles and Czechs.

Schörner was later accused of having left his troops the day after the surrender under circumstances similar to desertion. As the story went he had put on Lederhosen and a hat and had himself flown to Tirol in his Fieseler *Storch*. In reality he had found himself a dark suit. He did not buy the national costume until he was in Pinzgau – he was photographed by the Americans wearing this. At the time the photo was widely circulated through the world press.

Concerning the circumstances of the "flight" there are two versions. One says that Schörner was simply afraid of the Soviets and didn't want to fall into their hands. According to the other Schörner was acting on Hitler's orders – although Hitler was already dead. He said that on April 24, 1945 Hitler ordered him to take command of the Alpine Front and organize it as a waiting position.

Feldmarschall Schörner issued the last order to his armies on May 5. On May 7 he released his soldiers and his staff, as well as *General der Flieger* Seidemann, who was under his command. Then came the night of May 8/9, 1945. For the first time in more than five years all was quiet. But a new mission was waiting for Schörner. He believed that war between the Soviets and the Americans was inevitable.

Schörner:

"Since the route of flight necessary to take over the Alpine Front led over the region of the Czech uprising and the area of the known Austrian Red-White-Red resistance movement, and because a forced or emergency landing was possible at any time, it was an appropriate safety measure to carry out the flight, not in a field marshall's uniform, but in civilian clothes, so as to be able to get through in case of emergency.

"On May 8 at about ten o'clock, General Staff *Oberst* Meyer-Detring arrived at my headquarters accompanied by four American officers and delivered a directive from the Chief of the Wehrmacht Command Staff, *Generaloberst* Jodl, according to which the troops were to continue to offer resistance in the Erz Mountains for a certain time, in order to enable the eastern elements of the army group to escape to the west. I was to stay out of sight during possible resistance in the Erz Mountains beyond the deadline for the surrender.

"The waiting position of the so-called Alpine Front is to be seen in connection with a report by the American journalist Drew Pearson, who twenty-four hours after a secret meeting in the State Department on April 15, 1945 wrote: `It was decided to remilitarize Germany after the war and make it a bulwark against the Soviet Union.'

"When the Soviet intelligence officials interrogated me at the beginning of my ten-year imprisonment, they brought up the events of May 8, 1945 and said: `We know that you weren't taking a walk in the Alps. You were commander-in-Chief of the alpine fortress. That is a point which interests us greatly'."

At about three in the morning on May 9 Schörner flew south in his Fieseler *Storch*. The machine landed near Mittersil in Tirol, where *Generaloberst* Guderian was supposed to be located with his staff and elements of the OKH. But as Schörner soon learned, Guderian had been captured by the Americans in the meantime. Schörner realized the hopelessness of his situation and surrendered himself to the Americans, who handed him over to the Soviets.

Schörner was sent to Camp 27 Krasnogorsk near Moscow, where anti-fascist officers demonstrated against him in front of his barracks. Finally he came to the door and shouted to them in a biting voice: "Gentlemen, if you had shown the same energy at the front, then neither you nor I would be sitting here . . ."

Schörner's stay in this camp was brief. His tour of Russia's prisons was about to begin. In Lubyanka he was interrogated for hours by NKVD Colonel Abramov, in Butyrskaya he was forced to stand for days in knee-deep ice-water, in Lefortsovkaya he came to know the special methods of Soviet interrogation specialists. In Vladimir he was locked up with hardened Soviet criminals. Conditions improved somewhat after Schörner complained about the excessively degrading and humiliating way captured German women were treated, and to his amazement his own sentence, fifty years imprisonment for helping put down the communist uprising in West Germany in 1920 and for his resistance as a "Hitler General," was reduced to eighteen years. Fellow prisoners confirm Schörner's behavior in those years. He indignantly rejected every Soviet overture to join the "National Committee for a Free Germany."

In West Germany a persistent campaign against Schörner was staged while he was still in Soviet captivity. In books and illustrated magazines the field marshall was portrayed as the "monstrous product of inhumanity, narrow-mindedness and loyalty to Hitler." Assumption, speculation, conjecture – all the stories were fiction.

"Schörner exposed as Soviet agent." "Was Schörner a Soviet spy?" "Schörner working with the Soviets." "Schörner received by Stalin." "Schörner as Soviet marshall with special missions against the West." Then the press declared that Schörner had died. A few weeks later he was resurrected as the future Inspector General of the East German Armed Forces.

There was nothing in which Schörner wasn't implicated by the press. So-called factual reporters took diabolical pleasure in using lies, defamation, insults and character assassination in their attempts to morally finish a man who was in no position to defend himself and drive him from their community. According to them, wherever he went there were soldiers swinging from trees. He degraded officers, ripped off their shoulder boards and demoted and promoted them as he pleased. The trash journalists made him into a horror figure in uniform. In reality the whole thing wasn't so much about Schörner the person. The truth is, the campaign was begun at a time when the new *Bundeswehr* (federal defense force) was being talked about, planned and in its formative stage. The specially aimed attacks on Schörner were actually directed at German rearmament. Schörner was only seen as a tool with which to whip up feelings against the forces in favor of Germany maintaining armed forces. Identifying Schörner with the *Bundeswehr* was supposed to heat up the "without me campaign." The people steering the effort were in the politburo in Moscow and East Berlin, while the "useful idiots" were in West Germany.

Schörner's release from captivity took him completely by surprise. What awaited him in Germany, apart from the painful loss of his wife and son, was a wave of rejection in the press and finally a trial, in which he was sentenced to four and a half years in prison.

The attacks reached their climax when Schörner returned. His former Chief-of-Staff, *Generalleutnant* von Natzmer (the successor of General von Xylander, who died in a tragic accident), who twice held the same position as Schörner and who had always shown great loyalty toward the field marshall, gave inaccurate accounts of Schörner's "flight from the army group." These were corrected in court. Certainly Schörner had made mistakes, but the others had too. His drastic methods were rejected by most of his fellow generals. However the "hold out to the end general," as he was also called, had his reasons for holding on grimly in the final weeks and months – namely to enable the evacuation of women and children from the danger zone. Against a cruel enemy such as the Red Army, he had no other choice. Every day, in leaflets and loudspeaker addresses, the Soviet propagandist Ilya Ehrenburg exhorted the soldiers of the Red Army: "Soldiers of the Red Army, the German women are yours. Throw their children in front of your tanks!" Or "Soldiers of the Red Army, pave the roads to the west with the heads of the Germans! Drink the blood of the blonde brutes. Kill – kill – kill!"

The field marshall and his soldiers knew what they, and above all the women and children, could expect if they fell into the hands of the victory-intoxicated Soviet soldiers. In his excellent book *Der Fall Schörner*, lawyer Rudolf Aschenauer wrote:

> "They will never forget how Russian tanks which had broken through simply ran over women and children in our fleeing treks.
>
> They will never forget the German women who, pressing tatters of clothing to their bodies, fled before the bolsheviks or swam the Oder, desperate and begging for help.

Only one example:

The 100th Light Infantry Division, a very well led and disciplined unit, was transported out of the Neisse battle zone. Only half disembarked, it stormed the small Silesian city of Krappitz and the village of Burgwasser with the convent located there, and drove the Russians back across the Oder to the east, while suffering only minimal casualties.

The scene they found was as follows:

All the men had been shot, the women and girls raped, everything plundered, bestially defiled and destroyed.

The nuns had been driven into the convent church, where they were killed and their bodies terribly mutilated.

Everywhere such unimaginable acts were committed against German people on German soil.

"In this entire tragedy and experience the German Commander-in-Chief of Army Group Center was the sole responsible figure opposing these events. His duty was to stubbornly defend every foot of ground in Silesia, in order to save the German population from the fate to be expected from the bolsheviks. Given this weighty responsibility, he had to employ all the means granted him under the rules of war, where he felt it necessary, according to his knowledge of things, according to his conscience and according to his conviction.

This was the horrible reality which assailed the commanders and troops daily and which determined the rules of warfare in those hard weeks and months of the year 1945.

Schörner had come to know this hard, new type of war in the East well enough through his own experience: in the far north on the Murmansk Front, in the great Nikopol bridgehead, in the changeable battles at the Dniepr and the Dnestr, in the Riga battle zone and in the Courland, as well as finally with Army Group Center. The decisive event of his activity as a commander was that he successfully preserved his forces and their ability to fight through even the most difficult situations. He succeeded in this mission in Silesia in the same way, but under circumstances which, at the time the assignment was given on January 17, 1945, made its successful completion appear almost impossible."

In the end, of all the countless accusations against him, the only ones which stood up were one count of murder and two counts of attempted murder.

In the first case, at the end of March 1945 he had allegedly ordered the summary execution without court martial of *Obergefreiter* Arndt, who had been found drunk behind the wheel of a munitions truck.

In this trial *Feldmarschall* Schörner had one of the best defense lawyers in Germany, Dr. Rudolf Aschenauer, on his side. In later applications for a retrial, Aschenauer was able to provide witnesses who stated that Arndt had not been shot, but had been "let off" by another officer. The witnesses had come forward after reading of Schörner's sentence in the newspapers. Statements by the witnesses matched a description of Arndt perfectly. Nevertheless, on December 10, 1962 the denazification court rejected the application for a retrial.

The other two charges of attempted murder concerned the "Neisse Case." Schörner, who had been ordered to hold Neisse at all costs, learned that the city had been lost in the early hours of March 24, 1945. The 45th Volksgrenadier Division sent a report to the headquarters of XI Panzer Corps, which led to the conclusion that the field commander in Neisse was guilty of dereliction of duty. *General* Henrici ordered a legal investigation. The result was clear: *Oberst* Sparre, commander of the defenses, bore no guilt in the loss of the city, as he had been in a hospital following a severe heart attack and later was under ambulatory care.

Schörner was furious over the loss of Neisse. According to his information the field commander had failed and his deputy could not be found. However *General* Henrici informed him of the true state of affairs. Schörner nevertheless ordered *Oberst* Sparre and his deputy shot at once.

General der Infanterie Schulz, Commander-in-Chief of the Seventeenth Army, gave instructions not to execute the two men, contrary to Schörner's orders. *Generals* Henrici and Schulz then got in touch with Schörner, who, after listening to the arguments of the two men, cancelled the order.

Oberst Sparre's deputy, *Major* Dr. Jüngling, was taken prisoner by the Soviets. What the Austrian General Svetozar

Adamovic had to say about chief witness Dr. Jüngling in the Neisse Case is interesting: "First I would like to emphasize that I do not know *Generalfeldmarschall* Schörner and have never seen him apart from photographs. On the other hand, however, the person of *Major* Jüngling is known to me from my time as a POW in Russia. I met Jüngling in 1948 in the Morschin POW camp near Stryt in the Ukraine (formerly Galicia). At one time Jüngling was supposed to go home with a shipment of POWs, but was crossed off the list at the last minute. Afterward he went to the camp's NKVD officer and declared that as a former adjutant of the commander of the fortress of Neisse he had surrendered the fortress without necessity in the latter's absence. He had thus done the Red Army a great service and as a result had been stripped of his rank and sentenced to death. He therefore was no longer supposed to be treated as a staff officer, but as a simple soldier. Jüngling told the same story to witnesses in my presence."

Schörner could have avoided all this if he had accepted the Soviet government's tempting offer. But he refused. "I have nothing to be afraid of and will hide from no one. I want nothing more than to be treated fairly. My enemies are the bolsheviks!" he said, and added, "I stand completely responsible for everything I have done. I have only served my Fatherland and done everything to hold the front against the onrushing bolsheviks . . ."

CHAPTER XXIV

GENERAL HASSO VON MANTEUFFEL

W est Point. 1968. American elite cadets in parade formation. With drawn sword the officer an nounced a small man in civilian clothes who was accompanied by generals of the US Army. The former *General der Panzertruppe*, Hasso von Manteuffel, was guest of honor and speaker at the most famous military academy in the world. Who was this man, this *General* von Manteuffel, who had commanded a panzer army in the last world war and upon whom senior officers of the American army would bestow such an honor?

On the speaker's rostrum of the German Bundestag stood a deputy with grey hair. As he spoke he underlined his presentation with sparse gestures: "Wherever he stood, the German soldier fought properly and fairly in the First as well as the Second World War. The discrimination must end against German soldiery, a soldiery which can stand the test of history!"

The man who spoke these sentences was deputy Hasso von Manteuffel, former *General der Panzertruppen*, wearer of the Knight's Cross with Oak Leaves, Swords and Diamonds. He stood in the front ranks of those responsible politicians who had dedicated themselves to the rehabilitation of the German soldier and the release of the prisoners of war held by all the victorioius powers.

One could see at first glance that former *General* Hasso von Manteuffel was a cavalryman. Nothing changed after his transfer to the armored forces, in which he rose from *Major* to be the commander-in-chief of a panzer army during the war. He was seen as a cavalryman of the old school, was feared because of his readiness to strike and was liked because of the precise, extremely brief way he issued orders.

The name von Manteuffel has a favorable ring in Prussian history. The Manteuffels provided the soldier king and Frederick the Great with excellent officers and generals. Born on January 14, 1897 in Potsdam, the son of a guards officer, Hasso von Manteuffel was destined for the same career as his father, grandfather and great-grandfather: the life of an officer. After attending the cadet institute he joined the Zieten Hussars, which were based in Rathenow. There he became an officer candidate. The First World War saw Hasso von Manteuffel serve on the Eastern and Western Fronts. he was promoted to *Leutnant* in 1916. After the war he fought on, now in the *Freikorps* against the Spartacists. In autumn 1919 he was taken into the *Reichswehr* as a *Leutnant*. His duties included detachments to cavalry units. The enthusiastic rider seemed attached to his horse, and his name was closely associated with tournament riding. Among his awards were the German Reich Sports Badge in Gold (1939) and the German Rider's Badge in Gold (1931). As a jockey he enjoyed an outstanding reputation in the international turf world. Wherever he turned up, the small cavalryman with the hooked nose was the center of attention.

On April 1, 1934 von Manteuffel was promoted to the rank of *Rittmeister*. He had in the meantime been transferred to the 17th Cavalry Regiment (Bamberg) and, after volunteering in 1934, to a new branch of the army, the "fast troops." Von Manteuffel brought his former cavalry squadron to Eisenach, where it became the 2nd Panzer Division's 2nd Motorcycle Battalion. The German Armed Forces were to be made the most modern in the world. When, in 1938, von Manteuffel, now a *Major*, was transferred to the Army High Command (OKH) as advisor for motorization, he was already showing signs of what he would translate into reality in the field several years later: this officer went into military history as one of the most capable, brave and successful armor commanders of all time. From 1939 to 1941, as commander of the instructional staff of the 2nd Armored Forces School (Krampnitz, near Potsdam), he instructed officer candidates destined for infantry and armored reconnaissance units in courses lasting several months.

In May 1941, by now an *Oberstleutnant*, he took over II Battalion in the 7th Panzer Division's 7th Rifle Regiment. Von Manteuffel requested this post, even though his rank entitled him to command a regiment. In August 1941 he became commanding officer of the same division's 6th Rifle Regiment, with which he achieved noteworthy success. While leading the regiment von Manteuffel distinguished himself through his bravery and personal courage, and through his cold-bloodedness and decisiveness in situations which many would have considered hopeless. His ability to react quickly saved much blood in his own ranks and caused the enemy heavy losses. The small commander with the figure of a jockey became the terror of the Soviets.

The decisive phase of the first part of the campaign against the Soviet Union began on October 2, 1941. The Desna was crossed and Vyazma was the next objective. This city in Army Group Center's area of operations was the hinge point for the operations planned by the German armed forces command and lay on the road to Moscow. In spite of the heavy blows inflicted on them by the German forces, the Soviets recovered quickly and put up fierce resistance against the enemy advance. The objective of the German command was to reach the highway to Moscow north of Vyazma before the Russian winter set in. At that time von Manteuffel was still commanding the 7th Panzer Division's 6th Rifle Regiment. After piercing the Soviet lines von Manteuffel drove as far as the highway, exploiting the confusion which reigned among the defenders and at times advancing on the same road being used by the retreating enemy, and on the evening of the same day, October 6, 1941, entered Vyazma and prevented the enemy from breaking out. This action closed the pocket around the Soviets and created the consitions necessary for the subsequent advance on Moscow. All efforts by the enemy to break through the encircling ring by attacking from the west and east failed on the bravery of the battle group led by von Manteuffel.

Manteuffel preferred surprise attacks and audacious operations. He recognized immediately that the enemy could only be driven back by a disguised, surprise attack. Rifle in hand, he creapt toward the defenders at the head of his regiment. Surprise was achieved. Such was also the case near Jakroma, where von Manteuffel and his battle group stormed the bridge across the Volga-Moskva canal west of Moscow before it could be blown by the defenders and occupied the Kremlin's power station. For this he received the Knight's Cross on December 31, 1941 as well as a simultaneous promotion to *Oberst*. As the army command had no more reserves, the bridgehead east of the canal had to be abandoned two days later and the bridge blown. At the same point in time the Soviet forces launched their winter offensive north of Jakroma, as a result of which the front had to be withdrawn.

When *General* Model, then commander of a panzer corps, threatened to bring von Manteuffel before a court martial because he, acting on his own, had pursued fleeing Soviets with his battle group instead of carrying out another order, he answered curtly and tersely: "You can do that, *Herr General*, but not until I have defeated the enemy."

In fact Model pushed for a trial, but von Manteuffel's friends in the OKH stepped in to prevent a scandal. Years later, when the two faced each other – one as the commander-in-chief of an army group, the other as commander of an army – Manteuffel said on his first visit, "*Herr Generalfeldmarschall*, you can be certain of my loyalty." Model, curtly, as was his fashion, answered, "Thank you," and gave von Manteuffel his hand.

Hasso von Manteuffel was surprised, when in November 1942 he received orders to "help out" in Tunis. Promoted to the rank of *Generalmajor* in the meantime, he commanded the "Manteuffel Division" there. Prior to the surrender in Africa (May 13, 1943) he returned to Germany following a collapse due to exhaustion. In August of that year he assumed command of the 7th Panzer Division, the unit in which he had "grown up." He knew 90 percent of the officers and 50 percent of the NCOs there by name as well as their family affairs.

Von Manteuffel was an opponent of hastily-conducted withdrawal movements in the waging of mobile warfare. he saw no reason to give up ground as long as he still had reserves. On November 27, 1943 he recaptured Zhitomir from the Soviets in a surprising, audacious and tactically brilliantly-prepared and executed night attack. For this extraordinary act, which was associated with exemplary personal bravery, von Manteuffel was awarded the Oak Leaves on November 23, 1943. He was described in the divisional history as the "Hero of Zhitomir." The commander of the 7th Panzer Regiment, *Oberst* Adalbert Schulz, also distinguished himself in these battles, for which he was awarded the Diamonds on December 14, 1943.

In spite of the bravest defense the front could no longer be held. The commander-in-chief of the army group called for orderly withdrawal movements. The Soviets followed up immediately and tried to infiltrate into the resulting gaps, a tactoc of which they were masters. But they hadn't reckoned on von Manteuffel, who repeatedly halted their attacks in spite of the onset of cold and snowstorms. Thanks to the courageous actions of his forces, who revered him, the army group was able to conduct its withdrawal unhindered. Von Manteuffel's division had become indispensable in its role of mobile fire-brigade. Near Korosten the 7th Panzer Division took on an entire army. Here von Manteuffel gave an admirable display of the classic method of conducting warfare, coupled with clever and innovative counterattacks and outflanking maneuvers. His panzers turned up where the Soviets least expected them, while his grenadiers held the critical points at which the Soviets repeatedly attempted to break through. Thanks to the inspired leadership of *General* von Manteuffel the Soviets failed to break through the weak German positions. His skill in making the Soviets believe that he possessed much stronger forces than he actually did, in occupying pre-attack positions as inconspicuously as possible, and in attacking with lightning speed, guaranteed him great success.

In December 1943 von Manteuffel was ordered to Führer Headquarters, where he was placed in command of the *Grossdeutschland* Panzer-Grenadier Division and instructed to make it the most powerful panzer division in the army. Hitler agreed to von Manteuffel's suggestion that the division retain its former name, under which it had achieved great success and won acclaim. However the general requested that the new posting be delayed. His 7th Panzer Division was involved in extremely heavy fighting, and he feared that without the command it was used to, success could not be assured.

Von Manteuffel himself would prepare for a smooth handing over of the division to his successor. Finally, on January 24, 1944, von Manteuffel passed command of the division over to Adalbert Schulz, former commander of the division's panzer regiment and now a *Generalmajor*. Six days later, following his promotion to *Generalleutnant*, von Manteuffel took command of the *Grossdeutschland* Division. On February 2, 1944 Hasso von Manteuffel was awrded the Swords for outstanding achievements and his command of the 7th Panzer Division in the Battle of Korosten.

Von Manteuffel's fully-motorized grenadier units allowed the Soviets to advance, then attacked their flanks and formed small pockets behind the enemy front. This tactic created the impression among the Soviets that their attack spearheads had been cut off and destroyed. Their immediate reaction was to pull back their forces and regroup. But von manteuffel gave the Soviets no time. He attacked repeatedly, disrupting preparations for fresh attacks and giving the main body of the army group a chance to reorganize. When the order to pull back came he conducted out a fighting withdrawal, defeating all encirclement attempts by the Soviets.

Hasso von Manteuffel was a line officer. He didn't pass through the general staff school as one might have assumed from his talent in the tactical conduct of warfare. He grew up in the field forces. His skill as a commander, his daring and his bond with the soldiers were qualities which helped him achieve a high standing. When asked after the war why he had been so high regarded by Hitler, he replied, "Because I knew how to take him. I had no fear of him, and one needed to have no fear if he was to fearlessly speak his own mind to him."

Von Manteuffel's skill in commanding mobile forces led the Wehrmacht High Command to employ him in the western theater and entrust him with an army – which was accompanied by promotion to *General der Panzertruppen*. In September 1944 the OKH gave him command of the Fifth Panzer Army, which had previously been under the command of *SS-Oberstgruppenführer* Sepp Dietrich. Von Manteuffel was to use this army to break through the Anglo-American positions in the Ardennes Offensive. Hitler's aim was to destroy Eisenhower's troops south of the attack's point of penetration. He counted on the demoralization of the American forces, Eisenhower's inability to direct major operations and the longer supply lines on which his armies depended. This false assessment of the enemy, as had so often been the case on the Eastern Front, was to have tragic and shocking consequences.

In the struggle against the Americans Hitler childishly underestimated their materiel superiority. He refused to believe, indeed didn't want to believe, that the Americans possessed the best-equipped and most modern army in the world, and that they could produce literally endless quantities of materiel, munitions and foodstuffs, while his own forces sometimes received minute quantities of munitions, had no fuel and depended on a supply system which scarcely functioned at all any more. Furthermore the Allies enjoyed total superiority in the air. Hitler was incapable of seeing that the German armed forces were fighting a "poor man's war," especially on the Western Front, which should have been stopped long ago in order to spare human lives. Nevertheless, the bravery of the German soldiers was admirable and caused surprise and incredulity among the senior American command staffs. Anyone who held on under a hail of bombs and shells, defended and even went to the attack – as the Germans did – must be fanaticized. Thus, all of a sudden, Eisenhower's troops were fighting against "nazis," a term which became synonomous with stubborn bravery, fatalism, unpredictability, stubbornness and – quite unjustly – cruelty.

For von Manteuffel there was now only one mission: attack and defeat the enemy. His Fifth Panzer Army was the first to break through. As always the panzer general led from the front; small wonder that his Kübelwagen was three times shot out from under him. After initial success and rapid progress the attack bogged down before Bastogne, as it could not be adequately supplied with troops, weapons and munitions. The enemy, superior in personnel and materiel, had won the race for reserves. Furthermore the enemy air force harrassed all troop movements. Personal action and bravery at the focal points of the battle were no longer enough. Even von Manteuffel's most cleverly-contrived strategems could not turn the tide. For the services he had performed as commander of an army in spite of the unfavorable circumstances, von Manteuffel became the 24th member of the German armed forces to receive the Diamonds, on February 18, 1945.

A month later he took over as Commander-in-Chief of the Third Panzer Army on the Oder Front. Following a difficult fighting withdrawal, all the while under constant attack from Soviet tank armies, he reached Mecklenburg. Von Manteuffel knew that British troops were in his rear. He wished to surrender to them and not to the Soviets. In those days there was no longer a battle to decide, the war was long lost. What was at stake now was naked survival, escaping the clutches of the Soviets. For this reason, and only for this reason, von Manteuffel allowed his 300,000 soldiers to stream back through Mecklenburg, rather than toward Berlin as Hitler had ordered. There was nothing left to defend there, on the contrary, von Manteuffel's soldiers would either have been destroyed or taken prisoner.

The general negotiated with the British and reached an agreement whereby the bulk of his army was allowed to surrender to them. The welfare of his soldiers remained von Manteuffel's highest duty to the end. The men revered and respected him, because they knew that he did everything humanly possible to ease the burdens of everyday life in wartime.

At the time of the surrender von Manteuffel wished that the western powers would one day acknowledge that Germany's struggle against bolshevism had not been for nothing. During interrogation by British and American officers, he never stopped warning them against the Soviets, whom he characterized as Europe's enemy.

Von Manteuffel spent two years as a prisoner of war. He

was one of the few well-known army commanders not to appear on the Allies' "black list" of war criminals. Retired *General* Hasso von Manteuffel now faced the need to search for a civilian occupation. A friend helped him get a start, reccommending a large industrial concern. The manager had no qualms about taking von Manteuffel as an employee. He called a meeting of the works council, explained the former general's situation and reccommended that they give him a chance. The works council agreed. In a short time von Manteuffel became head of the export department.

The former general knew that public life needed capable men who were ready to accept responsibility. For this reason he joined a political party (the FDP) and sat as a member of the German *Bundestag* from 1953 to 1957. In a five-day jury trial which began on August 17, 1959, von Manteuffel was found guilty of murder and sentenced to one and a half years in prison. The trial caused a sensation among former soldiers. The court reached its decision, even though it admitted that the general had been loved by his troops because of his great concern for them, that he had been an outstanding commander and had personally been extremely brave.

What had happened? The 7th Panzer Division was engaged in heavy fighting in the Shepetovka area against an enemy enjoying a seven-fold superiority in numbers. It had been committed as a mobile "fire-brigade" by *General* Balck, commander of XXXVII Panzer Corps. Ceaseless attacks by the Soviets seemed to be wearing down the will to resist of the German soldiers.

The division moved into position on January 11, 1944. Shepetovka, important rail junction, and so to speak the rail terminus for the central front, was extremely valuable to the conduct of the war.

There was no longer a continuous main line of resistance; it had been replaced by individual strongpoints manned by infantry. There was a great danger that the Soviets might infiltrate into the open areas during the night. And as they were masters of infiltration, von Manteuffel issued orders for the troops to remain especially vigilant in their positions, particularly at night. According to the division medical officer there were more than a thousand wounded in Shepetovka, and their fate would be sealed if the Soviets were to take the town. In front of one company's sector there was a large haystack. The company turned it into a forward outpost, positioning a squad there commanded by an NCO. During the night a Soviet patrol with a horse-drawn sleigh approached the haystack. The NCO was outside at the time, and he and another soldier were captured by the Russians. Although two men manning another outpost saw what happened, they did not fire nor did they alert the unit so it could free the captured men. The next day von Manteuffel learned of the incident while visiting the command post. He ordered both soldiers arrested and convened the division court martial. This cleared one soldier, while the other, because he could not be accused of cowardice in the face of the enemy, was sentenced to two years imprisonment for dereliction of duty in the field.

General von Manteuffel requested the death sentence for the man sentenced to two years, the one who had stood by and watched his NCO being taken prisoner. He believed that the man had broken the unwritten rule, that every soldier, no matter what the situation, must be able to depend on his fellow soldiers to fulfill their duties to the full. He saw the danger, that in similar situations in the future men on sentry duty in the field might act as this man had done, and allow the Soviets to easily infiltrate their lines and pose a threat to the usual quiet time at night, which the men needed for rest and supply. He considered the act serious enough to make an example of the man and thus solidify the morale of his division. On January 13 the guilty man was shot.

Von Manteuffel was one to quickly disregard any Führer Order which went against reason. As a division commander in Tunis he had prevented the carrying out of one such order, the so-called "commando order," which decreed that enemy troops in German uniforms were to be killed. Nevertheless he was found guilty by a jury court of having caused the death of the soldier. He had intervened in an undecided hearing and had caused it to invoke the death penalty. His actions were based on the belief that Führer Order No. 7 entitled him to do so.

The court observed that, given the favorable assessments of his character by witnesses, there were no grounds to assume that the accused had consciously tried use an obligation to follow this Führer Order as an excuse for justifying his actions. According to the court's findings the accused was also unaware of the illegality of his actions.

The court also determined that von Manteuffel had pushed for the death penalty in order to help raise the fighting morale of his division in a critical situation. Futhermore he had seen the actions of the sentry, who allowed his NCO to fall into the hands of the enemy and possibly cost him his life, as an offense against the law of front-line comradeship. "He therefore acted out of sincere motives." (A quote from the judgement of the court.) He was also wrongly convinced that his action was justified by Führer Order No. 7. In justifying its decision the court further acknowledged that von Manteuffel had served meritoriously during the war, had shown concern for the troops under his command and had not spared his own life.

More than fifteen years had already passed, and as befitted the legal state of the limitations of criminal prosecution, the need for atonement was not as great. In the opinion of the jury court von Manteuffel had not acted out of dishonorable convictions.

The press was almost unanimous in declaring that it was asking too much of a court to expect it to delve deeply into a matter it had not experienced itself, after a period of fifteen years. The *Hamburger Abendblatt* wrote at the time: "He (Manteuffel), is also a tragic figure in this tragic episode. He has freely acknowledged this and has accepted responsibility – with one qualification: perhaps he erred."

The *Würmeler Tageblatt*: "It is our opinion that it is difficult, if not impossible, to weigh everything in such a way that it is done fairly, fifteen years after the fact... Trials against former concentration camp criminals are something quite different from one such as the Manteuffel trial. Those serve to restore conventional norms, this deals with what was then a valid norm, namely that a responsible commander must employ every possible means to protect his country from enemy troops. If we once again build up an armed forces we shall do exactly the same thing today. In this case a lack of discipline cannot go unnoticed. It's just that one sees it differently in peacetime than in war."

Von Manteuffel began serving his sentence in Landsberg in July 1960 but was released after two months. A number of prominent figures, in particular the former federal president Professor Theodor Heuss, had spoken out on behalf of von Manteuffel's release. One year Von Manteuffel received no pension. Later, by way of grace, he received a subsistance allowance, revocable at any time, by way of the president. Heuss: "It seemed to me that a truly tragic conflict existed when *General* von Manteuffel made his decision. From a humane point of view I would be pleased if in this case the supreme right of justice, mercy, was applied to a man whose professional life was otherwise above reproach and who demonstrated a noble ability in his common affairs."

Hasso von Manteuffel after the trial: "To me the decisive point seems to be: in crises and conflict situations such as this, especially in such 'borderline cases,' the mutual obligation of human loyalty forced the responsibility-laden military commanders in the east to take hard measures in the name of maintaining their credibility as commanders. For in my opinion those soldiers still willing to carry on and fight, who fulfilled their duty to their comrades-in-arms regardless of the threat of death or capture, had a right to expect that their military leaders would protect them by stepping in hard against those who failed. The obligation to human loyalty binds the responsible officer all the more, that is all the more forcefully, the higher his position and the greater his responsibility for the troops under his command. This is what the front-line soldier understands by 'comradeship,' and what separates the so-called 'good' divisions from the others. Every man, every NCO, every officer knows that he can count on his comrade to do his duty fully, especially in crisis situations. This is, was, and remains the immortal, timeless comradeship of the front, which for so many soldiers became a valuable experience of helping readiness to sacrifice. It is based on strict, pitiless necessities, not without fear by the way, and lives in the turning of one's path to death, sacrifice and selflessness. More than anything 'comradeship' means 'the ability to sacrifice' for the others!"

Following his release von Manteuffel was invited to go to America on account of his good connections with senior military personalities in the USA (forged while a member of the defense committee during his time in the German Bundestag). He made nine trips there, every year for about four weeks, speaking at West Point, at various universities and to the members of the McArthur memorial in Norfolk, Virginia, site of a NATO school for staff officers. Von Manteuffel received an invitation to meet former President Eisenhower and spent three days as his guest. He met with Generals Bradley and Bruce Clark several times. Later, following an invitation from Montgomery, he met the British field marshall. The Tactical Air Force placed an aircraft at his disposal, with which von Manteuffel flew back and forth across the entire United States.

General Westmoreland held a dinner for him in the Pentagon, and he formed a close friendship with General Abrahams, his opponent at Bastogne in January 1945. Von Manteuffel has been immortalized in wax in an American armed forces museum near Bastogne (Bastogne Historical Center). A book entitled *Panzer Baron* sold well in the USA and received favorable reviews in the press.

One day von Manteuffel was surprised to receive from General Bradley a neatly-bound set of photocopies of the briefs he had written in 1934. They had been in the Military Central Depot in Washington.

Hasso von Manteuffel died on September 24, 1978.

CHAPTER XXV

GENERAL
THEODOR TOLSDORF

He had had it with the hospital: In July 1976 he had broken his right leg, several years after suffering a fractured skull in an auto accident and soon afterward having his foot crushed by a falling beam. And this was after being wounded fourteen times in the Second World War, including being shot in the stomach and head and losing half a foot. Nothing could take the starch out of this man.

Theodor Tolsdorff, East Prussian, infantryman, became a general at the age of thirty-five in January 1945, commanded a division in the winter of 1944 and a few months later, following promotion to *Generalleutnant*, a corps. He was an extremely courageous officer, who never lost his composure and always found a way out, even in the most muddled situations.

Theo was five years old in autumn 1914, when he and his mother had to flee the Lehnharten Estate before General Rennenkampf's cossacks. The cossacks are coming! It was a cry of terror in German East Prussia eighty years ago.

Father Theodor Tolsdorff, a *Hauptmann* in the artillery, returned to the Lehnharten Estate after the war, but the war had left him a sick man and he was unable to leave his bed. Finally, on October 11, 1919, he died. Theo went to school in Königsberg. Later he became a farmer. Studying hard in night classes and winter school, Tolsdorff went on to become the administrator of an estate. His employers were very satisfied with his work. He was eager to learn, for a large estate awaited him at home. Tolsdorff soon recognized the crisis in which German agriculture found itself. He first wanted to complete his military service, then he would decide what to do. But Theo Tolsdorff never returned to the estate. When he joined the 1st Infantry Regiment in Insterburg as a volunteer in 1934, it was not his intention to become an officer. However on June 1, 1936 Tolsdorff was promoted from the ranks to *Leutnant*.

During the Polish Campaign Theodor Tolsdorff led the 14th (anti-tank gun) Company of an infantry regiment. His first feat as a commander occurred on September 2, 1939. The Poles were defending the Gora Kamienka, a bunker line, grimly and with unexpected tenacity. When Tolsdorff saw the German attack fail, he decided on a tactic which the enemy wasn't prepared for. In spite of heavy enemy fire and a total lack of cover, he and his company drove up in front of the Polish bunkers and opened fire with their 37mm anti-tank guns. The gunners kept firing until the Poles gave up. Tolsdorff was awarded the Iron Cross, Second Class for this action. Soon afterward a group of surrounded Polish forces tried to crack the German ring and break out. Spearheaded by a cavalry division, they launched a night attack on the German positions. Tolsdorff recognized the enemy's intentions and shot up the attackers from close range, preventing a breakout. His actions were rewarded with the Iron Cross, First Class. In the final days of the campaign Tolsdorff was wounded in the shoulder but remained with the troops.

After the campaign in Poland Tolsdorff's unit was transferred into the Rhineland as part of the army reserve. In the war against France his unit fought in Belgium, drove to the Flanders pocket then south past Paris to the Saumur area. Following the cease-fire he and his unit were transferred swiftly to southern France, where they remained as occupation troops in the Bayonne-Biarritz sector. At the beginning of August Tolsdorff's wounds broke open again, and he was forced to enter hospital. He remained there until October, when he rejoined his unit, which had meanwhile been moved to East Prussia.

When war against the Soviet Union broke out on June 22, 1941, Tolsdorff and his men stormed through the Baltic States.

Tolsdorff assumed command of a battalion when its commander was wounded. The attack would have ground to a halt had he not taken charge. The day's objective was reached, but *Oberleutnant* Tolsdorff was wounded. He was awarded the Knight's Cross on December 4, 1941 while in hospital. On April 20, 1942 he returned to his unit. Heavy fighting raged for possession of Schlüsselberg. Soon afterward, however, Tolsdorff lost half his right foot while leading a daring assault on the shore of Lake Ladoga. In June 1942 Tolsdorff's battalion played an outstanding part in the closing of the Volkhov pocket, for which he received the German Cross in Gold. On the last day of the battle he was wounded in the head by a bullet. Tolsdorff was forced to remain in hospital until September 20, 1942.

It was in the course of the Volkhov fighting that the Commander-in-Chief of the 1st Siberian Army, General Vlasov surrendered to the Germans. Vlasov later made a name for himself by forming a force of captured Soviet soldiers to fight on the side of the Germans. After the war Vlasov and his men were handed over to the Soviets by the western allies.

When Tolsdorff returned to his unit a bitter defensive battle was raging at Lake Ladoga. He and his unit helped fight off a major Soviet offensive in January 1943. The enemy were unable to crack the German front; instead they were met and driven back. The heavy losses which the Soviets suffered in this second battle forced them to halt. However in July they attacked again with fresh forces. The third and most difficult battle at Lake Ladoga began. After fourteen days of extremely heavy fighting the battalion had not lost a single centimeter of ground and had inflicted heavy losses on the Soviets. It had also participated in counterattacks in the neighboring sector, driving the enemy back and restoring the situation. On September 15, 1943 Tolsdorff was awarded the Oak Leaves for his role in the German defensive success at Lake Ladoga.

On New Year's Eve 1943 the 1st Infantry Division was transferred into the southern sector, the Vinnitsa-Odessa area, as the forces there were insufficient to repulse the enemy. In the course of the heavy fighting there, Tolsdorff took command of the 1st Infantry Division's 22nd Infantry Regiment after its commanding officer, *Oberst* Iffland, was killed. Then he was shot in the stomach from close range. In spite of the serious nature of the injury Tolsdorff was back with his soldiers after only a few weeks. They wondered where this man found the strength to overcome all the physical pain and the associated mental stresses. Theodor Tolsdorff was promoted to *Oberstleutnant* in Lublin hospital. After recovering from his wounds, Tolsdorff was sent to the officer cadet school in Metz as an instructor in tactics. The move was intended to spare him from further injury. However after only three days Tolsdorff requested a transfer to the front; the garrison atmosphere was not to his liking.

On June 22, 1944, on the exact anniversary of the start of the war in the East, and following a tremendous preparatory artillery bombardment, the Soviets launched a mighty offensive against Army Group Center. The Soviet objective was to break into the Reich itself, followed by an expansion of the offensive and the capture of Berlin. The thinly-manned front collapsed under the heavy blows inflicted by the enemy, and the Soviets neared the East-Prussian border. *Generaloberst* Reinhardt, commander of the Third Panzer Army, which had to fight off the heaviest thrust by the attacking Soviet spearheads and which lay in the focal point of the offensive, was the first to try and stabilize the confused situation. Together with *Generalleutnant* Heidkämper, its capable Chief-of-Staff, it succeeded in at least partly in turning the army's flight into an organized retreat.

In this situation Tolsdorff received orders to defend the city of Vilna. He scraped together alert companies and personnel on leave into a regimental-strength unit and set out toward the former Lithuanian capital. On the way, he determined that strong Soviet formations had inserted themselves between him and Vilna, too strong for him to break through with his limited forces. In Vilna, meanwhile, *General* Stahel was the battlefield commander. In Vilna were various hospitals containing thousands of wounded. Under no circumstances could they be allowed to fall into enemy hands. Tolsdorff received orders to form a pocket, in order to enable the evacuation of the wounded when the army gave the order to do so. After a few days the strength of Battle Group Tolsdorff was so diminished that the end was in sight. Tolsdorff informed the army: "It can't go on!" In this situation *Generaloberst* Reinhardt radioed: "Hold on. Coming with two divisions."

The *Generaloberst* came, leading the 6th Panzer Division and the *Grossdeutschland* Panzer Regiment. Both units had been in the process of departing for the West. At the last minute they were stopped and unloaded. While all of the 6th Panzer Division was committed, only elements of the *Grossdeutschland* Regiment took part in the battle. Diamonds wearer Hyazinth Count Strachwitz drove with the regiment's leading tanks as the attack unfolded. The Soviets immediately tried to encircle the German formations which had suddenly began moving east. They employed artillery and tanks in an effort to smash the attackers. It was not enough: units released from other sectors joined the German battle group. The two divisions under Reinhardt's command drove through the Soviet encircling ring just as it was beginning to take shape. The wounded remained in the center while Tolsdorff's men fought off the enemy assaults in a desperate rearguard action. This action resulted in his promotion to *Oberst* and the awarding of the Oak Leaves with Swords. Tolsdorff was the eightieth German soldier to receive the decoration.

Although the majority of the men had to swim across the Düna and its tributaries, losing uniforms and items of equipment in the process, a few weeks later Tolsdorff's soldiers were reclothed and back at the front. As a result of their efforts most of the wounded in Vilna were saved.

In early August, when Tolsdorff went to Führer Headquarters to receive the Oak Leaves with Swords, Hitler personally ordered him to go to Hirschberg for a division commanders course being given there. At the beginning of September, after completion of the course, Tolsdorff received orders from the OKH to go to Thorn, East Prussia, to oversee the formation of the 340th Volksgrenadier Division. In mid-November the unit was moved to the Aachen-Jülich area where it halted the American advance and prevented US forces from crossing the Rhine. In December the division was withdrawn from the front and moved into the Eiffel Mountains, where it made preparations for the Ardennes offensive. The division fought as part of the

Fifth Panzer Army, which was commanded by *General der Panzertruppen* Hasso von Manteuffel. Before Bastogne the 340th Volksgrenadier Division's attack was halted by heavy allied bombing. Afterward the division withdrew and crossed the Rhine near Andernach.

On March 18, 1945, Tolsdorff, who had been promoted to the rank of *Generalmajor* on January 30 at the age of 35, received the Diamonds for personal bravery and his division's outstanding accomplishments in the defensive fighting. *Generalfeldmarschall* Model sent Tolsdorff to Berlin to receive the decoration in the Reich Chancellery. There he was ordered by the OKH to immediately assume command of LXXXII Panzer Corps, which was stationed in the Amberg area in Bavaria. With the new command came a promotion to *Generalleutnant*. In the course of subsequent fighting the corps was forced to withdraw into the Alps before the advancing US forces. Tolsdorff's corps, whose command post was located in Eisenärzt, was attacked by strong allied forces. The American 7th Army included a French division, whose armored units lost a number of Sherman tanks to Tolsdorff's anti-aircraft guns.

On May 3, 1945 the chief of a flak battery reported to Tolsdorff that a civilian had appeared in front of his guns while firing was in progress. The civilian, who was carrying a white flag with a red cross in one corner, had waved to the French. The man identified himself as *Hauptmann* Holzey and claimed that he had orders from *General* Tolsdorff for the battery to surrender to the French. The flak soldiers warned the *Hauptmann* and demanded that he withdraw. "The French will string us up if they see you waving a white flag while we're still firing. They'll consider it a breach of international law."

The *Hauptmann* disappeared, but returned a few minutes later accompanied by a fourteen-year-old boy. This time he placed a white flag on a pole. Tolsdorff had *Hauptmann* Holzey locked up. The latter stated that he was on leave and had been asked to raise the white flag by the burgermeister of the town.

At the subsequent confrontation the burgermeister stated that he didn't know Holzey and therefore couldn't have asked him to raise the white flag. Eventually it was learned that Holzey had abandoned his unit. Holzey was immediately sentenced to death and executed. The execution of *Hauptmann* Franz Xaver Holzey was perhaps the most difficult decision in the life of Theodor Tolsdorff, who had distinguished himself in the war through personal bravery, comradeship and concern for his men, and there is little doubt that it had the gravest consequences. On account of his daring Tollsdorff's men called him "the great Tollsdorff," and during the heavy fighting in the summer of 1944 they dubbed him the "Lion of Vilna." Herbert Singer, once Tolsdorff's adjutant and wounded at the same time as he, said of him: "Tolsdorff was hard on others, but even harder on himself."

At the time of the surrender Tolsdorff was able to achieve one more success, in that his determined delaying tactics enabled tens of thousands of German soldiers to retreat from the Balkans to Reich territory.

When the Americans asked the highly-decorated officer to write down his wartime experiences, but then took away his decorations, Tolsdorff, like the Commanders-in-Chief of the Army and Navy and 250 other officers flatly refused to comply. On May 9, 1947 he was released by the Americans and made his way to Diepholz, near Bremen, where he drove a truck for his father-in-law's shipping company. Later he drove a bus on the Diepholz–Hannover route. Tolsdorff also worked as an attendant in a motor park. A brief stint as a "maid of all work" with a construction company also proved unsatisfactory. On December 7, 1952 Theodor Tolsdorff was unexpectedly placed under arrest. He had to answer for his actions in the shooting of *Hauptmann* Holzey before a court in Traunstein. The court initially sentenced him to two and a half years. A federal court overturned the decision and ordered the Traunstein court to hold a retrial. Finally, in September 1958, proceedings were dropped and on June 24, 1960 Tolsdorff was declared not guilty. The presiding judge of the Traunstein Regional Court, Friedrich Schmidt, vouched for Tolsdorff: "He wasn't a general who maniacally laid waste every area he passed through."

The same year Tolsdorff was hired by the German Asphalt AG and trained as a manager. A year later he was director of the branch in Karlsruhe. Tolsdorff held this position until 1969;

the same year he took over the branch office in Dortmund, and retired on December 31, 1974. Afterward Theodor Tolsdorff and his wife Lore lived in Wuppertal. His eldest son is a nose-ears-throat specialist in Bad Honnef; the youngest died in a fall in 1957. Once a year Tolsdorff and his war comrades met at their division's memorial in Wuppertal. He served as a managing director in the Organization of German Expellees, East Prussia. Theodor Tolsdorff died on May 25, 1978.

CHAPTER XXVI

GENERAL
DR. KARL MAUSS

A sign on the outside of the house at Osterkamp 3, Hamburg-Wandsbek, read: Dr. K. Mauss, Dentist. Only a few people knew that this man who ran a dentist practice had been a *Generalleutnant* in the war, commanded one of the most famous German divisions and had been decorated with the Knight's Cross with Oak Leaves, Swords and Diamonds.

Dr. Karl Mauss – dentist in Hamburg-Wandsbek, a man in a white dentist's smock, amputee – mastered civilian life just as he had succeeded as a soldier in uniform.

During the First World War, at the age of sixteen, he slipped away from school to the recruiting office. The enlistment board considered the boy too young. He made a comic sight in short pants and school cap, sitting in the changing room beside men with goatees and full beards. Highly embarrassed, Karl Mauss returned to his parent's apartment in Lübeck and told his father of his misfortune. The old man was loyal to the Kaiser and a patriotic man and the rejection of his son offended his honor.

"Wait a minute, I'll pull on my good sweater and go with you. That would be the limit if they wouldn't take my son under the Kaiser's banner. You will become a soldier, and that's that!"

The Lübeck senator for the army – Lübeck was then a free Hanseatic city – listened to the father's arguments and said provocatively, "Very well, your son will become a soldier. And you are going with him as a member of the veteran reserve!"

On the Somme the sixteen-year-old Karl Mauss became the youngest man in the division to win the Iron Cross, Second Class, after distinguishing himself as the best scout in his regiment. But Mauss badly wanted to become a flier and therefore requested a transfer. The regimental commander refused. He wanted to keep men like Mauss, who at the age of seventeen had already been promoted to *Leutnant* for bravery in the face of the enemy. And after the transfer of his division to the East, into the Carpathians, he was awarded the Iron Cross, First Class.

Mauss proved himself once more on the Italian Front. He and his company took several thousand Italians prisoner. His experience on the Eastern Front taught him to know the land and its people. This was to prove an asset in many difficult situations twenty-five years later. He continued his efforts to secure a transfer to the air force, until finally, after much pushing, he obtained what he wanted. During flight training the young officer almost drove his instructors to desperation. It was never high or fast enough for him.

One day during flight training in Schneidemühl, Mauss was supposed to fly as an observer, the final act in his training. After waiting in vain for the second man, he climbed into the aircraft alone, compensating roughly for the missing weight with field stones, and took off. At 3,800 meters he sensed that there was a problem with the aircraft's rudder. He maneuvered – but without success. The aircraft suddenly went into a dive. At 2,000 meters he was able to pull out briefly, but then the aircraft resumed its wild dive. There was a loud crash. Mauss felt the fuselage giving way beneath him and something struck his legs. In spite of everything he was lucky. The pilot's seat broke through the fuselage before the impact and Mauss had fallen out of the aircraft with it. Result: nine broken bones and a year in the hospital. An investigation of the crash revealed that the cause was tampering with the rudder control cable – sabotage! Mauss received his pilot certificate in his sickbed.

Following the unrest of November 1918 Mauss reported to the *Erhardt* Naval Brigade which, together with the *Freikorps Oberland*, battled spartacists, anarchists and communists and fought against the Polish uprisings which had sprung up in eastern Germany. In the battle for the Annaberg, the symbol of Upper Silesia, Mauss distinguished himself repeatedly. On October 22, 1921 he was promoted to *Oberleutnant*. Soon afterward he left military service.

Returning to private life, he initially tried to earn a living as a publishing and trade representative. Success eluded him, as was the case when he tried selling newspapers. In 1925 he enrolled in his Hamburg alma mater to study dentistry. On March 1, 1929, at the age of thirty, a dentistry degree was conferred upon him, and shortly thereafter he settled in his home city of Lübeck. His practice went well, but nevertheless his new career did not prove entirely satisfactory. Mauss was by nature a soldier. In 1934 he made his decision: on September 1 he had himself reactivated as a *Hauptmann* in the 6th Infantry Regiment in Lübeck. Soon afterward he and his men were transferred to hamburg-Wandsbek to form the basis of the 69th Hamburg Regiment. Promotion to *Major* followed on April 1, 1938.

Mauss took part in the fighting near Brest-Litovsk at the outset of the Polish Campaign. In September 1939 he was transferred to the 10th Panzer Division as a battalion commander. When the Western Campaign began the 10th Panzer drove through the Ardennes toward Sedan. His battalion was the first German unit to enter Calais.

The 10th Panzer Division fought as part of Panzergruppe Guderian in the initial stages of Operation "Barbarossa." It was under the command of *General* von Vietinghoff's XXXXIV Panzerkorps. *Oberstleutnant* (April 1, 1941) Mauss led an advance battalion. During a reconnaissance advance he captured a Soviet general, commander of an army corps. The following conversation ensued:

Mauss: "Further bloodshed is senseless. Order your corps to lay down its weapons."

Russian: "You're fooling yourself if you believe the war against the German Army is senseless."

Mauss: "Aren't you shocked by the losses suffered by your troops?"

Russian: "Are you aware of my fatherland's potential in men and material?"

Mauss: "That too will run dry. No army in the world can take such blows."

Russian: "Never! Not ours . . .!"

Mauss: "Then you intend to go on sacrificing your men?"

Russian: "Yes! For every hour, every day that we hold, and delay the German advance, is of supreme importance to our command!"

Mauss: "You mean, because then the rear area can be fortified and reserves moved up?"

Russian: "We still have several surprises for you."

Mauss: "You are very optimistic – and meanwhile your field forces crack under our blows . . ."

Russian: "It's not a question of cracking. You are facing only a fraction of the Soviet armed forces."

Mauss thought back to this conversation during the muddy period and the ice-cold winter, as well as in later years. He remembered the words of the Soviet general, even if he didn't want to believe them at first. The Russian's bluffing, he thought.

Battalion commander and *Oberstleutnant* Dr. Mauss drove through enemy-held territory into the Vyazma area. On October 11, after heavy fighting around Rusa and Istra near the old battlefield of Borodino, he resumed the drive on Moscow. This winter battle ended eighteen kilometers from Moscow in a totally-destroyed village.

The awarding of the Knight's Cross on November 26, 1941 for the holding of the bridgehead on the Ugra was small consolation for Karl Mauss. His forces had suffered heavily. After bitter fighting against Soviet elite units he wrote in his diary: "The tenacity of the enemy is astonishing when one considers that fifteen-year-old officer cadets are defending. They would rather allow themselves to be killed than surrender. Haven't seen any prisoners who were not wounded. Many have shot themselves."

Mauss learned from a captured Soviet captain that elements of the Siberian far-east army had arrived. He passed this news on to the division. A few days later his men were fighting against the well-equipped Siberians. It was an unequal battle, with the result that Moscow was not reached.

His superiors considered Mauss an outstanding leader, an example to his men. His decisions were well-considered but nonetheless quickly taken. To his men Mauss was one of them. Like them he ate from a mess kit and slept with them in the most pitiful hut. He was always with them under fire and never lost his cool demeanor, which was passed on to the men. Even the most furious snowstorm couldn't keep him in his Russian cottage. He had to be with his men, where the focal point of the attack was. In his diary he wrote: "Snow, snow, snow. The Russian attacks quick as lightning and withdraws. When we advance we find nothing."

He hated nothing more than the military routine. He concentrated on the enemy and always thought about how to inflict the highest possible losses on him. "What good are reports here?" he once called to his adjutant. "Tell division that Ivan won't get past me. I'm with my people, who need me now. Therefore I have no time for reports."

Karl Mauss was transferred to the 4th Panzer Division in March 1942 and on April 20 he was promoted to *Oberst*. He was now in command of the 33rd Rifle Regiment, a position he held until October. In May he was badly wounded near Orel but was back with his unit by July. He then stepped in for the division commander, *Generalmajor* von Saucken, who had been severely wounded. Encircled near Kursk, he led his forces out of the pocket with only minimal losses and all their vehicles. In recognition of this feat Mauss was awarded the Oak Leaves on November 24, 1943. Soon after he was transferred to the 8th Panzer Division as commanding officer.

In recognition of his bravery and because of his outstanding qualities as a commander, on January 28, 1944 he was entrusted with the famous 7th Panzer Division, Rommel's former "ghost division." His predecessor, Diamonds wearer *Generalmajor* Schulz, successor to *Generalleutnant* von Manteuffel, had led the division for only three days before being killed near Shepetovka.

Tirelessly and patiently, Mauss drove from unit to unit in his Kübelwagen, listening to the concerns of the men in the front lines. His superiors in the corps and army were not pleased with what they saw. His command post is too far forward, they declared. The unit must be led from the rear, otherwise there is the danger that Mauss might lose his perspective. But Mauss answered promptly: "The command post is where the shooting is and the commander where his men are. Tanks must be led from the front. The only time I lose my perspective is when I know where the enemy is solely from looking at the map!"

In the Carpathians his division was encircled without its supply units. The situation was doubtful when the Soviets attacked with strong forces. Radio intercepts revealed the presence of a Tiger battalion of the *SS-Leibstandarte*, and together with this Mauss fought his way out to the south.

As it was surrounded by strong Soviet forces, the moving pocket was supplied from the air. Mauss learned by radio that *General* Hube's First Panzer Army, also in a moving pocket, was approaching from the east. He immediately established contact, broke through the Soviet ring and united his forces with the First Panzer Army. Employing the 7th Panzer Division as spearhead, *General* Hube planned to break through the enemy encircling ring and veer south, where he expected to find German units. Radio sources confirmed that *Generaloberst* Raus' Fourth Panzer Army was in heavy fighting with Soviet forces. In a few hours communications were established with Raus. The panzer army's Commander-in-Chief signalled: "We're coming." The Fourth Panzer Army attacked and broke through the Soviet front. At the same time the 16th Panzer Division broke out of the pocket, advanced to Buchach, smashed the enemy and linked up with Fourth Panzer Army. Farther north the 7th Panzer Division overran the enemy positions, knocked out 53 enemy tanks, destroyed several guns and took several hundred prisoners. There, too, contact was established with Fourth Panzer Army. On April 9 *General* Hube said to Dr. Mauss, who on April 1 had been promoted to *Generalleutnant*: "It all would have turned out badly if we hadn't had you. Your men prevented the destruction of the First Panzer Army."

Only a short time later, in the summer of the same year, the major Soviet offensive against Army Group Center which had begun on June 22 was stopped at the East Prussian border. It was partly due to the steadfastness of IX Army Corps and the bravery of the 7th Panzer Division that the enemy was stopped near Raseinen. A great deal of the credit also went to the soldiers of the brave and battered 252nd Infantry Division.

The personal bravery and command skill of *Generalmajor* Mauss were known at the front. In those days his command post intercepted a Soviet radio message: "Attention, Mauss is back. Extreme caution recommended. The fellow can do anything." Mauss soon showed what he was capable of. On August 23 Mauss drove into the Raseinen from the north, drove out the Soviets and opened the way for accompanying elements of the 252nd Infantry Division.

On August 15 the Wehrmacht communique reported on the battle for Raseinen: "The battle for Raseinen has temporarily passed its peak. For days the Soviets have charged the corps' defensive front with tremendous masses of tanks, but in every case they were engaged and thrown back . . . The units of IX Army Corps distinguished themselves through their extraordinary bravery and endurance in the defensive fighting since June 22. The command and field forces have achieved their crowning success in the six-day battle for Raseinen, in the course of which two full-strength and well-equipped tanks brigades and two rifle corps were smashed with the loss of 345 tanks. With the vital assistance of the 7th Panzer Division under *Generalmajor* Mauss, an enemy breakthrough has been prevented in the area north of Tilsit and the conditions created for a further, successful defense of the East Prussian frontier."

The author had a personal experience with *General* Mauss during this battle for Raseinen:

"I was adjutant of an anti-tank battalion and had orders to establish contact with the 7th Panzer Division.

The reputation of *General* Mauss, Oak Leaves wearer and a dentist in civilian life, preceded him. I couldn't imagine such a mixture of soldier and medicine man. Thus I set out, full of expectation, to have a look at the 'prodigy' of the Raseinen front. The village in which 7th Panzer Division was assembled lay about 1 kilometer from Raseinen. Behind the protective white walls of a tidy farmhouse sat a command car. And behind it, on a bench, sat an officer, average height, with a scar across his cheek. I introduced myself. The officer on the bench turned around leisurely, examined me closely with two bright eyes as if he was trying to look right through me and murmured, 'Mauss.'

Quickly I repeated the division's instruction and the intentions of the battalion. The general listened quietly. Without interrupting he opened a map board and gazed at it.

Suddenly, without looking up, he said, 'You have a good memory.' A little confused, I stopped.

Then Mauss nodded and said, 'Go on, go on! Tell me where you stand. I'm to attack in an hour. First I have to have a look at what the Russian is doing.'

In brief sentences I told him of the breakthrough attempt by the T 34s.

'I was about to send my Panthers there as soon as I heard firing!'
he observed.

'We did it alone, *Herr General*,' I said.

'Excellent,' smiled Mauss, 'But come with me a minute.'

We drove up close to the main line of resistance. The terrain was hilly. There were many gardens and even more trees. We were able to observe the enemy undisturbed. The Russians were assembling tanks in broad daylight, something they never or only rarely did. The air shook with the dull rumble of motors. Clouds of smoke wafted beyond the city. We had a clear view of two T 34s, which disappeared into the cemetery.

'I'm going to attack here!' said Mauss, pushing his cap back on his head. Then he turned to me. 'Tell your commander that this sector is my preserve. He can do what he likes farther below. Boundary line: road to Raseinen'."

That was my first meeting with *General* Dr. Karl Mauss. I was to have a second the next day. The tanks of the 7th Panzer Division did not attack later that same afternoon as planned, but had to wait until seven o'clock the next morning. General Wuthmann, under whose command 7th Panzer was, wanted to strike the mass of the enemy with one blow.

In the early morning hours of August 23 the remaining artillery opened fire on the Soviet positions. The infantry climbed from its foxholes and overran the enemy. For the first time in weeks there were also German fighter aircraft in the air. They plunged like hawks on the assembled enemy tanks. Taken completely by surprise, panic broke out among the Soviets.

The cemetery now became a trap for the Soviets. Panthers and Tigers shot up the T 34s. Any which succeeded in escaping didn't get far. Our battalion's assault and anti-tank guns destroyed 80 tanks in a few hours.

By midday Raseinen was in our hands. Then the Soviets renewed their attack. They came from the east across the plain and drove from the north through forests and gardens, almost reaching the German positions. But waiting for them there were the tanks of the 7th Panzer Division and the anti-tank and self-propelled guns of the anti-tank battalion and 14th Company. Another 23 T 34s went up in flames. I saw Mauss in his car near my position while the attack was under way. Then two T 34s crawled out of the entrance to a farm not 300 meters in front of me. I saw Mauss duck. Just then I fired. Mauss' car stopped several meters from me. When the general recognized me he smiled and saluted. At the same time he remembered that the old military salute was no longer used. "Forgive me," he said, "I look like a prison guard when I raise my hand." After a while he said, "You did an outstanding job. My men tell me that you stepped in quite nicely. I'll mention that in my report. Thank you very much and good luck." Then he was gone, *General* Mauss, the prodigy of the Raseinen front.

On October 10 Karl Mauss was promoted to *Generalleutnant* and ordered to report to Führer Headquarters. The mood was depressed in the *"Wolfsschanze."* Courtiers had made themselves important, taking precedence over the real experts. Mauss was not pleased to have to surrender his weapon and undergo a search. These were additional security measures introduced after July 20. Hitler no longer trusted anyone, not even highly-decorated generals. Before Mauss was let in to see Hitler he had to spend the entire afternoon talking with *General* Burgdorf, the new head of the Army Personnel Office (*General* Schmundt had died of injuries suffered in the attempted coup), in a guest room.

"My dear Mauss," began Burgdorf. Then he explained what Mauss was supposed to tell Hitler and what he wasn't allowed to say. "The Führer must not be shocked. Please, no figures and no depressing speeches." When Burgdorf had left Mauss was taken to see Keitel. Once again he was admonished, only Keitel was much more forceful and radical than Burgdorf had been. He summed up all of Burgdorf's requests and instructions in a single order: "I forbid you to speak of things with the Führer which might be detrimental to his health. Furthermore you are to provide answers only about matters which you have been asked about. Should you nevertheless speak of other things then you will have to suffer the consequences!"

This was perfidy of the highest order. Mauss was confused. The man who never lost his head at the front was speechless, depressed and shaken. He was still unaware of the game being played in Führer Headquarters. Hitler, shaking, his eyes dull and his back bent, offered a lifeless hand to Mauss.

"You have fought bravely."

"Excuse me, *mein Führer*. My men have given their all."

Hitler looked up. Mauss thought he detected mistrust in his gaze.

"Our soldiers can't fight any more. There are only retreats . . ."

These words struck Mauss like a slap in the face. His men were no longer capable of fighting? Had they not proved year in, year out, how they committed themselves? "That's not true, *mein Führer*!" blurted Mauss. A disapproving look from Burgdorf, a gesture from Keitel. But Mauss had no intention of being silenced.

Hitler's mouth moved. "No morale . . . no will . . ."

"Who has told you this nonsense, *mein Führer*?"

At this point Keitel intervened. He bowed toward Hitler and tried to change the topic of conversation. However Hitler was obviously more interested in Mauss than his lackey. He turned to the commander of the 7th Panzer Division and said, "My generals visit the front and then report to me . . ."

"No one ever visited me! Most probably the generals drove to where there was no shooting!" Mauss replied sharply. Disgusted, he asked permission to leave.

"Do you have a personal request?" asked Hitler.

Mauss didn't hesitate. "*Jawohl*, I have one. I request 40 new Panthers!"

Keitel had already left. With Hitler and Mauss were Burgdorf and two staff officers. They were very much taken aback when they heard the division commander's request. No one had ever said that there. Usually they asked for leave, a withdrawal of their unit or some other favor. But Mauss wanted to keep on fighting.

To his surprise, Mauss received the tanks a few days later. They were badly needed, for the Russians attacked again in the Memel area and near Wolfsburg-Gumbinnen-Goldap crossed the German border for the first time.

Possibly by chance – even afterward Mauss could offer no other explanation – one day Hitler again summoned him to his headquarters. The upright and straightforward manner of this officer seemed to have impressed him. "Give me the situation. How do things look with you?"

Mauss took a deep breath and said in his own dramatic way: "If I may say so, shitty! My division lies smashed to pieces in the Memel area."

"And how does it look with the others?" Fear and suspicion lay in this question. But Mauss answered in typical fashion: "If we carry on like this, we might as well pack up and go home, *mein Führer*." It's unlikely that anyone had ever spoken so bluntly to Hitler. Burgdorf rolled his eyes, Fegelein froze, the adjutants stared awkwardly at the tips of their boots.

Hitler looked past Mauss. His lips moved, and he ran a trembling hand over his forehead. "If we lose this war then the German people deserve nothing less. The soldier has failed . . ."

Having let the cat out of the bag, Hitler thought a moment and then placed his hand consolingly on Mauss' arm. "I didn't mean you," he said, smiling.

"But you named soldiers in general."

"No! Only a certain group who don't want to fight any more."

Mauss had nothing with which to answer this dialectic. He gave up any idea of discussing the matter any further with Hitler.

On January 12 and 13 the Soviets launched a major offensive all along the Eastern Front. The defenses knew the date of the attack and had passed it on to the senior staffs. However, instead of abandoning the forward positions and allowing the attackers to swing at nothing, they didn't react at all or froze like a rabbit in the gaze of a snake. The results were catastrophic. The attack struck the 7th Panzer Division in the Ziechenau area. It soon became obvious that the Soviet objective was Berlin. Mauss fought a delaying action. North of Graudenz he was able to cross the frozen Vistula with all his men and equipment. Near Marienburg and Elbing he broke through into Prussian-Holland and tried to relieve *Generaloberst* Hossbach's Fourth Army. Once again it was to be his 7th Panzer Division which turned back the enemy.

Mauss launched his counterattack toward Elbing on February 2, 1945, just as Commander-in-Chief Hossbach and his Chief-of-Staff were relieved of their posts. In this phase of the defensive battle three more divisions were placed under his command, and with these Mauss was subsequently encircled in Gotenhafen. Then, while on a scouting advance, a direct hit killed all those riding with him. Karl Mauss was seriously wounded. His wounds were treated at the main dressing station; one leg had to be amputated. Following the amputation he ordered them to lay him on a stretcher, and from there he continued to issue orders to his units. But he couldn't keep this up for long. Four days later he collapsed. Mauss was transported from Hela to Copenhagen with thousands of evacuees from East Prussia and Pomerania.

General Burgdorf, the Head of Personnel in Führer Headquarters, couldn't believe his ears when a voice on the telephone said: "Mauss here, with one leg in Copenhagen."

"But that's impossible!"

"No, it's true."

"Is there anything I can do for you?"

"General Burgdorf, please don't leave my division in Gotenhafen. The boys will be killed or taken prisoner. God knows they don't deserve that. As a panzer division, perhaps it can still salvage something in Mecklenburg."

The scarcely believable happened: the 7th Panzer Division was evacuated from the pocket by sea. It subsequently fought on at the Malchin-Waren chain of lakes until the surrender, which was signed with the English.

Karl Mauss was promoted to *General der Panzertruppen* retroactive to April 1, 1945, and on the April 15 was awarded the Diamonds. He was the last commanding officer of the tradition-rich 7th Panzer Division, which had been commanded by three wearers of the Diamonds before him: Rommel, von Manteuffel and Schulz.

Following the surrender a British corps headquarters had Mauss brought to Ratzeburg and then Munsterlager in a convoy of three armored cars. There he was turned over to German military doctors for further treatment. His robust constitution and his unbroken strength of will saved his life.

In Munsterlager Mauss learned that his wife, the mother of their three children, had died. He asked the British camp commandant for permission to go to Lübeck for the funeral. His request was denied. He was told that he was a prisoner of war and that there were no exceptions. When he presented his request to the camp leadership in person, his written request was torn up before his eyes. They threw the pieces on to the floor and ordered him to pick them up. This was probably the bitterest moment in the life of the general, who in the course of two world wars had never seen a prisoner treated in such a demeaning fashion.

Following his release as a prisoner of war, Mauss' experience as a dentist stood him in good stead. For the second time he set about setting up a practice and making a living. In 1949 he remarried. A year later his son Dietrich was born. His greatest wish, to train young men in the newly-formed *Bundeswehr*, was not fulfilled. The Diamonds wearer submitted an application but was rejected. Dr. Mauss considered this rejection an affront against the front-line soldier, and he never got over it before his death. On February 9, 1959 the last commander of the famous 7th Panzer Division died of a heart attack following a lengthy illness.

CHAPTER XXVII

GENERAL
DIETRICH VON SAUCKEN

1 945 – April, May – the Danzig area – Hela Peninsula – the Soviets on the offensive – aerial bombs, artillery fire, rockets, machine-guns – German soldiers, bringing in food and taking women and children to waiting ships.

The man responsible for 300,000 civilians and soldiers, and who fulfilled this difficult task so well, was the Commander-in-Chief of Army Group East Prussia, Dietrich von Saucken. When orders came from above, instructing him to fly out of the pocket to safety, he refused, sending the following message: "Where my soldiers remain, I remain too." Before the German surrender he said to his soldiers, "I will go into captivity with you."

When the Teutonic Knights came to East Prussia in 1230 they found the Sauckens already there. 715 years later, in 1945, they were driven out by the Soviets. The Sauckens served the Teutonic Order in time of war, then the Prussian kings. Finally, numerous Sauckens lost their lives in the First and Second World Wars.

Dietrich von Saucken, who was born in Fischhausen, East Prussia on May 16, 1892, joined the 3rd Grenadier Regiment Friedrich Wilhelm I after leaving college and was promoted to *Leutnant* in 1912. In the First World War he served as a company commander and battalion, regiment and brigade adjutant. He took part in the heavy fighting at Verdun, in the Carpathians in 1916-17 and the March offensive of 1918.

Saucken was wounded seven times and earned both Iron Crosses, the Hohenzollern Order with Swords, the Austrian Military Service Cross and the Wound badge in Gold. His decision to remain a soldier after the First World War sprang from the conviction that he would be needed in the new army and love for his chosen career. His detachments to the brigade and later infantry command headquarters in Insterburg and to the 1st Infantry Regiment in Königsberg were concluded by a transfer to the 8th Cavalry Regiment in Öls, Silesia and from there to the 2nd Cavalry Regiment in Allenstein, Lyck, Osterode and Angerburg in his East Prussian homeland.

On April 17, 1927 Saucken was promoted to *Rittmeister*. Nine years later he became a *Major* and, following a period of detached duty at the military college in Hannover, received a promotion to *Oberstleutnant*.

From 1937 von Saucken was commanding officer of the 2nd Cavalry Regiment, garrisoned in Angerburg, East Prussia. In 1939, by now an *Oberst*, he and his cavalry regiment took part in the Polish Campaign, advancing across the Narew toward Warsaw. A number of successful engagements with minimal losses resulted in the Bar to the Iron Cross.

Soon afterward von Saucken and his cavalry were transferred to the German-Soviet demarcation line, west of the River Bug near Brest-Litovsk. At the end of September he gave up the cavalry regiment and assumed command of the 4th Panzer Division's rifle brigade.

In the autumn of 1941 – by now the war against the Soviet Union was in full swing – the commander of the Second Panzer Army, *Generaloberst* Guderian, achieved a surprise breakthrough in the direction of Moscow. As part of *General* Geyr von Schweppenburg's XXIV Panzerkorps, von Saucken smashed through the Soviet fronts. He was wounded during the crossing of the Dniepr. After the hard fighting for Orel and Mzensk the 4th Panzer Division with von Saucken's brigade bypassed Tula to the east to break the last opposition before Moscow. But Tula was not to be taken. The exhausted German troops of the Second Panzer Army were no longer capable of it. As well there was the pitiless cold. The temperature dropped to minus thirty.

Soviet workers militias put up determined resistance in and around Tula. They were extremely well trained for the defensive role. Encouraged by political commissars and ruthlessly forced to hold out, to the surprise of the German command and soldiers they fought to the last man. Stalin could thank their resistance for the fact that the Germans were forced to break off their attack on Moscow. Although the 4th Panzer Division blew the Tula-Moscow rail line and reached the Tula-Serpukov road, the strength of the troops was failing and there were shortages of fuel and ammunition. Unusually violent snowstorms paralyzed almost completely the German troops, who were totally, or at best inadequately, equipped for the winter war. The Soviet command recognized this German weakness and threw all its available reserves into the defensive struggle, from which they were soon to go over to the offensive. Fresh troops from Siberia were transported to the front. They came because Japan had refused to declare war on the Soviet Union. This released the Far East Army which had previously been tied down. In the end these elite units, which were committed in December, settled the fate of the German armies before Moscow.

Now, in 1941, the Soviets employed the same tactics and strategy against the Germans as they had to defeat Napoleon in 1812. Cavalry were deployed against the flank of the Second Army. Soviet troops infiltrated the thin German lines and appeared in up to division strength in the rear, in some cases sowing considerable confusion. Lightning advances by well-camouflaged tank units into the German front spread panic and chaos. All this took place in temperatures of minus 40-46 degrees. The German troops, weakened by numerous losses to frostbite, were forced to retreat for the first time since war began in 1939.

On December 25, 1941 Dietrich von Saucken assumed command of the 4th Panzer Division. Near Bolkhov, north of Orel, he blocked the advance of a Russian corps which had overrun a German infantry division. Von Saucken's unit halted and destroyed the enemy. In recognition of his successful leadership he was promoted to the rank of *Generalmajor* on January 1, 1942. Soon afterward he was wounded seriously. Fourteen days later *Generalfeldmarschall* von Kluge presented him with the Knight's Cross in his sickbed in Smolensk.

After recovering from his wounds von Saucken took over the "School for Fast Troops" in Krampnitz. On April 1, 1943 he was promoted to *Generalleutnant*. Von Saucken once again took command of the 4th Panzer Division and led it in the summer battles near Kursk and Orel. However the offensive from the Orel salient was broken off. Von Saucken's division was forced to veer southward moving by night, in order to head off a Soviet pincer attack against the Ninth Army. Von Saucken attacked the enemy from the move, stopped him and held. For this act he was awarded the Oak Leaves on August 22, 1943.

When contact with Army Group South was broken in the "wet triangle," the confluence of the Pripyat and Dniepr Rivers, von Saucken's division crossed the Pripyat and smashed an enemy bridgehead which had been established before the arrival of German forces. Fifty kilometers further south, near Chernobyl, the courageous 4th Panzer Division temporarily established contact with Army Group South. Then the enemy crossed the Dniepr near Rechitsa and broke through the northern wing of the Second Army. Von Saucken and his division were forced to change positions in an attempt to prevent a further breakthrough. He succeeded in closing this dangerous gap and restored contact with the Second Army. But the enemy assembled new forces, resulting in a several-day defensive battle in the Kalinkovichi area against a tenfold superiority. The 4th Panzer Division frustrated the enemy's plan to once again split the German Second and Ninth Armies. For this feat von Saucken was awarded the Swords on February 20, 1944.

Released from the Ninth Army, the 4th Panzer Division was once again sent to the Second Army and LVI Corps. The corps was caught up in the attack on Kovel and its mission was to halt Soviet forces which had infiltrated through the swampy terrain of the Pripyat. Kovel itself was surrounded by Soviet troops. LVI Corps was to relieve the city. After studying the maps carefully, von Saucken determined that the terrain around Kovel was impassable to tanks and vehicles – it was the middle of the spring muddy period. But a narrow strip of gravel, which lay behind the Soviet front, could be used to approach Kovel.

The first assault was therefore directed northward into the enemy's rear, in order to then veer south during the night and break through the encircling ring from the north, the direction from which the Soviets least expected it, and establish contact with the surrounded garrison. However the Soviets attacked again and forced von Saucken's forces back. He remained near Kovel until May 12, 1944, when he was called away to temporarily take command of III Panzer Corps.

On June 22, 1944 the Soviet armies launched a major offensive against Army Group Center. They broke through the German main line of resistance along the entire front, drove deep into the german rear, formed pockets and pressed ahead toward East Prussia. Von Saucken, now commanding XXXIX Panzer Corps, was given the job of halting the Soviet spearheads. There was heavy and bitter fighting as German forces withdrew across the Beresina, where the 5th Panzer Division held a weak bridgehead position. The German forces made a fighting withdrawal to Novgorodek, north of Minsk, but the Soviets were already behind them and cut off their avenue of retreat. Von Saucken made a surprise attack on the pursuing enemy, who were following up with strong armored forces, and achieved success, while in the west he simultaneously struck the Soviet forces in the Molodechno Narrows with the 5th Panzer Division's rifle regiment and drove them back. Von Saucken had retaken the vital retreat route. Inferior German forces initially prevented the Soviets from strategically exploiting the huge gap between the Third and Fourth Panzer Armies. *Feldmarschall* Model used the time thus gained to move in new forces, so that the great Soviet offensive of summer 1944 was halted at the Memel, east of East Prussia by the seven divisions of XXXIX Panzer Corps.

From the Memel, Headquarters, Ninth Army was sent to a position near Warsaw. The weakly defended Vistula was under attack by three Soviet tank corps. Although only half a division of paratroops and a weakened infantry division were initially available, following the dispatch of the 4th and 19th Panzer Divisions, the enemy's northern wing was destroyed in a battle north of Warsaw. The 4th Panzer Division, which was sent to XXXIX Corps from the north, seized the bridge over the River Bug near Wyschow. It was thus possible to move it into position in time to attack the flank of the enemy tank corps which was in the process of outflanking the weak German forces of the northern wing. In the nearly hopeless situation in which Army Group Center found itself, von Saucken's corps fought alternately as part of *Generaloberst* Raus' Third Panzer Army and in *Generaloberst* Schörner's Army Group North. XXXIX Corps had the task of closing a gap between Raus and Schörner. Von Saucken was unable to advance to Mitau with the weak forces available, but Shagarev was reached. The 4th, 5th and 12th Panzer Divisions, and the *Grossdeutschland* Panzer-Grenadier Division, all of which were under von Saucken's command, established contact with the "Kleffel Corps," which formed the southwest wing of Schörner's army group.

Von Saucken's units inflicted heavy losses on the Soviets. One hundred enemy tanks were destroyed. But each day the enemy added new equipment to their defenses. The commanding general's radio intelligence service listened to Soviet radio reports and learned how many tanks would be delivered by rail the next morning. Fighting under these circumstances seemed comparable to tilting at windmills. The Soviets were soon strong enough to break through the Raus Army, in spite of the bravery of the German troops, and push on to the Baltic. XXXIX Panzer Corps now fought a successful battle to secure the open southern flank of Army Group Schörner, until a continuous southern front was created. Although the corps was cut off, it was possible to bring out the 4th Panzer Division by sea as the year came to a close. Von Saucken and his staff were called away to East Prussia for other employment.

General von Saucken formed the *Grossdeutschland* Corps from the *Grossdeutschland* and *Brandenburg* Divisions. He was assured that his new corps would never be deployed divided. However in January 1945 the *Grossdeutschland* Division was forced to intervene in East Prussia, while the corps headquarters and the attached *Brandenburg* and 1st Parachute-Panzer Divisions were ordered into action west of Litzmannstadt. There the corps came under the command of the Ninth Army, whose front had already been broken by the enemy and which was on the retreat. Von Saucken's orders: Remain in the rear of the advancing enemy, unite with a battle group of XXIV Corps, which is still fighting as it moves among the Soviets, and afterward break through to the German front. This mission was accomplished in hard fighting by the *Grossdeutschland* Panzer Corps, which moved in a circular front, and XXIV Corps, which arrived later. In this phase von Saucken was transferred to the officer reserve on account of differences of opinion with the Army Chief-of-Staff. But on March 12, 1945 he was asked to a situation briefing in Führer Headquarters, where he was given command of the Second Panzer Army.

Lacking fuel and air support, von Saucken's battered army faced an enemy enjoying a tenfold superiority. The army's only contact with other fronts was by sea. Occupying a bridgehead around Oxhüft –Kämpe – Gotenhafen-Danzig and on the spit of land extending to the Frische Haff, it was supposed to deny the enemy possession of the named ports as well as the port of Hela. Ten-thousand refugees, who were following the movements of the German troops, were squeezed together in this tiny area. It was therefore also the duty of the Second Army and its commander to help these people, as well as feed them, evacuate them and save them from the clutches of the enemy. But the Soviets broke through toward Gotenhafen and Langfuhr. The cut-off western wing of the Second Army under General von Kessel was in a hopeless situation; Hitler ordered it to "hold to the last man." Von Saucken ignored the order and, in cooperation with the commanding admiral of the eastern Baltic, Admiral Thiele, brought the 40,000 men to the Putzinger Spit.

On the mainland, the bridgehead was reduced in size after the veering of the enemy from Zoppot an die See toward the east and the fall of Danzig. This was held to the end, however, while after the fall of Königsberg von Saucken was forced to take command of the German forces fighting in the Samland as well.

"Army Group East Prussia," as the remnants of the two armies were now called, could not prevent powerful Soviet forces from advancing to Cranz and rolling up the entire northern position on the Samland coast. Although von Saucken was able to prevent total encirclement, elements of his own southern wing were cut off east of Fischerhäuser Bay. Only a small part of this could be saved the following night, being evacuated across the bay in various types of vessels. During the heavy fighting on the spit of land called the Frische Nehrung, the German soldiers once again exhibited outstanding bravery. Their mission was to hold up the enemy until the 300,000 refugees and evacuees had been shipped out. But the Soviets attacked constantly with strong armored forces and unimaginable artillery fire. Although the 7th Bavarian Infantry Division succeeded in halting the enemy on the spit, the idea of evacuating all the refugees and troops by sea could not be realized. For the courageously-fighting soldiers and their Commander-in-Chief there was no way of avoiding capture.

The last *Kriegsmarine* vessel left at midnight on May 8 – the same day von Saucken was awarded the Diamonds by Hitler's successor, *Grossadmiral* Dönitz. The disappointed soldiers couldn't grasp the fact that there was no rescue for them. For years they had done whatever was required to avoid being captured by the Red Army. Now they faced an uncertain future. Von Saucken contacted his opposite number, Soviet Colonel General Byelborodov. With his authorization, von Saucken emptied the navy supply dump and distributed the food and cigarettes among the soldiers who were on their way into captivity. He himself was taken to Stettin, where he was interrogated by MWD officers while guards stood by with fixed bayonets.

On May 16, 1945 the Soviets flew him to Moscow. Von Saucken spent 32 months in notorious Lubyanka and later in various other prisons, some of it in solitary confinement. He could scarcely move in the small, narrow cell. He was allowed only one thirty-minute walk daily, in the prison courtyard or a corridor. Rations were pitiful: watery soup and a few grams of bread. Then his sentence was pronounced: 25 years forced labor. Vague charges were brought, then dropped and new ones invented. Finally the Soviets justified the 25 years with the pithy sentence: "Admits to having supplied troops off the land." When von Saucken replied, "The Russian Army is still living off the land today," the judge answered, "That's a lie."

Too little to eat resulted in severe dropsy, a common ailment among his fellow prisoners. Von Saucken was released in 1955. It took von Saucken years to recover from the ordeal of being a prisoner of the Soviets. After reestablishing contact with his family, which had fled East Prussia, he turned to his second calling: he painted and drew.

This second great talent possessed by von Saucken only seemed to be a contradiction of his profession as a soldier. He painted before he could read or write. He painted so well that he was allowed to skip art classes in school to go on nature walks and seek inspiration. During summer vacation he criss-crossed his East Prussian homeland. Von Saucken spent a great deal of time on the Kurische Nehrung, where he was able to watch and admire such well-known painters as Ernst Mollenhauer and Lovis Corinth at work in the Hermann-Blode guest house. His instructor, Professor Ellend, recognized young von Saucken's talent and provided encouragement. Had he not become a soldier, von Saucken would surely have been a successful artist. In his later years he drew and painted whenever he had the opportunity. A sketch book and colors were standard articles of equipment. Later von Saucken was one of the best known exponents of Sunday painting, and in 1962 became one of the co-founders of the association, Guild of Sunday Painters, in Munich. His paintings drew favorable comment at a number of exhibitions. Sitting in a wheelchair, the eighty-four-year-old painted pictures of shining beauty. His favorite subjects were motifs from his native East Prussia, which he painted from memory: dune landscapes, fishing villages, flowers, trees, portraits. Whether in oils, water-colors, pastels, red chalk, charcoal or ink – his pictures were technically complete and forceful.

Von Saucken was a man whom fate struck innumerable times: wounded thirteen times in two world wars, his eldest son killed in Russia, himself in a wheelchair – a consequence of his long years as a prisoner. But he remained unbowed, true to himself and loyal to those around him, just as he was in 1945 when he went into captivity with his soldiers.

Dietrich von Saucken died on September 27, 1980.

Chronological Award Listing

* Date of birth   †Date of death

	Knight's Cross	Oak Leaves	Crossed Swords	Diamonds
WERNER MÖLDERS *Oberst* * 18/3/1913 in Gelsenkirchen † 22/11/1941	29/5/40 Hauptmann	21/9/40 Major	22/6/41 Oberstleutnant	16/7/41 Oberst
ADOLF GALLAND *Generalleutnant* * 19/3/1912 in Westerholt	29/7/40 Major	24/9/40 Major	21/6/41 Oberstleutnant	28/1/42 Oberst
GORDON M. GOLLOB *Oberst* * 16/6/1912 in Vienna † 11/9/1987	18/9/41 Hauptmann	26/10/41 Hauptmann	24/6/42 Hauptmann	30/8/42 Major
HANS-JOACHIM MARSEILLE *Hauptmann* * 13/12/1919 in Berlin † 30/9/1942	22/2/42 Leutnant	6/6/423 Oberleutnant	18/6/42 Oberleutnant	4/9/42 Hauptmann
HERMANN GRAF *Oberst* 24/10/1912 in Engen/Hegau † 4/11/1988	24/1/42 Leutnant	17/5/42 Leutnant	19/5/42 Leutnant	16/9/42 Oberleutnant
ERWIN ROMMEL *Generalfeldmarschall* * 15/11/1891 in Heidenheim † 14/10/1944	26/5/40 Generalmajor	20/3/41 Generalleutnant	20/1/42 General der Panzertruppen	11/3/43 Generalfeld- marschall

WOLFGANG LÜTH *Kapitän zur See* * 15/10/1913 in Riga † 14/5/1945	24/10/40 Oberleutnant zur See	17/11/42 Kapitänleutnant	15/4/43 Kapitänleutnant	11/8/43 Korvettenkapitän
WALTER NOWOTNY *Major* * 7/12/1920 in Gmünd † 8/11/1944	14/9/42 Hauptmann	3/9/43 Hauptmann	22/9/43 Oberstleutnant	20/10/43 Oberst
ADELBERT SCHULZ *Generalmajor* * 20/12/1903 in Berlin † 28/1/1944	29/9/40 Hauptmann	31/12/41 Hauptmann	6/8/43 Oberstleutnant	14/12/44 Oberst
HANS-ULRICH RUDEL *Oberst* * 2/7/1916 in Konradswaldau † 18/12/1982	6/1/42 Oberleutnant	14/4/43 Hauptmann Gold: 1/1/45	25/11/43 Hauptmann	29/3/44 Major
HYAZINTH GRAF STRACHWITZ *Generalleutnant* * 30/7/1893 in Großstein † 25/4/1968	25/8/41 Major	17/11/42 Oberstleutnant	28/3/43 Oberst	15/4/44 Oberst
HERBERT OTTO GILLE *General der Waffen-SS* * 8/3/1897 in Gandersheim/Harz † 26/12/1966	8/10/42 SS-Oberführer	1/11/43 SS-Brigadeführer Generalmajor	20/2/44 SS-Gruppenführer u. Generalleutnant der Waffen-SS	19/4/44 SS-Gruppenführer u. Generalleutnant der Waffen-SS

HANS HUBE *Generaloberst* * 29/10/1890 in Naumburg/Saale † 21/4/1944	1/8/41 Generalmajor	17/1/42 Generalmajor	21/12/42 Generalleutnant	20/4/44 Generaloberst
ALBERT KESSELRING *Generalfeldmarschall* * 13/11/1885 in Marktsteft † 15/7/1960	30/9/39 General der Flieger	25/2/42 Generalfeld- marschall	18/7/42 Generalfeld- marschall	19/7/44 Generalfeld- marschall
HELMUT LENT *Oberstleutnant* * 13/6/1918 in Neumark † 7/10/1944	30/8/41 Oberleutnant	6/6/42 Hauptmann	3/8/43 Major	31/7/44 Oberstleutnant
JOSEF "SEPP" DIETRICH *Generaloberst der Waffen-SS* * 28/5/1892 in Hawangen † 21/4/1966	5/7/40 SS-Obergruppen- führer – General der Waffen-SS	31/12/41 SS-Obergruppen- führer – General der Waffen-SS	16/3/43 SS-Obergruppen- führer – General der Waffen-SS	6/8/44 SS-Obergruppen- führer – Generaloberst der Waffen-SS
WALTER MODEL *Generalfeldmarschall* * 24/1/1891 in Genthin † 21/4/1945	9/7/41 Generalleutnant	17/2/42 General der Panzertruppen	3/4/43 Generaloberst	17/8/44 Generalfeld- marschall
ERICH HARTMANN *Major* * 19/4/1922 in Weißbach † 19/9/1993	29/10/43 Leutnant	2/3/44 Leutnant	4/7/44 Oberleutnant	25/8/44 Oberleutnant

HERMANN BALCK
General der Panzertruppen
* 7/12/1893 in Danzig-Langfuhr
† 29/11/1982

3/6/40	22/12/42	4/3/43	31/8/44
Oberstleutnant	Generalmajor	Generalleutnant	General der Panzertruppen

HERMANN BERNHARD RAMCKE
General der Fallschirmtruppen
* 24/1/1889 in Schleswig-Friedrichsburg
† 5/7/1968

21/8/41	15/11/42	20/9/44	20/9/44
Generalmajor	Generalmajor	General der Fallschirmtruppen	General der Fallschirmtruppen

HEINZ WOLFGANG SCHNAUFER
Major
* 16/2/1922 in Calw
† 15/7/1950

15/1/44	27/6/44	30/7/44	16/10/44
Oberleutnant	Hauptmann	Hauptmann	Hauptmann

ALBRECHT BRANDI
Fregettenkapitän
* 30/6/1914 in Dortmund
† 6/1/1966

21/1/43	11/4/43	13/5/44	24/11/44
Kapitänleutnant	Kapitänleutnant	Kapitänleutnant	Korvettenkapitän

FERDINAND SCHÖRNER
Generalfeldmarschall
* 12/6/1892 in Munich
† 2/7/1973

20/4/41	17/2/44	28/8/44	1/1/45
Generalmajor	General der Gebirgstruppen	Generaloberst	Generaloberst

HASSO VON MANTEUFFEL
General der Panzertruppen
* 14/1/1897 in Potsdam
† 24/9/1978

31/12/41	23/11/43	22/2/44	18/2/45
Oberst	Generalmajor	Generalleutnant	General der Panzertruppen

THEODOR TOLSDORF
Generalleutnant
* 3/11/1909 in Lehnharten
† 25/5/1978

4/12/41	Oberleutnant
15/9/43	Major
18/7/44	Oberstleutnant
18/3/45	Generalmajor

DR. KARL MAUSS
General der Panzertruppen
* 17/5/1898 in Plön/Holstein
† 9/2/1959

26/11/41	Oberstleutnant
24/11/43	Oberst
23/10/44	Generalmajor
15/4/45	Generalleutnant

DIETRICH VON SAUCKEN
General der Panzertruppen
* 16/5/1892 in Fischhausen
(East Prussia)
† 27/9/1980

15/1/42	Generalmajor
22/8/43	Generalleutnant
20/2/44	Generalleutnant
8/5/45	General der Panzertruppen